The
Conventional
and
The Alternative
in
Education

John I. Goodlad

Gary D. Fenstermacher

Thomas J. La Belle

Val D. Rust

Rodney Skager

Carl Weinberg

University of California, Los Angeles

McCutchan Publishing Corporation
2526 Grove Street
Berkeley, California 94704

ISBN 0-8211-0611-2
Library of Congress Catalog Card Number 75-2780

Chapters 1-6 from *Alternatives in Education,* published by Jossey-Bass, Inc.,
Publishers. Copyright ©1973. Reprinted by permission of the publisher.

contents

preface

In recent years, the rhetoric of change has accelerated like change itself. In education, as in many other aspects of life, the rhetoric often outruns the reality, but the talk and even some of the action over the past two decades have been, at times, "heady."

The first half of the 1950s appeared to mark the end of an era. Criticism of "soft-headed," child-centered education was rampant, as 1953 produced a bumper crop of books attacking what was thought to be going on in our schools. The Progressive Education Association quietly closed its doors.

Then, in 1957, came Sputnik. What had been a somewhat academic debate over alternative value systems, "soft" versus "hard" education, was now in the public domain. Many educators even took up the cudgel against themselves to the point of masochistic self-criticism. Federal involvement in educational affairs "for the nation's interests" reached a high point with passage of the Elementary and Secondary Education Act of 1965.

Much of the federal support was for hard education, especially curricular reform in academic disciplines at the precollegiate level, with mathematics and the natural sciences predominating. Some single-subject projects received support of a million dollars a year. "Structure of the discipline" became a catch-phrase in the rhetoric of curriculum reform, although few knew what it meant. One was to sense the meaning intuitively.

This attempt to harden the fiber of schooling made some difference, more at the secondary than at the elementary level, but much of the intent failed to get inside the schoolhouse. Some of the substance and a little of the method of instruction changed. The system of schooling was little affected, however, by this so-called curriculum reform movement.

At the same time another movement was afoot in education. This one was much older than Sputnik, having roots firmly imbedded in the humanistic tradition. But this statement is an oversimplification, since humanism itself has had no single strand in human history, as Val D. Rust points out in Chapter 4. Likewise, the flowering of humanism afresh in the 1960s and 1970s was in no way a unitary phenomenon. The following chapters make this point clear. The authors approach their task from quite different perspectives, select quite different things as important, and disagree over how widespread the movement actually is. The movement to which they refer is that of alternatives in education—alternatives in schools and alternatives to schools—a movement which clearly is part of a larger social struggle for human emancipation and yet which also is perceived by some as only another effort in a long-term effort to make schools more humane. Alternatives in education mean different things to different people, meaning being a very personal thing.

Even while we were planning this volume the mountain of information on educational alternatives was continuing to grow. Education journals are now replete with accounts of free schools, open classrooms, schools within schools, and the like, and there must be millions of written words on organizational modifications such as nongrading and team teaching. We decided early in our deliberations not to add to the descriptive and certainly not to the "gee whiz" literature. Instead, we have attempted to place these efforts within a broader social, historical, and philosophical context.

While our interest is to analyze, not proselytize, our general bias toward opening up the system of schooling in a variety of ways shows through. At times, this bias is revealed in near-anger over what schools too often do to the humans in them. While differences in viewpoint are marked, we share a concern for utilizing all of our educational resources in creating alternatives commensurate with the diversity of human needs, interests, and potentialities within a given society. We see schools as we now know them as only one rather limited source of educational opportunity.

All the authors have participated in more than academic or scholarly ways in recent efforts to loosen up the educational enterprise. Thomas J. La Belle's interests in comparative education, with special emphasis on Latin America, have carried him into the problems of creating educational opportunities in countries where reliance on the schools alone is an unrealistic answer to educating all the people or even all the children in a foreseeable future. Where few schools exist, there is little deschooling to be done. Carl Weinberg, a sociologist turned humanist-philosopher, has been caught up in the trials and tribulations of creating an alternative school—putting his money where his mouth is, so to speak.

Val D. Rust, also a comparative educator, is attuned to recent educational reforms in Europe, getting the feel for change, however, in helping to create options for undergraduates at U.C.L.A. Rodney Skager, a psychologist and specialist in evaluation, has been practicing at least some of what he preaches here in attempting to evaluate an alternative school in Los Angeles, going in to see what goes on instead of waiting to measure what comes out. Gary Fenstermacher, a philosopher, has been coping with the task of creating alternative teacher education programs, all within the framework of one university. To these experiences of my colleagues I add a little seasoning by way of having tinkered with schools in quite a few places over the past thirty years or so.

In closing these introductory remarks, let me point out an interesting phenomenon. Throughout the century, change and especially the rhetoric of change have flowed in cycles in this country, concern for the soft superseding concern for the hard, the hard then replacing the soft, and so on. Today, however, both the hard and the soft make themselves heard simultaneously.

In recent reminiscences on what most of us would agree to be a life well spent, Carl Rogers said, "In all candor I must say that I believe the humanistic view will, in the long run, take precedence." B. F. Skinner just might disagree. It is rather handy to have two such able spokesmen around to disagree at the same time in human history.

John I. Goodlad

contributors

Gary D. Fenstermacher is an assistant professor of education and director of the Teacher Education Laboratory at the Graduate School of Education, U.C.L.A. His specialization is philosophy of education; his research interests include studies of the relationship between theory and practice, logic in teaching, and teacher education. He teaches both students preparing to be classroom teachers and those seeking advanced degrees in philosophy of education.

John I. Goodlad is professor and dean, Graduate School of Education, U.C.L.A., and director of research, Institute for Development of Educational Activities, Inc. He has been active in both research and innovation in this country and abroad, his most recent work concentrating on the change process in education. He is a charter member of the National Academy of Education and a past president of the American Educational Research Association.

Thomas J. La Belle is associate professor of education and assistant dean for research in the Graduate School of Education at U.C.L.A. He coordinates a five-year research program through the Latin American Center at U.C.L.A. on the analysis of alternatives to formal schools in Latin America. He is currently conducting research on nonformal education in Latin America.

Val D. Rust is an associate professor of comparative and international education and a faculty member of the Teacher Education Laboratory at U.C.L.A.

Rodney Skager is an associate professor of education in the Graduate School of Education at U.C.L.A. and director of the Program
for Research on Objectives-Based Evaluation at the Center for the
Study of Evaluation, a unit of the School funded through the National Institute of Education. The primary mission of the Center is
to contribute to the development of improved evaluation practices,
tools, and training materials. Professor Skager also serves as evaluation consultant to a variety of educational projects at the federal
and local levels.

Carl Weinberg is an associate professor in the Graduate School of
Education at U.C.L.A. He is attached to the philosophy of education specialization with an emphasis on educational humanistics.
(Humanistics involves the analysis of human values and definitions
of human beings that are implicit in educational theories and practices.) Besides writing about alternatives, he has helped to start a
school in Los Angeles based upon humanistic structures.

part i
perspectives

Our intent in the six chapters of Part I is to place the present interest in and drive toward alternatives in a broader perspective than marks most contemporary dialogue. Recently, much of the rhetoric equates "alternatives in education" with open classrooms, alternative schools, and free schools. But the canvas is much broader. It includes movement toward a variety of options within more traditional conceptions of schooling; programs or schools essentially freed from many traditional conceptions and restraints; and a variety of formal and informal educational enterprises having little or nothing to do with schools. Some schools that describe their programs as a return to the three R's also label themselves as alternative to modern "soft" pedagogy. It is clear that alternatives in education mean and include many different things.

Part of the perspective we seek to provide, then, pertains to this range of possible alternatives and meanings. We address, in addition, the common tendency to divorce what goes on in education and especially in schools from society as a whole. Society provides most of the contingencies motivating change and many of the restraints—especially in the realm of the more radical alternatives. A historical perspective reminds us not only of this fact but also that many present-day alternatives are but old ones revisited. For example, the so-called integrated day, much lauded by reformers in early schooling, was advocated by John Dewey and practiced in his laboratory school.

One of the most powerful restraints on actually implementing alternatives has been evaluation procedures linked to conventional goals. New practices have had to stand the test of evaluation geared to favor traditional ends and means. Serious interest in alternatives in education calls for serious consideration of alternatives in evaluation.

Part of our concluding perspective notes that today's alterna-

tives most likely will be tomorrow's conventions. This is partly because advocates of specific changes usually emphasize the countervailing rather than the optional character of what they propose.
Their rhetoric ultimately excludes other alternatives; what might
have begun as an option becomes "the" way. For options to have
broad impact, they usually must be institutionalized. But time and
the nature of social institutions ultimately tend to mold what was
initially deviant into convention. Those who would seek to change
institutions should understand this and other elements of their character. We have more to say about such matters in Part II.

a typology of educational alternatives

john i. goodlad

Education is a process through which behavior—ways of thinking, feeling, and acting—changes or is modified over time. (Some would say that feeling is a special kind of thinking but I shall not join this issue here.) Definitions almost invariably stress growth or expansion, processes requiring time. Consequently, any discussion of education must encompass the formulation of characteristic or dispositional behavior and the circumstances most likely to produce it. A formal curriculum or course of study may or may not be a part of the learning environment.

Usually, the educative process simply modifies emerging characteristics, but sometimes it completely replaces established ways of behaving or adds new behaviors to the existing array. There are, potentially, so many ways of behaving and of changing behavior that alternative ends and means for education are virtually limitless. For the welfare of individuals and humankind, it is important to keep the options open. When access to choices people see as desirable, for whatever reasons, begins to close down too tightly, the drive to

3

keep them open tends to intensify. Sometimes, new alternatives open up in the process. However, most efforts to create alternatives are post hoc responses to the perception that freedom of choice has become restricted.

Of course, access is not the only issue to be considered, as La Belle's paper will make clear. Another issue is whether existing alternatives are relevant to the needs and interests of the people. And then there is the question of efficiency, especially relative costs. Many recent innovations in schools in the United States, for example, are not appropriate for developing countries either because they are too expensive to maintain or because they are not addressed to educating more people at less cost (Coombs, 1968).

freedom is the issue

This chapter focuses primarily on the retention, restoration, and expansion of individual freedom to learn. Much recent rhetoric on openness, free schools, no schools, and the like takes this issue as its theme. This emphasis is understandable in light of the extent to which most schools seriously limit options and perpetuate certain inequities of a class-oriented society. Paul Goodman, John Holt, Edgar Friedenberg, Jonathan Kozol, Ivan Illich, and others have spoken eloquently to these realities. (Their names and their works are now too well known to require references.) In effect, they have given us new glasses with which to see at least a little way through the cultural smog surrounding us.

In another context, Norman Cousins (1973) states, "Human societies have gone into decline not because people were indifferent to dangers but because they were oblivious to signs." The erosion or limitation of personal freedom in education appears to bear a rather direct relationship to the requirement that large numbers of people learn what others have decided will be good for them and that a majority of these accept this situation as desirable or at least resign themselves to it. The so-called romantic and radical reformers see educational institutions as embodying this combination of conditions and as villainous accomplices in a continuing restriction of educational freedom—and, in fact, of freedom defined more broadly. Most are impatient with educational alternatives conceived only as better ways for schools at all levels to perform a narrow range of traditional functions, and, when pushed philosophically, they accept as legitimate only those processes and resources that help people learn what they want to find out (Holt, 1973). Since the discussion of alternatives today includes reconstruction of the schools as well as their elimination and the creation of other possibilities, this chapter deals with both.

Any consideration of individual freedom is dangerously incomplete, however, unless one is very careful to include the matter of collective or humankind freedom. Much of the individual-oriented agitation of the 1960s was a reaction to perceived overemphasis on manipulating motivation and shaping behavior through reinforcement mechanisms rather than a clear affirmation and articulation of alternatives. The critics stung like scorpions and then appeared to be husbanding their energies for the next attack. More thoughtfully argued proposals for change are now making their appearance, most of whose authors were not the most vocal critics. He who knocks the city down is not necessarily the best one to reconstruct it.

As an aside, one wonders whether our schools were victims of their own success. Following World War II, there was the to be expected return to valuing the individual, a reaction to sacrificing oneself for one's country. Emphasis on group dynamics techniques, forerunners of sensitivity training, was marked in the late 1940s and early 1950s, to be followed by emphasis on individual differences, individual problem solving, and creativity in the late 1950s and early 1960s.

Even if not much of this entered the schoolhouse (Goodlad, Klein, and Associates, 1974), the rhetoric was pronounced and eloquent; teachers were saturated with it and even practiced some of the techniques at their conferences. It is possible that their students picked it up and believed in it. Symbols, especially language, are powerful modifiers of behavior. The students may have learned well—may have been quite carefully taught, in fact—and so came to see the discrepancy between practice and rhetoric, not only in the schools but in the whole of society. They saw social engineering only as a liability and used the most available means, protest, to vent their feelings. As they were given little opportunity to participate in constructive change, much of the students' potential energy for reform was lost. Some of it went into efforts to recapture an imagined past or into various avenues of self-indulgent, often self-destructive, quick gratification. Our schools may have provided a superb half-education.

The other half has to do with the rights and welfare of peers, the aged, the unborn, neighbors, neighborhoods, fellow citizens, communities, the globe, humankind. Futurists have serious doubts about the welfare of all of these, and therefore of the individual, if the future is not planned or, if you will, shaped. And if the future is to be shaped, does this not mean that the individual must help shape it and in the process be shaped by it? Does this, in turn, imply that the welfare of the individual must be subjected to the welfare of all and thus, probably, to the direction of "leaders"? And that in order to prepare for future shaping an early stage of life must be instrumental to a later, the child a disciplined, platonic father to the man? Or is some kind of balance possible, a house with many mansions here on earth, where all may enter and enjoy individual freedom and dignity?

Clearly, the issues are as old as human history. Demand for alternatives seems to heighten as society suffers from what appears to be excessive concern for individual welfare on one hand or group welfare on the other. Progress often seems to be the residue of a balanced concern resulting from successive periods of excess. And an ahistorical approach is almost essential to the success of excess. Val D. Rust's backward look at alternatives in education (see Chapter 6) is not likely to become required reading for the disciples of educational revolutionaries.

visions and utopias

The classic issue of individual versus humankind welfare is nicely set in contemporary perspective by Bereiter and Skinner (who are, however, much closer together than the following quotes suggest, if my interpretation of the works from which the quotations are taken is correct). Bereiter (1972, p. 27): "To exert intentional influence on the course of children's development is to determine, in part, what kinds of people they turn out to be. It is to create human beings. It is, therefore, to play God. Method has nothing to do with it." And then (p. 25): "The God-like role of teachers in setting goals for the development of children is no longer morally tenable." Skinner (1971, p. 167): "The intentional design of a culture and the control of human behavior it implies are essential if the human species is to continue to develop." And (p. 160): "The issue is often formulated by asking: Who is to control? And the question is usually raised as if the answer were necessarily threatening. To prevent the misuse of controlling power, however, we must look not at the controller himself but at the contingencies under which he engages in control."

A mixed chorus of voices—legislators, curriculum makers, parents, school board members—would rise in outrage over Bereiter's contention that setting educational goals for children is immoral. (He even questions education as a viable, moral alternative and thus takes us beyond the issue of alternatives *in* education.) In fact, many would charge immorality *if adults failed to set objectives.* Skinner's *Beyond Freedom and Dignity,* by contrast, implies that stopping with individual freedom and dignity is immoral. Society needs to shape an environment which reinforces and, in fact, assures individual behavior conditioned to respect the freedom and dignity of all.

At this point, Bereiter (p. 37) joins Skinner: "Instead of trying to remake deviant people into socially acceptable people, try to alter conditions so that it is more advantageous to behave in a socially desirable manner than not to." Although in so stating, Bereiter adopts essentially a behavioristic approach, perhaps it will not prove disagreeable to the humanists, primarily because he omits controllers (who could be teachers). Many never seriously get into Skinner as a Utopian visionary because they are turned off quickly by their own visions of a person who claims authority over moral behavioral conditioning.

Perhaps this problem with Skinner mirrors our dilemma in trying to project alternatives that are more than attempts, in Fantini's words (1973, p. 15), "to improve a uniform nineteenth-century institution" yet do not become misguided opportunities for unbridled individual license. Our projections too often provide only exaggerated extensions of positions designed to countervail alternative excesses, not alternatives having broad appeal, if only because they protect against the excesses we have known. Consequently, one is inclined to say, when confronted simultaneously with neo-humanistic and neobehavioristic visions (to oversimplify competing positions with labels), "a plague on both your houses." Keniston's words (1965, pp. 3-7) provide the exclamation mark:

> As thinkers, Americans rarely if ever now attempt to construct an imaginary society better than that in which they

live; and at the same time, the faith that our society is in some sense a Utopia has surely disappeared. . . . But if we define Utopia as any attempt to make imaginatively concrete the possibilities of the future, Utopias have not in our own day ceased to exist, but have merely been transvalued. . . . Our visions of the future have shifted from images of hope to vistas of despair; Utopias have become warnings, not beacons. Huxley's *Brave New World,* Orwell's *1984* and *Animal Farm,* Young's *The Rise of the Meritocracy,* and ironically even Skinner's *Walden Two*—the vast majority of our serious visions of the future are negative visions, extensions of the most pernicious trends of the present.

Nonetheless, there are some attractive or at least encouraging visions. The logistics for attaining them are much less apparent. Despair arises out of wondering whether the best visions will grasp enough people soon enough, whether enough people will be motivated sufficiently to strive, or, if you will, whether powerful cultural contingencies can be induced quickly enough. For what? The attainment of our visions? Yes and no. Undoubtedly, any vision will change in our pursuit of it. Happiness? Probably not. Happiness is a very personal thing hoped for in Utopias but not assured by them. Happiness in pursuit? Perhaps.

Unfortunately, Utopias do not come on full blown. They must be worked toward, with all the personal trait development and self-discipline this implies. One may call this effort "creating environmental contingencies," if one wishes, but so saying does not change the fact that the desired, positive reinforcers may be in short supply during early, primitive stages of an evolutionary process. Even Rousseau's Julie in *The New Héloise* imposes some rules of conduct on her children during their early education. Then, if our Utopias are themselves to be evolving, requiring both commitment and individual growth, we come back full cycle to our initial definition of education, now extended to include groups of individuals—in fact, the whole of humankind. Of course, only individuals can be educated, in any meaningful sense, although inheriting in the process the whole history of the human race—indeed, as Teilhard de Chardin declares (1961), a share of the cosmos.

Our Utopia seems to become, then, a learning society supporting learning individuals. Hutchins (1968, pp. 134-135) defined it as one that had transformed its values in such a way that learning, fulfillment, becoming human, had become its aims *and all its institutions were directed to this end*. This is what the Athenians did . . . . They made their society one designed to bring all its members to the fullest development of their highest powers . . . . Education was not a segregated activity, conducted for certain hours, in certain places, at a certain time of life. It was the aim of the society . . . . The Athenian was educated by the culture, by paideia.

Hutchins's concept of the learning society embraces at once both what goes on as institutions seek to fulfill the educational functions assumed by them and what should go on in a society concerned with education as a way of life. The concept opens up the search for alternatives in education as being more important than the search for new modes of travel, heating, and entertainment. It even opens up the search, through educational processes, for alternative images of humankind, such as man as part of an ecological system rather than as exploiter of an environment from which he is somehow detached (Stanford Research Institute, 1973).

Another possibility is an evolutionary transformational process that is not just a linear extrapolation from existing societal trends—about which Toffler (1970) warns us in *Future Shock*—but a marked departure from them (as Toffler suggests for survival and growth). Hutchins's concept suggests that doing better what we are now doing in schools falls far short of the mark. It also brings to mind the old cliché that education is too important to leave to the educators—at least those now caught up in Ichabod Crane roles as keepers of America's schools. Such a concept also reminds us, soberly, of how threatening education properly conceived is to those in our midst who would keep educators stereotyped as Ichabod Crane. More than the educators, they know the power of education and are aware, intuitively perhaps, that properly conceived and conducted it is the most powerful tool for democratization ever conceived.

the morality of alternatives

The central educational issues in providing alternatives can be subsumed under two classical questions: (1) For what shall we educate? (2) How shall we educate? The significance of both has been at least implicit in the foregoing. This chapter now proceeds to a kind of typology of alternatives in education. First, however, a further word on the "how" is in order, the central issue here being the one raised in the quotes from Bereiter and Skinner.

The issue is a moral one. I assume that attaining a learning society requires the commitment of a substantial number of citizens to it. They understand and value it; they are fully aware of its importance to their own individuality and the welfare of humankind. Presumably, their own development has provided a means of transcending self to embrace others and of transcending society to become autonomous. Presumably, such dual transcendence is both learnable and educable. Is a philosophy of learning adequate that embraces as legitimate only those processes and resources that help people learn what they want to find out? Are there phases of life during which such transcendence is more easily achieved? Is it fair to the individual not to intervene at such times, even when he or she senses no need for such learning and has no awareness of its significance?

Up until the preceding paragraph, I had endeavored to keep out of part of the issue raised by Bereiter—namely, whether it is moral to do anything to anyone else in the name of education (that is, to educate). Now it becomes essential to take a position, and my position is that both learning and being educated are necessary at this time—and into an indefinite but not necessarily infinite future. I am not ruling out the possibility of a learning society's bringing "all of its members to the fullest development of their highest powers." But that society is not now here. To deprive one of "being taught," therefore, may be as immoral as to impose one's will on another. In effect, I accept education as a moral alternative, and consequently, method has a great deal to do with it, and alternative ends and means become exceedingly important.

With Frankena (1972, p. 396), I rule out one common set of alternatives: indoctrination or "the use of example, habituation, suggestion, exhortation, propaganda, and sanctions like blame and punishment in such a way as to inculcate certain rules or virtues and with the purpose of insuring behavior in conformity with them, not of preparing the way for reflection and spiritual freedom." With Frankena (p. 395), I endorse "a more properly educational way" of "promoting the achievement of reflective, personal autonomy, self-government, or spiritual freedom, even if this leads the individual to criticize prevailing ideals, principles, or rules (in a way, this aim has two parts: autonomy and reflectiveness)." I accept education as a moral alternative and regard alternatives in education, both ends and means, as a priceless freedom.

forwarding and supporting options

The ideal circumstance for continuously modifying one's dispositional ways of thinking, feeling, and acting is a direct interface between oneself and opportunities for such modification. The simplicity of this observation quickly disappears, however, the moment the word "desirable" is interjected. It can be and is interjected commonly with respect to "desirable" ways of thinking, feeling, and acting (goals for the individual); preferred processes (with desirable usually meaning efficient); and better opportunities (with desirable meaning relevant). And so we are right back into our central issue: Are such interjections (and, therefore, by implication, interventions) moral?

Whether or not they are, we must pay some attention to what people in communities or societies do. They endeavor to legitimate aspects of the interface. This is a political-social process by which individuals and groups seek to move their particular interests through the political structure so as to affect the array of choices available at any time. Power in the form of money, prestige, connections, and personal charisma usually thrusts one option ahead of the others. Similarly, considerations of practicality or efficiency cause one to flourish and another to wither. Thus, posing and forwarding an alternative may result in no more or even fewer options. When one option is thrust aside by another of no demonstrated greater validity, the outcome is akin to censorship.

There appear to be at least three major societal approaches to ordering this process of forwarding and supporting alternatives. One is societal abdication of all such censorship roles and functions. Another is virtually the opposite: a single alternative, modified to some degree for individual conditions, is endorsed and maintained by controlling agencies on behalf of a sanctioning body or a promulgated ideology to assure the "cultural essentials" for all. The third is the widest possible promulgation of options satisfying criteria pertaining to several alternative images of humankind.

At this point in history, the first is an "academic" alternative, worthy of discussion and Utopian conceptualizations. At its best, it is the learning society referred to earlier. At its worst, it is a jungle populated by unscrupulous hawkers seeking to impose their wares on the ignorant and then to enfeeble critical powers through the certainty of cult. Power pushes aside many of the options. In the United States, hucksterism limits the television options; creating noncommercial alternatives is an uphill battle. In Israel, with one channel and limited viewing hours, someone or some small group decides between "Sesame Street" and "Ironside." The option to leave the set turned off remains but resisting the young child's plea to stay up to 8:00 p.m. one night per week for "Ironside" is not easy. Would "Sesame Street" be better? Who decides? Is the opportunity to leave the set off freedom of opportunity (to learn)? Is refusal to modify individual behavior more or less moral than leaving environmental contingencies the way they are—that is, not denying support to some, not providing support for others, and not creating new ones?

The second is a somewhat academic alternative, too. Societies simply are not successful in holding exclusively to *one* ideology. Success begets failure; affluence is a monumental threat; national pride in accomplishment seeks new worlds to conquer, and exposure to them promotes adulteration; the celebration of success suggests atrophy, and zealots foment revolution. Human beings have a way of defeating or altering the circumstances. The *kibbutz* which employs people to operate its plastics factory is a far cry from the early commune, and only a few *kibbutznicks* would want to turn the clock back—mostly only those who were not part of the evolution.

No, human beings seem to want to order their lives and events, whether by reaffirming or reinterpreting principles of faith and how to live by them or by imaging their destiny or the nature of man and devising criteria to live by. In so doing, the individual is part of the process. Herein lies an important principle: freedom to create options is as necessary as freedom of access to the options available. The importance of participating in the evolution of oneself and one's society causes the third alternative to have powerful appeal. The truly compelling Utopia is one in which the contingencies bespeak and foster the pursuit of Utopias.

the classification of goals and methods

It would appear necessary, then, in the name of freedom, to keep all three possibilities open. The search for *the* approach is not ruled out, but it is the search that is important. The goal must remain elusive. In education, there appear to be four classifications of practice and potential practice:

1. common ends and common means
2. common ends and alternative means
3. alternative ends and alternative means
4. self-selected, open ends and means, including the freedom of not deliberately choosing.

The total array of educational resources and decisions, in turn, may be classified (Goodlad, 1966) as *instructional* (tutors, teachers, books, responsive machines, for example), *institutional* (institutions whose primary function is designated as education), and *societal* (aspects of living having potential for serving an educational function). This kind of classification gets us around the problem of drawing a line between schooling and education, since education is a process and a function which can go on at many times, in many ways and places, including schools. It also avoids some invidious problems of stereotyping and judging by association. Thus, teachers in public schools are, by some strange processes of stereotyping, considered less humane than teachers in private homes, ski instructors, and the like. Similarly, schools are deemed malignant while homes and job-related educational activities are benign—notwithstanding the high incidence of parents beating and mutilating their children and the need for child labor laws. These are matters frequently passed over far too lightly by some of our romantic reformers.

If one opts truly for openness (Anderson, 1973) in regard to alternatives, the two-dimensional grid implied above takes us somewhat away from popular either-or distinctions, as well as away from the error, noted earlier, of judging, for example, "free" schools as necessarily and logically more humane than the little red schoolhouse of yesterday or P.S. 2002. Leondar (1971, pp. 14-15) speaks feelingly of life in so-called counterschools she visited:

> Whether for the sake of principle or necessity, counterschools often promote a relentless sociability. Where this produces openness, tolerance and cooperative enterprise, it can scarcely be faulted. But just as often it operates to deny privacy, silence and sustained purpose. Or if not denied, these luxuries must be protected by a system of rules no less onerous for being self-imposed.

Figure 1 presents the grid, with the cells a *tabula rasa*. Filling them in is a task of monumental proportions going far beyond the dimensions of this paper. Literally dozens of items could go in most of the cells except those under "common ends, common means." The possibilities for varying the *what, who, where, how,* and *when* of education are virtually limitless. Even when the educational system promulgates a single set of ends and means, societal decisions about *who* is to be educated *when* sharply restrict or considerably expand the options. In developed countries, the vastly greater expenditures per student for tertiary over primary education represent an interesting value choice. Pervading alternatives of substance, place, and time are the philosophical aspects of *how*.

Alternative Groupings of Alternatives in Education	Instructional	Institutional	Societal
Common Ends, Common Means			
Common Ends, Alternative Means			
Alternative Ends, Alternative Means			
Self-Selected, Open Ends and Means			

Figure 1. Two-Dimensional Grid for Classifying Educational Alternatives

There are proper and improper educational means in the human sense. Schools that foster or permit the tyranny of older children over the younger have lost their way, whether or not "free"; just as surely have schools whose mechanistic, straight-line reinforcement techniques contribute equally to cheating and reading skills, whatever their results in achievement scores. Similarly, the teaching of literature is no more humane than the teaching of physics simply because one is classified under the humanities and the other under the natural sciences.

common ends, common means

One cannot speak of common ends and common means except in an approximate or relative sense; there is no such thing. In a society committed to the inculcation of cultural imperatives in the young, even prodigious efforts to specify substance and praxis (there are countries with syllabi spelling out in detail precisely how daily instruction is to be conducted) are modified, distorted, and changed by vagaries of pupil mix and teacher personality. And so it is even with the chosen tribal functionary and the group of boys he inducts into the privileges and responsibilities of manhood.

The alternatives built into a common ends-common means concept of education tend to be of an either-or sort. In the classroom, there are pass-fail marks (or more differentiated systems such as A, B, C, D, F) and promote-nonpromote decisions with respect to moving through the system. For the institution as a whole, it is "out" or "in," a decision often made early, followed by a waiting game until age 14, 15, or 16 (depending on school-leaving laws). For society as a whole, the alternatives are the determination of when to begin (usually with more alternatives for the affluent), when to leave, and a sorting process regarding eligibility for subsequent noncompulsory segments of secondary and tertiary education. Motivation for going on is maintained by requiring educational credentials for entry into the economic system.

The maintenance of a schooling system with such limited alternatives, many of them punitive, seems to require a good deal of accompanying baggage directed to rationalization, justification, legitimation, and the like. Testing systems develop, and external examinations hang on long after considerable opposition to them has arisen. These frequently are used as weapons against innovation. When an innovation is suggested, there is a sudden interest in what research (based on test results) has to say about it, even before it has been tried. But there is a corresponding lack of interest in research questioning the system: for example, research on the effects of failing marks and nonpromotion. The dissemination of such information is offset by increasing rhetoric regarding the dangers of "soft" education and the need to protect a common cultural heritage (even when it is by no means common!). In effect, when the system is threatened, the ceremonial rain dances pick up speed.

In the United States, we are experiencing a fascinating inten-
sification of these rain dances. It will not be the last hurrah before
the myths collapse but the increasingly elaborate paraphernalia required to maintain some of them assure their ultimate demise. One
such set of paraphernalia is represented by those aspects of the accountability movement which simply shift responsibility for the
system's Procrustean character from pupils or students to teachers.
The primitive carrot-and-stick psychology which proved virtually
useless in adjusting children to the system is now being applied, at
great cost, to their teachers.

When we put together such a concept of accountability with
performance-based teacher education, we have a rather elegant
piece of rational bureaucratic folly. The rationality is the notion of
holding teachers responsible for stating and achieving their objectives (presumably derived from the common ends of the system),
identifying their successful behaviors, and then teaching these behaviors to future teachers. The folly was stated conversely long ago
by Aristotle when he cautioned that it is the wise man who knows
the degree of rigor to apply to the circumstances. The interlocking
system called for implies a predictive, scientific, or theoretical base.
No such base exists; in fact, we are not even close to establishing
one. Studies on the differential effects of various methods of teaching reading, for example, have not established one method clearly
over another. Even when much time and money are spent in introducing an alternative approach, the differences in pupil achievement
are minuscule. What are teachers to do, then, when shown the low
reading scores of their pupils?

The admonition is to learn this or that currently popular set
of performance skills. Not being as deviant as one might wish (perhaps selection already has assured a certain conformity and adaptation in most teachers and, if not, the press of the school system
will), most teachers dutifully learn what is required of them. If the
new skill were simply one more string to the pedagogical bow, this
learning probably would be desirable. However, the cant and rhetoric of the current fad encourage either-or (not both-and) approaches
to improvement, reinforcing one alternative over the others.

An inquiry into the time and money spent on activities conducted in the name of accountability by school districts and their
personnel under the combined goading of rhetoric and legislative
acts is dismaying. But quite apart from reservations one might have

about these face-validity cost data, the moral question nags. Is it moral to use teacher time in this approach to accountability? Is this the way teachers would want to go, and is this the way teachers would want to use resources if given freedom of choice? The moral question aside, it is difficult to see sense and reason behind an approach to accountability which makes teachers responsible yet restricts (if only by exhortation) the alternatives they may employ. In effect, responsibility is assigned at one point but authority reserved for another (a neat way, perhaps, for those retaining the authority to sidestep the Peter Principle). It is a sad commentary that in such a field of uncertainty we seek laws to force conformity and to create an aura of certainty when, in fact, none exists. This is one form of censorship, a little more subtle than most.

common ends, alternative means

Most reform efforts in this century, and especially during the past two decades, have been directed toward finding alternative (hopefully, better) ways of achieving a set of educational aims deemed essential for all. Proposals have far exceeded trials or implementation. The literature on these alternatives is so extensive and so well known to most readers of educational journals that there is no point in citing sample references. Likewise, most of the ideas and forms are sufficiently well known to negate the need for definition and description.

Instructional alternatives include programmed instruction through books, nonresponsive machines and responsive machines such as computerized television consoles; pedagogical approaches such as problem-solving techniques, small group instruction, individual pupil diagnosis and prescription and multimedia presentations; and an array of individualized alternatives for pupils requiring very little or no teacher intervention. Institutional alternatives include simultaneous operation of several distinctly different models of curriculum organization (single-subject structures, integrated subjects, activity oriented to student interests, and so on); introduction of multigrade, multiage, and nongraded patterns of school organization; various ways of grouping pupils or teachers or both, including team teaching; use of modular scheduling or less complicated variations in length of class periods, timing of recess and lunch periods. Societal and systemwide alternatives have included experimentation with greater decentralization of authority and resources; creation of out-of-school activities; performance contracts with educational consulting firms; and even so-called alternative schools freed of systemwide requirements regarding means.

All of these fit into one or more of just a few basic kinds of manipulations: varying time available for learning (by mastery learning and nongrading, for example), varying place (leaving the school for some educational purposes), varying pupil mix (pupil grouping), varying teachers (team teaching), varying external restraints (decentralization), varying approach or style of learning (changing teaching methods). Many of these have now become rather standard ways of proceeding. Several have become *the* standard way in some schools, thrusting aside what was there before and thus replacing monolithic practice with monolithic practice.

Those innovations which have been most successful in gaining acceptance are the ones requiring only minor deviations from long-established practices or those most readily modified and homogenized so as to be palatable. The most acceptable innovations are those requiring little or no modification in teacher and administrative behavior. In effect, they are not changes at all. Nothing changes but the appearance of change (Sarason, 1971). Very often, the innovation as conceived is powerful enough but its significant elements are lost in a process of smoothing out the potentially indigestible lumps—a process of immaculate adoption. As one superintendent remarked to principals and teachers, "Innovate all you want but don't change anything."

The desirability, validity, and morality of unresearched alternatives are as relevant to this discussion as to the previous one regarding common ends and means. Is not the absence of research support here as much of an indictment as their absence in the previous discussion? The answer is "no." In order to secure relevant data on the relative effects of alternatives, we need alternatives. These need care and feeding until they are strong enough to warrant comparison—and then on criteria relevant to both the new and the old. (Usually, the new must stand the test of criteria relevant only to the latter.) What I was objecting to earlier is legislative or administrative fiat designed to legitimate one practice over another as though there were, indeed, unequivocal evidence to support it.

But how can the promulgation of unproven alternatives be defended? The answer lies in eschewing enforcement of their use by

laws and various mechanisms designed to punish for nonconformity or to reward for conformity. We are back to freedom again. It is one thing to insist on single practices for teachers when there is powerful evidence for them, quite another to prescribe by law or protect by fiat when no such support exists. In a field of human endeavor lacking such evidence in almost all areas, it is the better part of wisdom to create alternatives, publish their strengths and weaknesses for various purposes, and encourage teachers to use whatever seems to work best under the circumstances.

Teachers, like other human beings, tend to respond positively to such a challenge, especially when they have nonthreatening opportunities to learn, to exchange ideas with colleagues, and to advance professionally as a result (Bentzen and Tye, 1973). Encouraging the use of alternatives should be accompanied, of course, by sustained study of their effects in both experimentally controlled and field situations, research far in excess of anything we have known to date.

Despite some rather exciting reforms of curriculum, organization, and instruction, the common ends-common means orientation to formal education hangs in there tenaciously. Maintaining this system of education protects many elements of stratification and segregation in our society. Planned change is, at best, difficult. But when problems of logistics are complicated by the implications and consequences of threatening what exists, which is always the case, effecting change becomes no way of life for the inept or faint-of-heart.

alternative ends, alternative means

Although the implementation of alternative means regarding the what, how, where, who, and when of education has been disappointing, the importance of and need for innovation are broadly accepted. The moment one introduces the concept of alternative ends, however, debate quickens. Fears range from concern that "the tools of the human race" will not be taught to apprehension about the promulgation of ideologies threatening to "the national interest." Much of the controversy centers on how much choice shall be available to individuals at various stages in the educational or life cycle.

In current practice, a picture of educational freedom might

resemble an inverted triangle, narrow or limited at the bottom and broadening as one progresses upward in time. Generally, the goals are common for all at the primary level; one may explore a few options at the secondary level; and selection of scientific, aesthetic, or literary goals is more or less open at the tertiary level. This is not a steady, even progression, however. In general, kindergarten offers more alternatives than the second grade (Goodlad, Klein, and Associates, 1974); for most students, the senior year in high school is more open than the freshman year of college; and, although choice of a profession is open to many college graduates, professional education itself is usually sharply prescribed. Nonetheless, the system operates on the general assumption that increasing freedom of choice is a right earned through earlier mastery of a narrow range of core goals.

Regarding these core goals Hutchins (1972, pp. 210, 211) has the following to say:

> The barbarism "communication skills" is the contemporary jargon for reading, writing, figuring, speaking, and listening— arts that appear to have permanent relevance . . . . They are the indispensable means to learning anything. They have to be learned if the individual hopes to expand his individuality, or if he proposes to become a self-governing member of a self-governing community. Learning these arts cannot be left to the choices of children or their parents.

This position is a far cry from that of viewing as legitimate only those processes and resources that help people learn what they want to find out. It is the common position in this country and in most, if not all, others.

In general, the drive for alternate goals has had two foci: balance or emphasis and timing or placement. Today, virtually any listing of aims for American education would be encompassed by the following categories: intellectual development, enculturation, interpersonal relations, personal autonomy, citizenship, creativity, aesthetic perception, self-concept, emotional well-being, physical health, and moral and ethical character. Free schools, alternative schools, and the like are created, frequently, because people perceive regular public schools as neglecting or underemphasizing several of these.

There is a great deal of controversy about whether some of

these categories are more important for one stage of personal growth than another; whether there is greater psychological readiness at one stage rather than another and, consequently, a potentially more compatible fit between teaching and learning; and whether it would be more appropriate or efficient to emphasize a few goals at a time rather than this whole range of commitment, but still touch on all of them in the course of a year or two. Such innovations as modular scheduling, single courses taught in great depth and breadth over a semester, and "schools within schools" in which students enroll for exclusive work in a field or cluster of fields for several months or even longer are directed at this last concern. Regarding the second controversial issue, Hunt (1964) and others have argued for early intervention in the cognitive development of children, especially when a disadvantaged milieu is likely to cause retardation. Thinking of this kind has resulted in a recent "educational discovery" of the young child (Goodlad, Klein, Novotney, and Associates, 1973).

In regard to the first, I have been developing a "phases" concept of schooling, in which nongraded phases of from two to four years in length overlap each other in a series of progressions from early childhood through all the years of formal schooling (Goodlad, 1967). Each phase has dominant or priority functions, each of which is derived from assumptions about the nature of the developmental-environmental interface and its implications for educational ends and means. For a decade, the University Elementary School faculty at U.C.L.A. sought to define and conduct such a phase-oriented program.

Even though educational programs based on the common ends-common means approach differ markedly from models providing differential selection of ends and means, all seem to be on a continuum from rigidity to increasing flexibility. Regardless of where a program fits on this continuum, however, it appears to retain certain conventions. We hang on to the conception of school as a place, for example, and of education being something that takes place in school buildings during certain hours. In the United States, at least, even career education generally is pursued in a school when it probably could take place better in other work settings. The final cell in the grid, self-selection of ends and means, is the first to break with this continuum as it contains more radical alternatives. Fenstermacher takes note of this in Chapter 6.

self-selected, open ends and means

Some educational innovators would argue that self-selection is an option in some of the alternatives already mentioned. One's response to this observation depends on what is meant by self-selection. Admittedly, many open and alternative schools allow and even encourage pupil choice among alternatives. Yet in nearly all instances, there remains a set of implied norms with respect to choice. For example, when a teacher says, "What shall we do today?" the intended options are drawing, dancing, reading, story-telling, or perhaps hunting for insect creatures in fields or ponds. If there were, indeed, no restrictions regarding choice, then self-selection (within the general option of school) would be operating. But most advocates of self-selection do have a set of norms in mind, norms internalized by children at an early age. Even in the schools so much lauded by reformers—namely, the British Infant Schools—the available range of alternatives quickly becomes apparent, and one is seldom surprised by radical departures. Eisner (1973) reports an absence of group discussion and planning in the schools he visited.

True self-selection of goals as well as means demands societal and institutional alternatives going far beyond the largely instructional freedom so commonly recommended by reformers in recent years. The voucher system, for example, although it appears to provide maximum freedom of choice to parents and their children, really allows them to choose only among places still bound by the conventions of schooling referred to above—and this choice, in turn, is sharply defined geographically for most people. A major argument for the voucher system is that it will encourage innovation through free enterprise. There is little or no evidence to support this assumption for education (and one must even question its validity for aspects of business and industry—witness, for example, the rigidity of the automobile industry in this country). Our private schools are not markedly deviant. Private nursery schools are about as free as one could conceive schools to be, and yet they resemble each other and public nursery schools very closely (Goodlad, Klein, Novotney, and Associates, 1973).

We will approach a situation of true self-selection when one may choose among options (which might or might not include schools) whether or not they offer a core of "cultural essentials." This means that school in any form no longer would be compulsory. Likewise, none of the options would be supported by special sets of coercive contingencies. But such a situation must not be confused with freedom, because the available range of options still might not parallel the range of human needs and interests. Presumably society would move toward such a fit, however. Nonetheless, this would not satisfy those who, with Hutchins, believe that the choice of learning those indispensable arts of the human race is too important to leave to children or their parents. Skinner most certainly would want to include in the learning society those contingencies most likely to assure the learning of those arts at the propitious time.

Realization of a society supporting self-selection of ends and means would require a radical change in the role of schools. Futurists usually speak of two possibilities. One is a narrow, sharply delineated program for teaching the fundamentals of reading and writing (Hutchins's indispensable arts) for a relatively short part of the total time spent in educational activity. Those in this camp usually lean toward the use of behavior modification to assure efficient learning.

The other alternative is essentially a fusion of schooling with education—school becomes a concept rather than a place. There could be, indeed, places resembling classrooms where various kinds of dialogues and small group activities would go on, but the community (in fact, society) constitutes the learning milieu. Interestingly, in utilizing the city as a school and viewing everyone in the city as a potential teacher, Rusch still found the typical classroom to be the best place for some forms of education (Biederman, 1972). By cutting ourselves away from schools experimentally, we may discover those elements worth including in a learning society.

summation

Figure 2 summarizes the preceding discussion regarding ends and means, with several examples in each cell. This typology is admittedly arbitrary. The distinction between institutional and societal is not always precise, for instance, largely because there is no clear-cut delineation in our society as to what should be left to local, institutional autonomy and what decisions should be retained by centralized, controlling agencies (Goodlad, 1966). Likewise, an innovation such as nongrading could be placed in three of the four

Alternative Groupings of Alternatives in Education	Instructional	Institutional	Societal
Common Ends, Common Means	intraclass ability and achievement grouping; promotion or nonpromotion; marking systems	interclass ability and achievement grouping; suspension and expulsion criteria and procedures	ages for entering and leaving; matriculation requirements
Common Ends, Alternative Means	individualized and small group instruction; variety of learning modes; programmed instruction; mastery learning	team teaching; nongrading; multiage grouping; modular scheduling; variable patterns of curriculum organization	decentralization of decision-making; out-of-school options; performance contracts; alternative schools; curriculum guides suggesting varied approaches
Alternative Ends, Alternative Means	organization of learning groups around expressed interests; selection from an array of individualized stimuli (for example, programmed instruction in literature rather than math)	phases approach; successive emphases, geared first to one set of goals and then another; schools within a school; partial voucher plans	free schools; voucher plans; some alternative schools; easing up of requirements for entering tertiary education or economic participation in society; public E.T.V.
Self-Selected, Open Ends and Means	no required instructional program; choice of teachers and areas of emphasis (the instructional program now becomes entirely personal)	no institutional requirements; learner does or does not take advantage of it with no fear of punishment or retribution other than personal consequences	vast variety of formal and informal institutions committed fully or partially to education; school as a place might or might not be one of these; a learning society

Figure 2. A Typological Grid of Educational Alternatives

institutional cells. Consequently, no cell should be regarded as necessarily fully discrete.

Further, it could be argued that the alternatives suggested for the common ends, common means category belong under common ends, alternative means, since no alternatives whatsoever are possible under the former. But this strict interpretation destroys the approximate intent of the analysis. Its purpose is to suggest a flow from utmost rigidity to utmost freedom in a learning society as one moves downward on the chart. Space limitations prevent further discussion here or depiction of the many more examples that could readily be entered into most of the cells.

transition

Most reform-minded observers of our educational practices, institutions, and systems come away depressed. So much of what they see is as it was when they went to elementary or secondary school. And yet, there has been change, even in so brief a time as the past fifteen or twenty years. Most of it has been in attitudes. In the early 1960s, well-known elementary educators were endeavoring to close ranks in a futile effort to stay the demise of the self-contained classroom. Today, most of them applaud open classrooms, with their teams of teachers, multiage pupil grouping, and so on. The frontiers of what are worth considering as viable alternatives have been pushed out.

The movement toward implementing alternatives is slowed by problems of logistics and a considerable ignorance regarding how to change social institutions or create new settings (Sarason, 1972). We have assumed that we know what goes on in schools and how they function but we know surprisingly little. The possibility that individuals and institutions can become self-renewing is tremendously appealing but how they are to become so remains largely a mystery. The educational agenda for the next decade or so is to translate much of what we have been saying into functioning reality. The days of entrenched resistance to the idea of more alternatives, greater openness, and increased humaneness in the conduct of education are largely behind us, despite stubborn pockets of resistance.

But another contest among ideas looms. As suggested earlier, the route from the little red schoolhouse to alternative and even free schools is linear, even if rambling and circuitous. In fact, a few free schools appear to represent a nostalgic return to the one-room school. But some proposals would make a complete break with the past many remember or have heard about from grandparents. Among them are: doing away with mandatory schooling, dispersing educational functions among an array of formal and informal institutions and media, and deschooling society. The views of Illich on this last have brought forth an impassioned response even from many persons regarded as educational reformers. The public schools recently have acquired some unexpected friends.

These ideas are threatening, even incomprehensible, to most educators and citizens in countries moving toward universal schooling. They are much less frightening to nations in which schooling still is for the few; they have little to lose. Perhaps the role schools play in this country is too recent a part of our history to withstand radical modification. Were we to do away with them, we probably would re-create them very much in the mold of the past. But if we are successful in implementing relatively soon the more modest alternatives already gaining acceptance, perhaps those more radical proposals now threatening to tear at our roots will be taken in stride in the ongoing transition to a learning society committed to educating the complete person (Faure and others, 1972).

references

Anderson, R. H. *Opting for Openness.* Washington, D.C.: National Association of Elementary School Principals, 1973.

Bentzen, M. M., and Tye, K. A. "Effecting Change in Elementary Schools." In J. I. Goodlad and H. G. Shane (Eds.), *The Elementary School in the United States*, pp. 350-379. Seventy-Second Yearbook of the National Society for the Study of Education, Part II. Chicago: University of Chicago Press, 1973.

Bereiter, C. "Moral Alternatives to Education." *Interchange*, 1972, *3*, 25-41.

Biederman, P. W. "Mobile School Uses the City as a Classroom." *Summer Reporter*, 1972, *8*, 1-2.

Coombs, P. H. *The World Educational Crisis.* New York: Oxford University Press, 1968.

Cousins, N. "Watergate and Hiroshima." *World*, 1973, *2*, 12.

Eisner, E. W. *English Primary Schools.* Stanford, Calif.: Stanford University, 1973.

Fantini, M. D. "The What, Why and Where of the Alternatives Movement." *National Elementary Principal*, 1973, *52*, 14-22.

Faure, E., and others. *Learning to Be.* Paris: UNESCO, 1972.

Frankena, W. K. "Moral Education, A Philosophical View of." *The Encyclopedia of Education.* Vol. 6. New York: Macmillan, 1972.

Goodlad, J. I., with Richter, M., Jr. *The Development of a Conceptual System for Dealing with Problems of Curriculum and Instruction.* Los Angeles, Calif.: U.C.L.A., 1966 (out of print).

Goodlad, J. I. "The Educational Program to 1980 and Beyond." In E. L. Morphet and C. O. Ryan (Eds.), *Implications for Education of Prospective Changes in Society.* Denver, Colo.: Designing Education for the Future, 1967.

Goodlad, J. I., Klein, M. F., and Associates. *Looking Behind the Classroom Door.* Revised edition. Worthington, Ohio: Charles A. Jones, 1974.

Goodlad, J. I., Klein, M. F., Novotney, J. M., and Associates. *Early Schooling in the United States.* New York: McGraw-Hill, 1973.

Holt, J. "A Letter from John Holt." *National Elementary Principal,* 1973, *52,* 43-46.

Hunt, J. M. "How Children Develop Intellectually." *Children,* 1964, *11,* 83-91.

Hutchins, R. M. *The Learning Society.* New York: Praeger, 1968.

Hutchins, R. M. "The Great Anti-School Campaign." In *The Great Ideas Today,* pp. 154-227. Chicago: Encyclopaedia Britannica, 1972.

Keniston, K. *The Uncommitted.* New York: Harcourt, Brace and World, 1965.

Leondar, B. "The Counterschool Approach." *New Leader,* 1971, *54,* 14-15.

Sarason, S. B. *The Culture of the School and the Problem of Change.* Boston: Allyn and Bacon, 1971.

Sarason, S. B. *The Creation of Settings and the Future Societies.* San Francisco: Jossey-Bass, 1972.

Skinner, B. F. *Beyond Freedom and Dignity.* New York: Random House, 1971.

Stanford Research Institute. *Changing Images of Man.* Menlo Park, Calif., 1973.

Teilhard de Chardin, Pierre. *The Phenomenon of Man.* New York: Harper & Row, 1961.

Toffler, A. *Future Shock.* New York: Random House, 1970.

cultural determinants of educational alternatives

thomas j. la belle

Following the often negative and critical appraisals of schools which characterized both the professional literature and the popular press during the late 1960s, it was perhaps inevitable that some dissatisfied educators, parents, and students in the early 1970s attempted to conceptualize and develop educational alternatives. Because of the variety of rationales, assumptions, methods, and goals inherent in this quest for alternatives, however, we need to take a broad view of the movement in its social and cultural framework. In an attempt to offer such a view and to bring together these various perspectives on alternatives, I discuss the movement in terms of three broadly conceived and inductively generated categories. These classifications are not meant to be mutually exclusive or to represent a single theoretical or methodological approach to alternatives. They are, instead, heuristic devices designed to bring some order to a rather confusing field of study and activity.

three alternative aims

The various approaches to alternatives taken by scholars, prophets, and critics during the past ten years may be divided into three general categories, according to their primary objective: (1) relevance, or educational responsiveness to human needs and problems; (2) efficiency, or fiscal responsibility; and (3) equality, or equal opportunity to gain access to societal resources and to participate in societal decision making. Although these three goals are imbued with the usual questions about educational purpose and method, their advocates tend to be characterized by particular conceptual orientations and value premises.

The educational-relevance category is perhaps best represented by alternative schools. Such schools, often known as "free schools" or "new schools," cater primarily to middle- and upper-class youngsters seeking a less structured, more individually oriented learning environment where student initiative is encouraged and humanistic studies are stressed. Other alternatives based on the relevance criterion include innovative curricular programs inside traditional schools which are designed to build on or promote continuity with the sociocultural background the student brings with him to school (such as ethnic studies, bilingual and bicultural programs); to take advantage of community resources (for example, street academies, occupational training and placement, ecological studies); and to attend to particular interests and needs of students based upon current knowledge of child growth and development. The main principle underlying these alternatives is the individualization of experiences by making them meaningful to a particular individual or population or to the resolution of a particular problem.

In the second category are those concerned with the enormous financial investment in education as it relates to both dwindling economic resources and learning outcomes in students. They argue that the worldwide crisis in available funding for education, accompanied by increased population growth and thus increased demand for schooling—along with rapidly rising teacher salaries, building costs, and other supplies and material expenses—necessitate alternatives which will be less expensive, more efficient, and more beneficial to the individual and society. The use of the mass media (including radio, television, and satellites), computer-assisted instruction, self-instructional curricular packages, educational vouchers, and administrative reorganization are some of the most common alternatives designed to increase efficiency.

The third group of alternatives is concerned with equalizing access to societal resources through education. Although some of the programs and methods mentioned above also apply to this goal, the major objective here is to address the overwhelming impact of the student's socioeconomic status on his achievement in school. Economically poor individuals tend to be at a disadvantage in relation to traditional curricular, methodological, and achievement-testing practices based on middle- and upper-class norms. Because the empirical evidence on the positive relationship between socioeconomic status and academic achievement is so profound throughout the world, the alternatives discussed in this context are often alternatives to the school rather than the substitution of one kind of school for another.

This "equalization of access" category of alternatives is the most radical of the three orientations in that it raises seriously the issue of using out-of-school resources for educational purposes and thus is closely related to "deschooling." Basically, the deschooling proponents stress the individual's freedom to pursue the learning of his choice without the institutional constraints embodied in credentials, grades, or diplomas. They encourage each person to take advantage of a wide network of learning resources available in the community through other individuals and institutions. Although one might adopt the deschooling position for a variety of objectives (such as continuous, lifelong learning), the notion of deschooling arose primarily in the context of equality of opportunity, and thus I have chosen to place it in this third category. The argument, originally presented by Ivan Illich (1971), is that schools produce and reinforce two social classes based on the amount of schooling completed, creating an educational caste system through reliance on diplomas and credentials. Thus, like the occupational marketplace, schools are viewed as reinforcing and rewarding individuals who come from middle and upper socioeconomic backgrounds while at the same time alienating and constraining those who deviate from such patterns (see, for example, Berg, 1970).

In Illich's view, reforms within the educational establishment will not suffice. In effect, he and his deschooling colleagues are raising questions about the nature of our society, specifically the social hierarchy, the system of production and consumption, and the values that support them. Thus, diminishing the importance of or eliminating schools is only one aspect of the total revamping of our culture and society advocated by the deschooling critics.

One type of alternative aimed at producing equality of access, but not likely to satisfy proponents of deschooling, is the short-term, out-of-school program that gives occupational training to people of low socioeconomic status who either have dropped out of school, have had no opportunity to go to school, or have some schooling but desire experiences which will provide skills and guarantee employment. Normally, such programs are adapted to specific needs in particular sociocultural contexts, are locally administered, and depend more on performance than on certificates or credentials. In addition, compensatory education programs such as Head Start, although basically social-pathological in orientation, attempt to provide greater equality of access and opportunity for achievement and thus might be considered "equality" alternatives.

The various alternatives I have mentioned illustrate current programmatic attempts to revamp the educational enterprise. As can be seen, some require rather far-reaching institutional reform and substitution necessitating some sociocultural change, while others are rather traditional options within schools, affordable only by those populations that have met such basic human needs as health, literacy, and housing. Besides Illich, however, only a few have gone beyond educational reform to ask profound questions about the nature of society (see, for example, Reimer, 1971).

socioeconomic influences on public demands

Alternative programs depend on what particular sectors of the population want of the educational system. The relatively higher order demands by middle- and upper-class families for humanistically oriented schools differ from the relatively basic demands for equal opportunity by lower-class families. Although presumably everyone would like to make an educational system relevant, efficient, and equitable for all sectors of the population, what satisfies one group is unlikely to be the same as what satisfies another. In other words, since the probability of finding success in school and subsequently gaining access to societal resources is considerably greater for a middle-class youngster than for a lower-class child, their educational needs and expectations are different. Thus, when educational services are planned and implemented for the total population, it would appear safe to assume that the basic human needs for food, clothing, and shelter have been met by the middle and upper classes, who therefore want optional approaches that make life as meaningful as possible. Although there is no reason to believe that lower-class people do not also desire a more meaningful life, in order to concentrate on that goal more immediate needs must first be satisfied: survival precedes humanism.

This does not mean that the relatively successful history of schools with middle- and upper-class youngsters obviates their need for alternatives. But finding alternatives to the school probably will not have high priority. Instead, attempts to refine existing schools and develop alternative schools for the middle and upper classes will continue. Thus, their educational choices will probably remain in the domain of "free schools" and "learning networks," designed either to be more humane in orientation or to provide access to knowledge for those already able to take advantage of the opportunities offered by schools. Also, these options are likely to be accompanied by renewed emphasis on reducing costs and increasing effectiveness within schools. In a sense, middle- and upper-class people, at a time when choices can be afforded in the pursuit of excellence, are and will continue to be concerned with relatively luxurious options.

Are there cultural limitations or constraints on the development of educational alternatives? If such limitations exist, how are they manifested in the conceptualization and implementation of alternatives? These questions are unanswerable in the absence of social and cultural data. When such data are available, they demonstrate that in almost any sociocultural system educational programs tend to reflect the educational norms established by the most politically and economically advantaged sectors of the population. Therefore, the amount of freedom permitted for educational experimentation by the total population depends on the attitudes of these groups. One might refer to this freedom as the sociocultural space available for innovation. Although it can be assumed that the more complex the culture, the greater the space available, the educational norms established by the most powerful sectors, irrespective of the complexity of the culture, may still dictate the nature of the programs accepted.

the components of culture

One way to assess the complexity of a given culture is to analyze the number of options available to a population in terms of technology, value orientations, and institutions. (See, for example, Honigman, 1959.) A complex culture fosters differentiation in life styles and thus in the goals and means by which individuals and groups satisfy needs and interests. This pluralism accompanying complexity may be marked by the decline or emergence of institutions, by the adoption of new or more syncretic moral and ethical standards, and by the use of a number of energy sources.

As the United States moves further into the nuclear age, the technological foundation on which production and consumption are based alters both value orientations and the types of institutions created to respond to those values. Likewise, as either values or institutions are altered, the nature of the other two components of culture undergo change. The analysis of educational alternatives must necessarily take into account these components of culture as changes in technology, values, and institutions give rise to questions about how the educational enterprise should be conducted. The role and function of educational programs, after being examined in relation to the complexity of the culture, must then be viewed in terms of the demands made by the population (relevance, efficiency, equality).

Demands for alternatives to the traditional school are multifaceted. They are a result of a combination of sociocultural changes which must be responded to in both institutional and noninstitutional ways. No single alternative will meet the requirements of the total culture since the rationales for seeking alternatives do not come from a common source. These multiple expectations, embodied in the three conceptual categories focusing on relevance, efficiency, and equality, emanate from particular subgroups in society. Thus, social institutions emerge in response to these various reference populations, which because of ideology (values), socioeconomic status (institutions), and available skills and knowledge (technology) make certain demands.

In this interface between the complexity of culture and the demands made by the population the educational planner must be able and willing to find common ground. Without compatibility between each of the multiple approaches to relevance, efficiency, and equality, on the one hand, and the complexity of culture, on the other, there is little likelihood that new educational programs will have anything but momentary existence and impact.

relevance

Examples of cultural influences shaping educational relevance are numerous. On a nation-state level, for example, the educational systems for Protestants and Catholics in Northern Ireland, for Arabs and Jews in the Middle East, and for Hindus and Moslems in Southeast Asia are considerably different and often oppose one another. In the United States, such issues as cultural identity, occupational placement, religious affiliation, and roles dictated by sex and age are value-laden and often elicit arguments about what is or is not deemed relevant in educational programs.

One way to assess these influences is to examine the schooling processes developed by ethnic minority populations within the United States. Like all educational activities, such programs are designed to provide continuity, or relevance, in cultural learning from birth to death. In other words, they try to control the external influences impinging on an individual by building on the family and extended-group value orientations so that the individual learns to identify himself primarily with only one group. The intent is to avoid any discontinuity in the maturation of an individual's values by blocking out competing influences. Although a case can be made that most public schools in the United States also promote the cultural continuity of their clients with middle and upper socioeconomic backgrounds, it is perhaps easier to identify efforts to achieve educational relevance by looking at ethnic minority populations which attempt to isolate themselves partially or completely from the remaining population. I have chosen two such examples, the Amish and the Black Muslims, to discuss in this regard.

The Amish. One of the most complete patterns of lifelong education and value continuity among minority populations in the United States exists among the Old Order Amish. The Amish, descendants of the Swiss Anabaptists, came to the United States in the late eighteenth century and settled in Pennsylvania. Today, small communities exist throughout the Midwest and Northeast. The Old Order Amish, primarily organized in church communities,

place a high value on communal obligation and the development of
a Christian character. Despite some variability in customs across
communities, the Old Order Amish are generally recognized
through their use of horsedrawn carriages, adoption of the Pennsylvania German dialect, distinctive dress and grooming, and their
complete avoidance of electricity, telephones, and automobiles. The
Amish forbid formal education beyond the elementary grades.

Hostetler and Huntington (1971, p. 4) identify five cultural
themes which distinguish the Amish and are important for understanding their socialization practices: "separatism from the world,
voluntary acceptance of high social obligations symbolized by adult
baptism, the maintenance of a disciplined church-community, practice of exclusion and shunning of transgressing members, and a life
of harmony with the soil and nature."

To solidify further the bond between the individual and the
community, the Amish run their own schools to reinforce and guarantee "the cultivation of humility, simple living, and resignation to
the will of God" (Hostetler and Huntington, 1971). The Amish establish schools within each community so that the children can
mature in an agricultural environment and assist with farming
chores. Each community selects one of its members, committed to
Amish values, to act as teacher. They reject outside schools and cre-
dentialed teachers because they wish to prepare their children to
live in the church-community, which does not recognize worldly,
external criteria of success. Amish children aspire to occupations
needed by the community. Through providing opportunities for
work within the community, the culture is reinforced and the educational process prepares children for a secure and predictable future.

The Muslims. A second subgroup with unique educational
goals is the Black Muslim community. Although somewhat less integrated and isolated than the Amish, this separatist religious organization, based on the teachings of Islam, has distinctive racial, social,
and economic characteristics. The movement is an outgrowth of the
blacks' struggle against oppression. Using principles of black nationalism and religious ideology, the Muslims have been able to identify
themselves as a group and develop a new and distinct status hierarchy separate from the white majority (Clark, 1969). The Muslims
believe that the black man is the original man, that he is part of

Allah, that he is divine and supreme. They advocate the segregation of white from black and the practice of a strict moral code which includes abstaining from alcohol, gambling, profanity, and drugs (Lomax, 1963). They also adhere to a strict diet akin to that of Orthodox Jews. The Muslims' most essential goal is economic independence, an objective they feel will foster both freedom and power.

Within these cultural themes, the Black Muslims articulate a ten-point social program which identifies the nature of the society they wish to bring about. One point specifies the type of education they desire (Randle, 1972): the Muslims want schools that separate boys and girls and that are taught and administered by people who adhere to Black Muslim values of righteousness, decency, and self-respect. The black nation demands that members send their children to Black Muslim schools wherever possible.

Within such schools, the day is divided between secular and religious instruction. Students are taught Muslim duties, dietary laws, character development, the history of the black man and the Muslim movement, and both English and Arabic. Other aspects of the curriculum include mathematics and the physical and social sciences. The objective of a Muslim education is "to re-educate the so-called Negro, who has been the victim of centuries of mis-education . . . to attain his rightful place in the sun as a Black man. . . . a cardinal fact of its teachings is to give the students a feeling of dignity and appreciation of their own kind" (Lincoln, 1961, p. 126).

The Black Muslims are just now graduating the first generation of youth completely schooled in the Muslim doctrine. The result is men and women living in accord with the teachings of the Messenger of Allah in an interdependent, segregated black nation and community. Although still in the first stage of development, the Black Muslim movement is also trying to secure economic independence through ownership of both production and commercial enterprises, thus attempting to guarantee a continuous segregated life cycle.

Both the Amish and the Black Muslims use schools to foster a sense of identity through reinforcing certain behaviors and excluding others. Because the populations the schools serve are already socialized into a particular way of life, the schools build on existing orientations and extend the influence of the family and community. In effect, they are relevant to the ideological, technological, and institutional components of the sociocultural systems to which they belong. This relationship between culture and education is clear when the society is well integrated, as is the Amish, and somewhat less clear in the Muslim movement, which because of its relative youth must react to the influence of predominantly white institutions in order to bring together its membership. In both cases, the school is an integral part of the total culture. The school does not compete with the family; instead, all cultural components are mirrored in the school's everyday policies and procedures.

Although it is perhaps easier to see what is meant by relevant education in these small isolated societies, one can readily grasp the principle that the school reflects particular cultural biases by entering any school in any community, state, or nation. The personnel that operate the school and the community that supports it must necessarily select their policies and practices from a limited number of options. Many of their operations are implicit rather than explicit. Thus, they are based upon tradition-bound methods and attitudes, often not consciously held, adhered to because they reflect the current social order. Although the parameters within which to choose principles and practices are normally wide, those acceptable to the community to which the school belongs often are extremely limited. This referent community sets the rules or norms by which the school operates.

In areas where there are several potential referent communities, the school is dominated by the most powerful economic and political population. Thus, the school serves the middle-class or upper-class Anglo in this country in much the same way as the Amish and Black Muslim schools serve their respective populations. They are continuous with the family and community and reinforce the external life style. For members of the Indian, Chicano, black, or Anglo lower-class populations, however, the public school in the United States is discontinuous. In many cases it is as discontinuous for these children as an Amish or Black Muslim school would be for anyone not a member of these communities.

Where discontinuity exists between the school and the referent community, there is competition in the socialization of the young. Assume that an Amish child is forced to attend, without option, a public school. One can readily see that the middle-class Anglo school based on a work-success ethic, on a future-time orientation, and on independence and individualism as well as puritan morality would be at odds with the background of this child. The typical public school based on these and other principles would, however, reinforce and extend the values held by a majority of the population of the community, if not the country.

This brief view of two rather homogeneous societies demonstrates the overwhelming impact of a referent culture on the role and function of educational institutions designed to reflect and support rather than change the social order. There is no reason to believe that schools, or any other educational institution or mode, using either public or private funds, will function in a way that does not support the interests of their relevant populations. One need only look at the turmoil created over such issues as sex education, creation and evolution theories, corporal punishment, and pornography in the nation's public schools to realize the constraints which the referent culture places on both educational content and process. If this assessment is correct, a basic principle in designing educational alternatives within schools or alternatives to schools is to test their relationship with each of the components of culture. Without such an appraisal, alternatives, like schools, will simply be prevented from functioning in any way which threatens to destroy long-held behavioral patterns in the referent culture.

efficiency

That long-standing concern of educators, efficiency, is currently receiving renewed and more concerted attention. Part of this concern over efficiency is expressed by curriculum and instruction specialists, administrators, and evaluators inside the education profession, while part rests with economists, legislators, and the public at large. The issue is the amount of resources expended for each unit of learning produced: in other words, output divided by input.

Educational alternatives to achieve efficiency may include qualitative improvements in curricular materials, pedagogy, and management, or they may use new resources such as television, radio, and communication satellites. In addition, such traditional options as daily and yearly scheduling (often by computer), manipulation of class size, and team teaching are also employed to reduce the unit costs of educational outcomes. Although increased efficiency can be achieved through such approaches, the nature of the priorities and goals established is what dictates the means and, therefore, the resources needed to produce desired outcomes. If such objectives are quantifiable, and thus measurable, the problems inherent in achieving more efficient outcomes are lessened, since the assessment process requires identification of both resources and obstacles and depends on the use of statistical analyses.

The goal of efficiency is clearly reinforced by the components of the culture, especially by technology. Whereas the demand for relevant alternatives is most influenced by people's ideology, those who desire efficient alternatives are looking to technology to achieve them. As is well known, our society places great hope in technological progress as a source of social benefits. In pursuit of this aim, the machine supplants manpower, assembly lines create products and advertisers create consumer demand, and investment and profit become sacred. Clearly, our culture's ideology and institutions support the stress on efficiency, affecting the ways available energy sources are harnessed and used. By looking at contrasting cultures, such as the Amish, with their disdain for electricity, automobiles, and telephones, we can view our own positive orientation to the same material objects.

Given this stress on technology, it should not come as a surprise that efficient use of scarce resources is of prime concern to everyone who delivers social services. Yet this very concern often conflicts with achieving the kind of services that are planned. The strain is perhaps best seen in the contradictions between relevance and efficiency. In education, these principles tend to be treated as opposites because the former champions individual liberty while the latter often demands more conformity and cooperation. Thus, while individuals in a complex and heterogeneous society want schools to respond to the current interests and needs of students and to present reality, they also value efficiency, an objective which forces individuals to cooperate in order to agree on common needs and interests. Individual creativity, initiative, and achievement are prized and rewarded, yet only if they are accomplished within temporal and financial limitations so that they do not waste precious resources and become an impediment to their productive use by others.

Thus, self-realization through the individualization of educational experiences is not the only goal, for society demands that such liberty also shall result in the betterment of all individuals, who thereby become more productive workers and better citizens. The stress on efficiency, therefore, often leads to standardization and conformity in terms of educational outcomes. The educator's problem becomes one of efficiently satisfying standardized norms, most often externally imposed, while individualizing relevant experiences for learners.

Frazier, in B. F. Skinner's *Walden Two,* expresses this relevance and efficiency conflict in another way:

"Now, you can't get people to follow a useful code by making them into so many jacks-in-the-box. You can't foresee all future circumstances, and you can't specify adequate future conduct. You don't know what will be required. Instead you have to set up certain behavioral processes which will lead the individual to design his own good conduct when the time comes. We call that sort of thing 'self-control.' But don't be misled, the control always rests in the hands of society" [1948, p. 100].

Although the goals of relevance and efficiency need not be contradictory, they seem to be so in most of the educational institutions we know. For example, most traditional schools group students by age or ability. The rationale underlying such organization may be efficiency: if students are grouped in ways that enable the teacher to find commonalities among them, instruction is more likely to produce expected outcomes and time is saved by not having to work with each student individually. However, one can also argue for grouping using the relevance criterion if the groups are formed around an important, agreed upon characteristic, such as sex, age, or reading level, which is believed to relate to meaningful learning.

The efficiency-relevance opposition is also evident in the scheduling of educational experiences. Such experiences may be meaningful to students, but the daily schedule of classes, the school calendar, and the systems of security aimed at assigning individuals to certain areas at certain times tend to operate against relevance and in favor of the overriding concern with efficiency. In our culture, when production and group goals conflict with consumption and individual liberty, the former appear to outweigh the latter.

In planning educational alternatives one is always aware of the need to use available resources efficiently and somewhat less likely to be concerned with the relevance of those resources. In this emphasis lies, perhaps, the major cause of the "free school" and "new school" movement, since what it champions is not the systems analysis, input-output approach to education but the more individualized and laissez-faire approach advocated by humanists who want a meaningful education for their children.

In effect, such a movement expresses disenchantment with externally imposed criteria and norms and rejects a value system which holds efficiency to be a major determinant of educational success. As has been suggested, however, the growing crisis in the availability of financial resources for educational programs, including those for free schools and new schools, makes it necessary to attempt a more viable compromise between these oppositional principles. Can we use existing resources in the community such as the family, the work place, and the church to provide educational experiences that are both efficient and relevant? Are there ways to reach large sectors of the population through various combinations of media, ways which will respond to individual needs and interests yet involve minimal standardization and conformity? Can we foster educational programs that offer multiple, lifelong opportunities for individuals to pursue relevant experiences without exclusion on the basis of prior experience, age, or financial resources? Educational alternatives must confront the efficiency-relevance issue. The successful options will, in some way, resolve the problem through balanced compromise.

equality

The egalitarian ethos in the United States permeates much of the thinking underlying educational programs. We know, however, that the freedom and equality granted to each citizen in such documents as the Constitution are not necessarily manifested in the population. Other societal values and beliefs appear to foster prerequisites for the achievement of educational equality (as well as other types). Some of these prerequisites are material, like money; some are attitudinal, like "hard work results in success"; and some are cognitive, like the values associated with school and school diplomas.

Because actual behavior is the real test of a culture's values, one can easily note the conflict between what is said or written down and what is actually done. The judicial and legislative systems in this country have thus been doing battle with prevailing value systems, attempting to enforce the written word as it conflicts with practice. Although the results have been mildly successful where law enforcement agencies are at the ready, the results have been less than satisfactory when the people themselves retain decision-making power. Even though the desegregation of schools is perhaps the most noteworthy result of this ongoing battle, it is a more explicit example of the equality-inequality contradiction than I wish to raise here.

The most pervasive inequity present, and one that can best be seen in the institutional component of our culture, is the uneven distribution of power and status. In effect, this impedes equality of access to society's resources for bettering the quality of life. Although in many quarters it is popular to believe that such access is almost totally dependent on individual initiative and hard work, there is growing evidence that access is governed more by the socio-economic status and ethnicity of an individual's family background. It is rather easy to demonstrate statistically that such a relationship exists in large groups, while it is more difficult to do so at the individual level where exceptions can be found.

The schools' role in bringing about equality of access, opportunity, and achievement indicates the influence of background factors on occupational and income attainment (Blum and Coleman, 1970). There is growing evidence that success in school primarily depends on conditions outside it. Studies in more than a dozen so-called developed countries found that approximately two-thirds of the variance in school achievement was explained by family background as opposed to one-third by in-school factors (Central Advisory Council on Education, 1966; Coleman, 1966; Husén, 1972). Additional confirmation comes from the RAND Corporation's review of research on the determinants of educational effectiveness. The authors of the report conclude that available evidence fails to "show that school resources *do* affect student outcomes," although the "socio-economic status of a student's family—his parents' income, education, and occupation—invariably prove to be significant predictors of his educational outcome" (Averch, 1972, p. 148).

Schools are only one example of our society's inability to design institutions that give everyone a chance to take advantage of general resources. Political, judicial, medical, and economic institutions are likewise characterized by their lack of response to lower socioeconomic populations since their operations primarily represent the values of those who control those resources. The school, because it functions as a selecting and sorting institution for society, tends to reinforce a class hierarchy. It usually promotes and advances those who accept and perform in accord with externally imposed academic achievement standards while it alienates and discourages those who do not. Those who meet the criteria for school success are more likely to have grown up in middle- and upper-class homes.

The problem appears to rest with the lack of correspondence between the school as an institution and the lower-class portion of its clientele. The referent culture of these students is at odds with that of the school. They expect the school to make them vertically mobile by credentialing them, but the conceptual style, language, and values such clients bring with them to school do not coincide with those behavior patterns expected by the representatives of the school's middle- and upper-class referent culture. The resulting discontinuity means that many students are unable to take what they want from the school.

The equality advocates believe alternatives to the school are needed by members of the lower socioeconomic classes for whom the school has been shown to be ineffectual on most criteria. A major obstacle to such options is the wider values associated with the kinds of credentials one needs to pursue a career. In other words, if a community begins to discover or invent alternatives to the school for these clients, will it provide them with the legitimate credentials which the wider society demands for sharing its resources? Or will such alternatives simply relegate the individuals who participate in them to the lower status positions in society and thus do little to alter their resource base?

Clearly, our society uses the school to legitimate certain experiences. We often call these experiences "courses of instruction." Successful manipulation of such instructional activities results in appropriate grades, credentials, and diplomas. Without possession of such indices of "success," individuals will have a difficult time convincing others that they in fact have some requisite level of competence to secure access to wider resources. It appears that to change such indices we must either alter the cultural values which support this credentialing process—and thus society's criteria for judging success—or radically change the concept of the school. To accomplish the latter would require, again, alterations in the cultural criteria for achievement and in what people expect educational institutions to provide.

Eliminating social classes by placing control over the means of production in the hands of the workers is, as Gintis (1972) suggests, one way to alter such values. Economic change through political action such as that occurring in China and Cuba, and more recently in Chile, is based on policies which, in the ideal or normative form, are attempting to reduce hierarchical relationships and consequently to change those values associated with credentialing.

Although there is probably no realistic way of altering the educational values of a given population, short of such socio-political-economic change, it is conceivable that out-of-school alternatives in countries which embrace capitalism might produce greater immediate benefits for individuals from lower socioeconomic-status sectors. Although the school is not likely to be eliminated, even though it supplies little more than ritual activity for many of its clients, it currently is the exclusive provider of legitimate and sanctioned learning. Presently, out-of-school learning is nonsanctioned, as we lack mechanisms to categorize and legitimate such experience. Out-of-school education seems to be legitimate only for those individuals who have achieved within the school. Thus, the "successful" person is one who has had the requisite formal schooling plus other out-of-school educational experiences. Social permission to substitute these "other" inputs for the formal school's activities is not likely to be given soon. If anything, worldwide population growth and concomitant needs for some semblance of order and stability will probably bring more, not less, institutionalization in society.

Rather than stressing academic achievement or career preparation, why should educational alternatives not provide healthier and happier places for children to be? Many people feel that an improved environment is sufficient reason to seek new options. But advocates of equality are dissatisfied with humanistic educational programs that fail to prepare individuals for the inequities encountered outside such programs. Furthermore, they argue that in our society success is based not on humanism but on power and resources, which are more likely to be socially and culturally transmitted than to be achieved through educational programs. Thus, if alternatives fail to provide learning outcomes which make a difference in terms of securing access to resources, the equality proponents believe that the traditional school, albeit less than satisfactory, must suffice.

Thus, out-of-school education may prove beneficial and popular only with those who have already achieved some success through the formal system. It may do little in the long run to foster greater access to resources among people of lower socioeconomic status or among those who have not been effective in manipulating the formal schooling process. If the goal is to approach status parity among all socioeconomic sectors, then encouraging this marginal population to pursue out-of-school activities is unrealistic.

The question which needs empirical testing, therefore, is whether or not the advantages obtainable from out-of-school activity include equality of opportunity and whether such experiences should be perceived as substitutes for the "legitimization" benefits accrued through the formal school system. Out-of-school education for the lower socioeconomic sectors probably will produce short-term benefits, enabling the unemployed to join the labor force as skilled and semiskilled workers and permitting the entrepreneurs to secure a greater financial return on their investments. The target population for such programs is likely to be youth and adults who have failed to meet the legitimated educational criteria already established. This sector includes the small farmer, the urban semiskilled and unskilled, and the unemployed. The programs are likely to be formal and short-term giving small returns. How much an individual can improve his status without reentering the formal system is questionable. In other words, since the school controls most legitimate credentialing, does it become more important in terms of mobility as an individual desires more status?

In an ideal relationship between formal schooling and out-of-school activities the individual could secure school credits for experiences acquired outside school. Although this credit-granting is theoretically feasible, in practice the schools are normally organized too rigidly to sanction it; no established "open" categories are likely to exist within the formal curriculum. James Coleman (1972), implicitly recognizing this dilemma, suggests that all youth in the United States should secure both cognitive and technical vocational skills, the former in schools, the latter through experiences on the job. By requiring all youth to pursue this pattern, Coleman feels that in-school tracking of students will give way to an emphasis on the amount of time they are exposed to different experiences; such a step should help control the influence of socioeconomic status on success indicators.

conclusions

In this chapter I have attempted to bring together several perspectives on educational alternatives and relate them to a model of culture. I have tried to show how these approaches to the study and implementation of educational options are directly related to the components of culture and to the space they allow for educational experimentation. The categories of relevance, efficiency, and equality, like the cultural components of ideology, technology, and institutions, were not presented as mutually exclusive but as overlapping and interrelated. I argued that each category has its counterpart in culture (that is, relevance is associated with values and ideology; efficiency with technology; and equality with institutions) to demonstrate the importance of isolating an approach to education and viewing it in a more limited cultural perspective. My intent, however, was to point out how culture determines the nature of educational processes and how education, whether informal, nonformal, or formal, reinforces the culture. The principles of relevance, equality, and efficiency are themselves culture-bound and might not be priorities among the Amish, let alone in cultures outside the United States. Thus, as alternative educational programs are sought, the need to know one's culture and the limits it sets on acceptable institutional and curricular configurations remains as yet another challenge and obstacle for the educational planner and practitioner.

references

Averch, H. A., and others. *How Effective Is Schooling? A Critical Review and Synthesis of Research Findings.* Santa Monica, Calif.: RAND Corporation, 1972.

Berg, I. *Education and Jobs: The Great Training Robbery.* New York: Praeger, 1970.

Blum, Z., and Coleman, J. "Longitudinal Effects of Education on the Incomes and Occupational Prestige of Blacks and Whites." Report No. 70. Baltimore: Center for Social Organization of Schools, Johns Hopkins University, 1970.

Central Advisory Council on Education. *Children and Their Primary Schools.* London: Her Majesty's Stationery Office, 1966.

Clark, J. H. *Malcolm X.* New York: Macmillan, 1969.

Coleman, J. S. "How Do the Young Become Adults?" Report No. 130. Baltimore: Center for Social Organization of Schools, Johns Hopkins University, 1972.

Coleman, J. S., and others. *Equality of Educational Opportunity.* Washington, D.C.: Government Printing Office, 1966.

Gintis, H. "Towards a Political Economy of Education: A Radical Critique of

Ivan Illich's Deschooling Society." *Harvard Educational Review*, 1972, *42* (1).

Honigman, J. J. *The World of Man*. New York: Harper, 1959.

Hostetler, J. A., and Huntington, G. E. *Children in Amish Society, Socialization and Community Education*. New York: Holt, Rinehart, and Winston, 1971.

Husén, T. "Does More Time in School Make a Difference?" *Saturday Review*, April 29, 1972.

Illich, I. *De-Schooling Society*. New York: Harper and Row, 1971.

Lincoln, C. E. *The Black Muslim in America*. Boston: Beacon, 1961.

Lomax, L. E. *When the Word Is Given*. Cleveland: World Publishing, 1963.

Randle, S. "Education and the Black Muslim." Los Angeles: Graduate School of Education, U.C.L.A., November 21, 1972. Unpublished manuscript.

Reimer, E. *School Is Dead: Alternatives in Education*. New York: Doubleday, 1971.

Skinner, B. F. *Walden Two*. New York: Macmillan, 1948.

the meaning of alternatives

carl weinberg

To talk about meaning is to undertake the difficult assignment of unraveling multiple realities. Persons find their meaning within the context of their social and psychological lives. To discuss the subject of meaning independent of the contexts within which it takes hold and free from the behavior of the people involved becomes an academic exercise.

My intention in this paper is to approach the subject of meaning from several directions. Hopefully, the totality will be close to the whole. The subject is alternatives. More precisely, it is the meaning of alternatives in education. Where, then, does one begin when one understands that the meaning of something, actually anything, exists in the minds of those whom the phenomenon affects? The easy way out, and I intend to take it as a first step, is to remove the question of meaning temporarily from the realm of individual minds and describe the phenomenon of alternatives from a number of different positions that are quite familiar to academics. These are the sociological, psychological, and philosophical contexts. In this particular realm, meanings take on the perspective of a convention. That is, they derive substance from the references and concepts that are particular to each discipline. Although it is true that a subject loses its own life in this kind of transformation, it is nonetheless helpful to those who wish to understand the foundation or structure of a phenomenon to begin here. My purpose is ultimately to restore the life of the concept of alternatives by talking about them in their own terms: how they are used, particularly by persons involved in the business of doing alternatives, not merely studying them.

Let me begin by making certain distinctions between "alternatives" and other labels that have been used to describe ongoing educational practices. Such terms as "free," "humanistic," "open," and "natural or organic" unfortunately convey a spirit of radical or revolutionary assaults on the mainstream of schooling in which many persons have a vested interest. The term "alternatives" is much more acceptable to educators at all levels because its lack of specificity allows everyone to believe that they are part of the innovation or at least that they can find something acceptable in it. School administrators, for example, can latch on to technological innovations as alternatives and thereby join the legions of educators who pride themselves on being open to something new.

The alternatives discussed here do not include new ways of doing old things, nor do they refer to changes as change per se. Unless the active or proposed change does incorporate an element of a comprehensive, total system of educating children, no matter how rude or unformulated, the change does not achieve the status of an alternative.

Defenders of the status quo and educational "liberals" (those who believe change is necessary but are antagonistic to extreme or dramatic overhauls) find the word "alternative" less loaded than those terms which imply that present schooling is inhuman, closed, and hopelessly tied to the most despicable aspects of bureaucratic life. My intention here is to avoid implicitly contentious or polemical writing and to focus on a wide range of meanings that educators can examine within a variety of contexts, without the need to feel defensive or to protect their special or unique interests.

the movement

The movement toward alternatives in education should be thought of, in the most general sense, as a counterpart of similar occurrences in other institutional segments of our society. When someone speaks of "the movement," he is referring to liberation struggles on the part of alienated members of our society. These struggles are well known, usually classified as civil rights' movements, and involve a range of activities and events from black sit-ins to student demonstrations to the establishment of private independent schools that stand ideologically opposed to the system of public education in the United States.

These liberation movements have a number of common goals, and some description of their aims can provide a base for understanding the actual structures and strategies that go into creating alternatives.

Equality. This is the goal of creating an environment in which persons share in both the power and the responsibility, particularly the decision making in matters that directly affect their participation.

Autonomy. This is the goal of establishing channels for individuals to create a life or work that is free from the intimidations and manipulations of others who base their authority on conventions of superiority and control.

Opportunity. This is the goal of guaranteeing that individuals can manage the system equally with other members who are striving to achieve within this same system.

Openness. This is the goal of managing a system or institution so as to provide a maximum variety of ways for persons to achieve gratifications from or in it.

Integration. This is the goal of dealienating an environment in order that each individual is and feels like an integral, worthwhile member of the community.

These, then, are the broad goals of liberation struggles across a number of different but related group movements. Educational alternatives, as patterns sought by a host of persons both professional and lay, seek the same goals, but in forms that are specific to schooling, and that is my subject. But before beginning an analysis of what alternatives are, a few words about what they are not might be helpful. The overall reformist movement in education includes those who seek to modify the present system without disturbing most of the major structures, as well as those such as Illich (1971) and Reimer (1971), about whom I will say more later, who call for a complete elimination of schools as they are. The point here is that the word "alternatives" does not refer to the destruction of schooling as we know it, but to a broad spectrum of criticism and suggestions for improvement emerging from a wide variety of sources. The moderate position is that different kinds of schools are good for different kinds of students. A "free" school, like a conventional school, might not be good for everyone.

We can talk legitimately, then, about alternatives in education coexisting within separate organizations or even within a single organizational structure—a school district or an individual public school. In the City of Los Angeles, for example, there are at least five alternative schools and hundreds of what we might call alternative classrooms in otherwise conventional schools.

One further delimitation of what is not meant by alternatives. Many flourishing private schools have emerged in the past decade to capitalize on the difficulties facing public education. Problems of finance, of racial tension or busing, of the elimination of so-called soft or hard curricula—depending on one's prejudices—have influenced thousands of parents to place their children in private schools where they can get a jump on their peers in the race for the most prestigious careers. This kind of education underlies some of the most central and typical processes in American society, core in its values, instrumental in its process, and alienating in its outcome. When I speak of alternatives, I am referring to patterns of schooling that differ from conventional patterns not only in the form of schooling, but in the values, goals, and processes on which they are based.

the language of alternatives

Meaning is often revealed in the language employed. Those who wish to create alternatives usually realize, whether they work in bureaucratic organizations or as independent political organizers, that they must first communicate their objections and intentions. Although innovators are seldom understood, few are unintelligible. The words are familiar, but what they refer to specifically is seldom clear. A term such as "freedom," for example, has occupied long dissertations. The idea of an "open" classroom is interpreted very differently by different people. The notion of "participatory democracy" has similar problems. I am not going to explore these terms here, but one concept, "consciousness," is crucial to any understanding of the meaning of alternatives. The women's liberation movement, for example, sees the process of "raising consciousness" as essential to achieving its goals. Through a set of educational activities they hope to reveal to persons who exist in some kind of a disadvantaged state of being that their circumstance need not be the way it is. People must be shown that conventional patterns are arbitrary and might be otherwise. Black and brown members of society need not be service workers, women need not assume full responsibility for household chores or child raising, successful students need not be professionals, formal organizations need not be so formal, and students need not be subjected to the arbitrary whims of teachers or administrators. Consciousness, then, as I use the concept here, is a state of awareness of one's circumstance and of the ways it might be modified or changed.

Most persons in various social contexts are socialized to believe that the patterns to which they are expected to comply have some kind of inherent validity. They act as if the rules by which their personal, social, or even educational lives are directed are somehow right simply because they exist. Raising consciousness, the main thrust of the liberation curriculum, means dislodging persons from those beliefs and values which confine them to restricted possibilities.

Perception of alternatives, then, in education as elsewhere, is based on altering a state of acceptance and raising to awareness another set of possibilities for consideration. Beyond this awareness exist the political processes by which one can achieve alternatives and the educational process that enables one to understand and adopt alternatives. It cannot be too strongly emphasized that the fundamental meaning of alternatives in education and in life is to be found in the way the human consciousness conceives: first, that things need not be as they are; second, that alternatives to conventional patterns are possible and available; and third, that these options can be generated and described.

meanings in contexts

Meaning always inheres within a particular context. At best, if people understand each other at all, they are able to because they have attained a given level of competence within a specific context. As members of a particular group or society, they have learned the references that give words their meaning. Contexts are those areas in which persons share the same references for words. A sociologist, for example, uses the word "competent" to refer to the ability of a member of a group to function normally in that group. A psychologist may use the word to refer to an individual's ability to function without anxiety or neurosis. A boss on a machine crew will mean that a person can do his job as he, the boss, expects. A wife may be referring to her husband's economic or sexual capacity.

Within the academic community, contexts take on a more complex and elaborate configuration in which meanings evolve from a particular way of viewing the world. Historians and geologists are looking for different things, and a psychologist working in a School of Business or Engineering focuses on phenomena different from those of his colleague in a School of Education. The issue is perspective: members of one discipline or subculture do not see things the same as persons in other disciplines. This distinction is critical to an understanding of the remainder of this paper in which the meaning of alternatives is run through the mill of different perspectives. The goal is to aid understanding and, at the same time, give those who have a special interest in learning about or teaching about alternatives a framework for doing so.

At a time when radical educators are joining their brothers and sisters in a variety of social movements, it is imperative to improve communication so that unnecessary battles and misunderstandings do not obstruct the business of improving schooling for students.) The problem that we need to circumvent can be illustrated by an experience of mine that could have been more costly than it was. (A few years ago, while driving across the Rockies with my two children asleep in the back of the station wagon, I came to a fork in the road. It was late afternoon, and I had been driving for many hours. About one hundred yards away, I noticed a woman painting a landscape. I approached her and asked for directions to a particular city. She said that if I continued on down the road (on which I had begun), I would arrive at my destination. I then asked her if it was a good road.

"Good," she replied, "it's a beautiful road."

I thanked her and set out on one of the most hazardous, frightening, and dangerous rides of my life. The road was so treacherous and unprotected that, after better than an hour of slow progress, I returned to the original fork. I then confronted the woman who had given me directions.

"I didn't say it was safe," she said innocently. "I only said it was beautiful. It's one of the most beautiful stretches of scenery I have ever painted."

The perspective of the artist versus the desperate perspective of a tired driver. Words take on very different meanings. Let us begin with the sociological viewpoint.

the sociological context

Sociologically, alternatives must be viewed as alternative structures for those patterns which have been established to fulfill important social functions. These functions will be considered in relation to five principal aspects of educational operation: (1) attendance, (2) organization, (3) adaptation, (4) socialization, and (5) integration.

Attendance. Currently, American children must go to school from about age six or seven to fifteen or sixteen. Termination of compulsory attendance varies from state to state. Some exceptions are made for adolescent students, depending on work arrangements that may be substituted for school activities. Attendance requirements regulate not only school attendance but attendance in classes. Proposed alternatives range from suggestions to do away with all compulsory attendance to such variations as a mixture of compulsory and voluntary attendance, compulsory attendance in school but voluntary attendance in classes, and contract arrangements whereby students agree to attend some activities but not others. The meaning or assumption which underlies alternatives to compulsory attendance is that students will benefit from schooling to the degree that they volunteer to participate in available activities. Advocates want to move from a highly controlled environment, in which students' lives are determined and ordered by monolithic forces, to a system of voluntary action in which the students' will and interest influence the extent to which they take advantage of school offerings.

Organization. Most schools in Western society are bureaucracies. Positions of authority and decision making are arranged hierarchically, with students standing (or sitting) at the bottom of the ladder. This standard organizational pattern is also characterized by formalism. Schools are formal places where interpersonal relations are governed by role expectations. Students and teachers relate to each other in terms of conventions that accompany roles. Administrative roles are explicitly spelled out, and their occupants have little leeway, and usually less motivation, to depart from historical precedent. School relationships are guided by normative prescriptions, and any violation of these prescriptions is always accompanied by sanctions appropriate to the institution. Students are punished with detentions or poor grades, teachers may be promoted, fired, and sometimes moved horizontally (from a ghetto to a suburban school, for example), and administrators either move up or remain static, and occasionally are replaced. At the level of interpersonal relations, a host of conventions cue members to the way others are addressed (first name, Mr., Dr., Professor) and the extent to which persons are available for personalized communication dealing with individual problems.

Alternatives in this structural area might be variations in patterns of authority and control, new ways to determine sanctions, and possible shifts in the way school participants relate to each other. Egalitarian decision making and informal personal relationships are two possibilities.

A third element of the organizational structure which provides room for speculation about alternatives is the division of labor. Bureaucratic roles usually carry not only prescribed authority but substantive responsibility. Administrators make fiscal decisions and supervise staff, teachers teach and evaluate, students do what they are told—presumably learn something. The basis for maintaining this prescribed division of labor is usually conventional wisdom, and extensive innovations in this area are possible. Might not teachers supervise each other, students teach, administrators assist teachers as resource persons?

The Adaptive Structure. The concept of adaptation, borrowed from Talcott Parsons's formulation (1951) of the functions of a social system, applies to the patterns related to training and allocating students through the various school curricula to the job market. A primary component of adaptation is the structure of efficiency on which educational processes are based. The importance given to efficiency in conventional school systems is made more evident by the dominant adaptation of alternative schools, which generally take the opposite tack. Whereas public schools organize their resources and accomplish their tasks on a cost-budget basis, alternative schools often advertise a low student-teacher ratio. This ratio is not always (actually seldom) a result of being able to afford more teachers; rather it derives from a different approach to organizing students for learning. That is, small groups on a volunteer basis may engage in a lesson, while others under the supervision of a parent or an older student are doing other things more or less on their own. In conventional structures efficiency is paramount. What this means is known to every parent, teacher, student, and administrator: schools must be organized to transport the maximum number of students through the grade system for the least money. In the classroom, this means that the student group is usually taught as a unit —presumbly on the assumption that all students are capable of learning as a group in the same way. The principle of individualized instruction, as any student of schooling knows, has seldom advanced to the stage where students are allowed to learn in their own way, only at different rates of speed, and even this modification of routine is the exception rather than the rule.

The goal of efficiency is also the rationale for constraining both time and space in conventional settings. A field trip to the zoo once a year for elementary school students is usually the one typical and token variation from the pattern of keeping children confined in single spaces for clearly specified time units. Alternatives to this structure would be to vary the locales of learning and to achieve some flexibility in scheduling. Efficiency sometimes takes the form of group management and control, and while it is probably true that maximum numbers can be controlled more efficiently with time and space limitations, alternative plans are founded on the assumption that time and space should not be used as control mechanisms.

Another characteristic of the conventional adaptive structure is what is sometimes called a product (as opposed to a process) orientation. The student's learning is considered a product, whose quality is measured at various stages, and at each stage students are allocated differentially to different curricula according to performance scores, ratings, and informal teacher evaluations. The product model assumes a number of stop and start points, called semesters, in which students are expected, as a group, to know so much of a given subject as outlined in curriculum guides. For larger time units, conventional school systems have established a number of certification points which approve students to move to a higher level—from junior to senior high, from high school to college, from college to graduate school, from graduate school to a particular job.

Alternatives based on the process model, on the other hand, attempt to move away from certification at specific points, as well as to liberate learning from limitations of time, place, or grade level. Alternative structures for processing and certifying students claim legitimacy on the grounds that they remove constraints on learners, and also on teachers, even though their task is more complex and control of the process more difficult. But many schools and classrooms have come to grips with this problem and have developed strategies to deal with it.

Socialization. One function that all educational systems adopt, in partnership with such other institutions as the family and the church, is to produce moral and reliable citizens. Reliable means skilled and committed. People must have skills to man (or woman) the various posts that are required to keep the society running, as well as the commitment to assume these positions. The school's task has been to produce the skills and instill the values that the larger society considers necessary and appropriate. The skills taught by most schools in Western society are compatible with industrial modes of social life. The values, as Max Weber (1930) correctly established, are also those which maintain a capitalistic industrial mode. Such values as industriousness, respect for property, upward social mobility, punctuality, loyalty, and patriotism are prominent. Once goals and strategies have been chosen, a legion of motivations and sanctions is institutionally instilled in order to assure compliance by students. All schoolchildren quickly learn the intentions of the school in which they are captives for the kind of socialization they are to receive. Teachers use a set of punitive and rewarding acts to force children to behave as if they believed the values even if they do not.

Established values and skills need not remain so, of course, and many alternative structures already exist in alternative schools. Instead of accepting the notion that all children must learn how to read, write, and figure, some schools deemphasize such "basics" and allow children considerable time and choice to gain these skills. Possible alternative values are as obvious as the ones that now prevail. All one need do is to consider the core values that are present in the school and classroom and reverse them, or at least reduce their power. For example, instead of industriousness, laziness (although an opprobrious term now) could be converted into a respectable value if it connoted the capacity of persons to relax, daydream, play, or even to avoid hard work until something worthwhile came along. Alternative structures also have been developed to open up the kinds of abilities that children can develop beyond those that are suitable to an industrial society. Such courses as plant raising, animal care, guitar and folk singing, and even silent, under-the-tree daydreaming are available in some alternative schools.

The main thrust of alternative structures is to avoid the hypocrisy that is often implicit in the way schools go about implanting values. They teach the value of trust and do not trust students; they teach democracy in an authoritarian manner; they stand on their belief in equal rights and equal opportunities regardless of race or sex, but every sociologist who has ever inquired about these phenomena has detected racism and sexism almost anywhere he (or she) looked.

One last point about socialization. All status systems are founded on values. If all good things were available to everyone regardless of effort, Western civilization would witness a thorough revamping of its value structure. But in industrial society as it exists, people are socialized to aspire to and compete for the differentially valued rewards of that society. This competition is the core of the structure used to socialize students. Every teacher who has ever worried about control and trying to get students to do what he or she wants recognizes the motivational value of competition. It is precisely here that alternative structures stand in juxtaposition to the mainstream of schooling. If alternative classroom teachers can bring off educative experiences without resorting to the various rewards for competition (grades, prizes, smiles), then a whole new consciousness about motivation can be developed.

Integration. The structure of integration is the means whereby persons discover their relationship to others in the system, both in terms of formal requirements and informal relationships. To accomplish most tasks, people divide the labor and work together in an organizational structure. But once roles and statuses have been defined, each component must begin operating as a whole to achieve the goals of the institution. Within this total operation exist individuals who possess different social characteristics—age, sex, race, socioeconomic status, and ability. How do schools integrate these individuals? What is the basis of this integration? The patterns are well known. The alternatives should be equally obvious. The conventional method is to group children according to ability and segregate them along lines of age, sex, race, and socioeconomic status. Perhaps the first, ability grouping, accounts for much of the other. Children learn that the performances expected of them depend on their age, sex, race, and ability. They learn (or at least *we* have learned—Coleman, 1966) that differential facilities are available to them depending on their skin color.

Within mixed (not integrated) schools, social research has uncovered a lengthy history of differential rewards based on social class or socioeconomic status (the latter being a measure that makes extensive and in-depth studies unnecessary). Although some comprehensive surveys of sexist practices in schools are beginning to appear (for example, see Willard, 1972), one need only recall one's own school days to realize the infinite number of ways that educational structures use to keep boys and girls from being anything but mysteries to each other (lines, gyms, bathrooms, cooking versus woodshop, entrances and exits, health classes, lockers, and a heavy emphasis on noncommunication in classrooms).

The problem facing alternative schools is to figure out how to use social and personal differences in the educational task, rather than purely in motivational (grouping) or ecological arrangements. The community school implies homogeneity and guarantees segregation.

Real integration would mean that persons, regardless of those characteristics I have discussed, would have access to the same resources—both the school's offerings and each other. No one questions the educational value of informal contact between students. If this exchange were institutionally encouraged, even arranged, a genuine alternative to the segregated structures of much of present-day schooling would emerge.

Another important goal of integration, a most radical departure from present structures, is to reduce private gain seeking. Classrooms are usually divisive in that one student's success may mean another's failure, and students learn to associate grades, awards, honors, successes, and failures with private rather than communal gains or losses. If one can imagine an educational context where the highest gratification occurs when another learns something that I, as student, already know, then one is ready to conceptualize a communal rather than a private basis for education.

the psychological context

Psychological perspectives on alternatives should be understood within the context of applied approaches to learning. These approaches conceive of the learner as a particular kind of being. It would be misplaced confidence in our intellectual theories to assume that most teaching, conventional or alternative, is based on any coherent or research-based rationale. But this does not mean we cannot supply such a rationale, even though it is after the fact to the theoretician and probably superfluous to the practitioner.

The important contrast between conventional and alternative views of learning derives from assumptions about the nature of the learner. One perspective is associated with classical conditioning and behavioristic paradigms of how humans learn. The other, to which we can link alternative definitions, is more associated with Gestalt psychology and its younger brother humanistic psychology. According to the former theory, the learning being can be manipulated almost infinitely. The only problem for the behaviorist is to discover the appropriate operants, or natural behaviors, to be conditioned and the conditioners (gratifications and rewards) to which the organism will respond. In this view, humankind is not considered qualitatively different from lower order animals. The definition of the human being that emerged out of the behavioristic tradition was one that had to be fitted to the natural science model of inquiry adopted by learning psychologists. This model was able to establish confidence in itself by claiming that objects of study contained no inner existence. The physical and biological sciences did not need to worry about their subjects acting independently, or thinking, in ways that could not be measured with scientific instruments. Once educational psychologists took the major step of presuming that this model was appropriate to the study of human beings, they established both the grounds for proceeding and the basis for a debate that has blossomed into a healthy questioning of the whole enterprise. The question that is asked is, "Is the human being an appropriate subject for the natural science model of inquiry?" (For an extensive analysis of this question see Georgi, 1970.) Those who subscribe to the alternative or humanistic perspective have grave doubts. These doubts are based on a belief that human beings possess a core phenomenology, that is, a unique, individualistic way of viewing the world that cannot be derived by any of the psychological tools that exist or are likely to exist.

The key concepts in the alternative perspective are *experience, potential,* and *growth.* Human beings experience the world, and if they are not the same as each other, they experience it differently. Scientists can only approximate this experience, and even these approximations are probabilistic. Phenomenological psychologists, working within the conventional rules of their discipline, have tried to cope with this issue in the laboratory by attempting to derive people's experience from what they report their experience to be. But this is still a controlled situation, and people typically react to these controls with stereotyped responses. Anthropologists sometimes claim that naturalistic observation solves the problem, although this technique too has methodological shortcomings in that persons may behave differently when they know they are being observed.

R. D. Laing (1967), the radical British psychoanalyst, has achieved much notoriety and success among the antiscientists with his essays on the impossibility of studying human behavior in any way short of entering the world of the subject, a very difficult process at best. Abraham Maslow suggested that we conceive the human being not as he or she is but in the light of what he or she might be. The "becoming" notion, discussed earlier by Gordon Allport (1955), fits nicely the existential, phenomenological model of humankind that forms the basis for a new theory of education. The idea that humans possess a potential, unknown and unlimited, if taken seriously by educators, argues against any controlled or directed educating that sets goals or objectives for learners that are not grounded in the idiosyncratic potentiality of each individual.

Any educational practice contains some theory or set of assumptions, even if the practitioners cannot articulate them. To put it simply, we must believe something in order to proceed in a particular manner. Otherwise, why one way rather than another? If the answer is tradition or conventional wisdom, we must still assume that a set of assumptions underlies such "wisdom."

Somewhere in the culture one can find the basis for the

practical tactics that are formulated. If we wish to understand the meaning of alternative ways of viewing the learning person, it would be a mistake to consult the works of Maslow, Carl Rogers (1969), or Fritz Perls (1971), even though these men and others like them have articulated a humanistic psychology in which a theoretical model of education could be grounded.

The real source of contemporary educational alternatives— and here I am speculating—is "pop" rather than academic psychology. It is sensitivity training, encounter groups, Gestalt therapy, growth centers, meditation, yoga, and a host of other means through which desperate human beings are trying to discover who or what they are after the layers of bureaucratic, depersonalized, chauvinistic wraps are unwound.

Nevertheless, the earlier discussion of academic psychology is not irrelevant, for a similar struggle is occurring in that field—to work within old mythologies or create new ones. The mythologies of educational practice are the same in form, although not in intent, as the mythological conventions of academic psychology. Those who break the mold of conventional practice because they see no basis for loyalty to the old rules are performing the same action that humanistic psychologists engage in in order to advance understanding of the human personality and how it learns.

The psychological assumptions that underlie most educational alternatives might be summarized as follows:

People learn in a free environment. Freedom, as part of a psychological process, involves individuals in the task of making decisions or choices. This often involves risks, but the process itself is assumed to lead persons into growth patterns that are unavailable in closed or unfree environments. Psychological growth occurs when people gain confidence in their ability to make decisions on their own and discover that freely made choices allow them to move in directions that are compatible with their interests and personal styles of learning.

People learn by experience. Persons learn best when they are totally involved in experiences that interest them. Experience, in this context, refers to participation in activities which convey to each participant what knowledge, skills, or styles he needs to be effective in the kind of tasks he has chosen. This learning-by-doing notion assumes that learners discover the processes operating on them by becoming immersed in them. For example, they learn best what democracy is by doing it, not by reading about it. Humanistic educators respect experience because it involves the whole person, not only the cognitive processes that are evaluated on examinations.

People learn by taking risks. To take a risk is to undertake potential learning experiences without being able to predict the outcome. The important dynamic that underlies risk-taking is change. Persons do not change by participating only in comfortable routines. This assumption works in conjunction with the other two —making free choices and experiencing. In order to learn, we must try new things, risk possible damage to our egos. In the real lives of children, risk-taking means attempting activities in which they feel no skill or ability, such as painting or music or athletics. Many a child has been shocked out of every form of participation in these pursuits by teachers who are overly harsh or critical of his abilities or talent. Teachers encourage risk-taking only by withholding judgments until the student has given activities a good try, and even then judgment must be communicated in such a way as not to frighten the student into totally withdrawing from activities he likes, even if he possesses no special abilities.

Persons learn cooperatively. This assumption has dual foci. It says first that people learn "better" in the absence of competition. When competition is present, students learn the strategies to compete (such as how to take tests) rather than examining the ideas for their own sake. Further, it says that losers develop negative self-images which also work against their efforts to learn. If the only value of learning is what one wins, instant losers will see very little value in trying. Cooperative learning, conversely, expands the range of possible inputs and capitalizes on the psychological support available in the group.

People learn through their human qualities. Modes of learning appropriate to human beings differ, in some areas, from those we have observed in dogs and white mice. Of course, the reverse is also true. We would not teach a dog to sit or stay by lecturing to it. Human qualities are thinking, reflecting, sensing, and a number of variations that seem normal at particular ages. Children play, and adults work. Unfortunately, school teaches children as if they were small adults.

Alternative ideas on this theme can be broken into several components. First, *human beings are unique.* Because all humans grow up in different environments with different dispositions, they develop as unique beings. Therefore, they need individualized instruction, not just in terms of speed rates, but also in terms of learning styles. Each child has a unique configuration of such characteristics as sex, age, race, size, and so on, all of which affect the way he experiences himself in making learning decisions.

Second, *the learner is a feeling person.* Students have feelings about what they experience. These feelings are part of the learning context, but are seldom used in the instructional task. Strategies to utilize this affective component can be developed.

Third, *the learner is part of the human experience.* Human beings are born, grow, have sexual experiences, work experiences, and death experiences. Yet students are seldom exposed in any meaningful ways to these processes. We shield children from the realities of their own existence, perhaps because we, as teachers, have no confidence in our own abilities to treat these subjects well and honestly. But we miss the great opportunities to reduce anxiety and promote learning if we fail to discuss these essential aspects of daily life.

Fourth, *the learner is a social being.* Children study roles in order to understand society, but they seldom study about themselves to the same end. Schoolchildren are already deeply enmeshed in role-playing, and we can help them see how society operates by focusing on the way they learn to deal with the world.

In conclusion, whether these psychological assumptions can be supported empirically is not an academic question, although it is really only a question for academics. Persons engaged in creating alternative schooling operate as if they are true. And so far, because research is so sketchy (research support being generally unavailable) and because evaluation models for alternatives lag far behind models based on conventional practice, the credibility of those who support the alternative movement remains low in the academic community. Nevertheless, growth psychology is having a considerable impact on the larger society, which does not operate as rigidly in terms of conventional rules and paradigms as do academics. For this reason, educational alternatives are currently viable beyond the empirical evidence in their defense. The future, however, looms bright, for formal institutions sooner or later move in the direction of the general culture.

the philosophical context

Any discussion of the meaning of alternatives must encompass certain concepts that have traditionally belonged to the philosopher's domain: those of freedom, values, and knowledge or understanding. As I try to relate these ideas to the meaning of alternatives I will first discuss each separately, then integrate the three, and finally apply this integration to educational practice.

Freedom. The idea of freedom takes the form of assuming that human beings are born free as opposed to the contrasting hypothesis that they are born to fulfill some purpose, usually interpreted in theological terms. Freedom, as a supporting notion for educational alternatives, is conceived as the natural state of humankind, and freedom of choice is a moral right, even responsibility of each individual.

The ramifications of the belief in freedom are considerable. If one assumes that freedom is good, one must examine what kinds of freedoms are possible for individuals and appropriate in communities. That is, if we are really free, what choices do we have? If we do not know what choices exist our freedom to choose is still limited. To take this idea to its logical conclusion, the awareness of alternatives would have to include those which are known as well as those which are unknown. In practical terms, if a student does have freedom, that freedom involves the possibility of changing directions or choices whenever heretofore unknown alternatives become known to him.

In a learning community, or any other, the consequences of acting freely can be conceived as real or imaginary, as inherent in the rules of the social system or as psychological realities resulting from either a definition of a situation or an ethical belief. Both types of consequence influence free action, yet do not render the personal choice less free—only more or less difficult. Alternative educational systems ordinarily come to grips with this situation by arriving at a set of principles or guidelines that spell out those circumstances in which persons are constrained from acting in ways that are detrimental to other individuals or to the collectivity. A representative rule is one that says an individual may choose any course of action as long as this choice does not interfere with the learning opportunities of another or others. Most teachers operating within such a structure are required to make difficult judgments about the effects of a student's choice of action. Sometimes, if schools or classrooms are run totally as participatory democracies, the whole group may arrive at a set of rules to handle situations which are deemed harmful to others.

Freedom is an alternative to unfreedom and can be described nonevaluatively in terms of possibilities and constraints. Among humanists, however, freedom is also very much a value and is posited as a central condition of growth. Let us look now at some other contemporary values in relation to those of humanism.

Values. Current norms within the school reflect the goals of efficiency and respect for social and personal styles which are derived from achievement and ascriptive patterns inherent in the larger society. Achievement values are one-dimensional and universalistic. That is, all students must compete for rewards along a single dimension of performance, which is evaluated according to only one criterion. A grade of 90 or above is an A. The achievement that counts is ordinarily academic and cognitive rather than personal and affective. Getting the arithmetic problems right carries more weight than befriending another student or coming to understand one's motivations and prejudices. The concept of universalism refers to the fact that all students are evaluated in relation to the same set of achievement scores regardless of their starting points or differential learning styles.

The favoring of persons who come closest to adhering to the moral standards of the learning community is called ascription. A student who works hard at something receives approval even if the task displeases him and is antithetical to humane considerations. Respecting the teacher's authority is usually rewarded even though compliance to unjust rules may be a questionable action. Many Americans in the last decade—Martin Luther King is an outstanding example—have used civil disobedience to question the morality of a system that rewards conformity and punishes deviance, even when such deviance arises from an independent judgment that it is less moral to comply than to protest. Freedom is only possible to the extent that people realize they need not comply with unjust rules or compete with peers for goals which merely conform to established values.

The question of standards involves an analysis of how standards emerge and how they control behavior. The latter issue is known to all who have achieved mobility within a competitive social structure. The question of source raises a more basic issue. Most students of anthropology have little difficulty linking standards to characteristics of different cultures, and when we realize that standards vary we begin to grasp the idea that most standards are arbitrary and vary from society to society. The social science deduction from these analyses is that standards are neither right nor wrong but simply different—varying on the basis of unique qualities within cultural systems.

The philosophical perspective saves us from such inconclusive relativism by raising fundamental questions about right or wrong. It does not take us very far to say that Nazi standards and Communist standards differ. Any set of practical activities, such as education, must have a rationale to support the standards that guide members' behavior. As I suggested above, most traditional schooling values competition, efficiency, control, authority, conformity. Humanism provides an alternative rationale. The basic value propositions that guide humanistic endeavors are that harmony in human relationships is good, life is good, change is good, growth is good. In the absence of an ethic based on principles derived or accepted from supernatural sources, humanism bases its propositions on natural sources and the process of maintaining these natural conditions. If life and change and growth are natural conditions, then a system of human relationships that protects them is the logical consequence of accepting the goodness of these natural states. Any behavior that threatens life, change, or growth is to be avoided; that which enhances these conditions is to be sought and developed. In educational terms, a classroom which seeks to enhance growth, for example, is one that has achieved a structure that allows persons to grow in relation to the growth potential of individuals within that classroom. If changes are required, and they always are, the system adapts to those changes. The humanistic position is complex, but the basic premises have been stated. Once we accept these, we have an idea of the grounds on which a system of learning can be elaborated. Some questions that face proponents of this perspective are these: How do we know that each individual needs to grow? How does that individual know? On what can decisions be based? These questions take us to our third issue, knowledge and understanding.

The Question of Truth. In the present discussion the question of truth involves principally the assessment of the kind of evidence that individuals require to make choices or decisions about how to act in support of their own growth potential. In popular life as well as educational life, the alternatives, polarized for the purpose of analysis, are objective or subjective data. Most of Western society has a product consciousness. That is, only if actions produce an observable outcome can their worth be assessed. Such outcomes constitute truth, at the level of belief, when we can look at some concrete product that our decision or activity has produced. For this reason, we are willing to pour more money into space travel than education because we can witness a sky lab rising from Cape Kennedy but cannot assess the educated person. A student's graduation is the only sign of learning that concerns us since it is observable. In the same way, when parents say they will support their child's education, they really mean purchase a degree, for the symbol has replaced the reality of learning.

Because the society operates on a product model, so logically do the schools, as their many tests and certificates proclaim. The alternative is to assume that the truth of what occurs in the learning exists in the subjective consciousness of the person who experienced it. This issue strikes at the heart of the evaluation problem which Rodney Skager grapples with in Chapter 5. That is, if we do not utilize product data, like scores, then how do we know that a person is growing, and if we do not group and diagnose and prescribe on the basis of hard data, what then can we use?

The humanist perspective tries to make a case for subjective truth. This line of thinking has a long history, from Pascal (1941) and William James (1909), who were talking about God, to Kierkegaard (1959), who was talking about both God and knowledge, to Husserl (1962) and Polanyi (1958), who are talking about knowledge. To simplify the assumptions in order to reveal the philosophical basis of alternatives rather than to present the substantive argument, which is not the purpose of this paper, we need to consider a few basic ideas.

The first premise is that within the human organism exists a mechanism which knows the individual being as well as the outside world. This mechanism is capable of cuing the individual at the level of motivation about the kind of behavior that would produce growth or understanding.

Second, only the intuitive process avoids the problem of mythologies or relativistic systems that cue persons about how to make decisions. People who are caught up in mythologies which work against their basic well-being live in a state of alienation, or self-estrangement, where they feel that even when they seem to make their own decisions, they are simply guided by rules they have neither made nor had a chance to reject.

Third, the argument proceeds on the assumption that experience teaches in a way that detached reports of facts or the way things are do not. What it teaches is both qualitatively and quantitatively different from what can be learned from books or objective information. I understand differently and better, and I can apply my understanding to myself. I know something because I have had to deal with it as an experiential reality. Experience teaches better in the sense that what I know about myself guides me to decisions that will implement that understanding. If learning is to be incremental and consistent, then only the individual can know where he has to go and when he is ready to go in that direction. The child's experience forms the foundation on which other educational experiences are based.

Fourth, a distinction is made between knowledge and understanding; knowledge is what is known, and understanding is the way it is known. Full understanding encompasses those aspects of the phenomenal world that persons grasp in relation to their experience. Knowledge includes those facts, such as scientific information, that allow persons to describe processes within systems of knowledge (mathematics, biology) that cannot be grasped in a way that people know as part of their own experiences.

Fifth, the question of truth or understanding is directly related to the basis on which personal choices are made. Decisions about how to live, work, learn cannot be based on objective data, except as these give people information that can be checked out with the intuitive self.

Finally, subjective or intuitive knowledge has become a foundation for educational alternatives because persons involved in the movement have been able to assess the destructive power of objective bases of decision making, particularly since monolithic authority systems always accompany the establishment of observable facts as the basis for controlling the lives of others. This relationship has existed in all organized religions, political systems, and schools.

An Integration. The credibility and the applicability of each of the major concept areas, freedom, value, and truth, depend upon an integration. It does not help much to know the truth about oneself if one does not operate within a system that values it or if one does not have the freedom to move in directions that are compatible with the understanding. The belief in freedom as a paramount existential state of being requires a congruent value structure in order for persons to make decisions compatible with felt truths about how and where they must proceed. The development of a set of standards to guide systems such as schools is an inevitable consequence of collectivities coming together in a mutual enterprise. When the premise underlying such standards is that expectations must be consistent with natural processes such as growth, the direction is clear. Organization policy is sharpened when an experiential base is deemed necessary to produce this growth. Students are given freedom to act on their intuitive sense of what will be productive for such growth, and the institution establishes standards to protect this process and encourage it.

In these terms, philosophical perspectives on alternatives have practical meaning. The points of view on each of the three dimensions are interrelated and prescriptive, and presumably mutually supportive. Although counterarguments may be presented for the validity of objective truth, for the real absence of freedom in the human purpose, and for standards based on assumptions of other realities, this is not the place to air and contrast all positions. My purpose has been to link ideas with a particular educational policy, specifically alternatives, in order to increase understanding of what lies beneath practical adaptations in education.

alternatives in the real world

While all of the analysis and intellectual dialogues go on within the profession of education regarding alternatives, many who function outside academic environments have been implementing alternative structures in the everyday world of schooling. Over the past decade, a number of qualitatively different yet related programs have been tried, many are still being tried, and many programs are on the drawing board.

In the backwoods of Brazil, Paulo Freire (1968) put his theory of alternative ways of educating into practice among illiterate workers. Because of the political repercussions of his efforts, he was soon expelled from his homeland, yet he has continued to serve the alternative community well—through UNESCO and through the many speeches and contacts he has made, as well as the writing he has circulated in many countries.

Illich and Reimer have made similar contributions to the thinking of persons involved in seeking alternatives to conventional schooling and have established their own operation in Cuernavaca, Mexico. All three, Freire, Illich, and Reimer, give meaning to alternatives by emphasizing the social class biases of conventional education systems and recommending a revision of all those structures (discussed earlier under the sociological context) that maintain conditions of privilege for the economically advantaged and paths of failure for the economically disadvantaged.

In the United States, over the past dozen years, a mounting number of efforts have been marshaled against conventional education. The efforts began as criticism and for many have led to the institution of new educational structures in various contexts. Jonathan Kozol, whose *Death at an Early Age* (1967) enjoyed widespread popularity, has been actively engaged in implementing alternatives in minority communities, and his most recent writing articulates notions similar to those propounded by the Marxian educators Freire and Illich. The major difference between Kozol and these other critics is that Kozol differentiates between counterculture schools and alternatives aimed at improving educational opportunities for the economically disadvantaged. This distinction is uniquely a phenomenon of the United States and some European adaptations and has no meaning in Latin American contexts, where counterculture movements do not yet figure in the overall picture. This distinction requires some explication, since it points up some basic disparities in the way the educational revolution is understood by groups with different social characteristics.

On the one hand, the movement toward educational alternatives has been spearheaded by persons, usually of affluent middle-class backgrounds, who established so-called free schools within both rural and urban settings. On the other hand, some alternatives conceived within inner-city communities are aimed at a more humane education contained within the conventional framework of basic skill training. Although both prongs of the movement are attempting to create alternative conceptions of schooling, their directions are different. Some spokesmen, Kozol in particular, assert that our energy should be turned toward equalizing opportunities for all North Americans, before we implement alternatives that further augment the differences between the classes and the races. Roszak (1969) pointed up the dilemma for the alternative school movement when he commented that the lack of cohesiveness in confronting the establishment (political or educational) exists in the reality that minorities want into the system and middle-class dissidents want out. Kozol's emphasis seems to suggest that before persons can be said to possess freedom to make choices, they must begin with the same opportunities to move in either direction—to make it within the system or to opt for alternative paths and life styles.

This conflict is not likely to be resolved, and the meaning of alternatives must be sought within the collective consciousness of the separate groups. It boils down to two basic positions: one, which is economically based, calls for alternative educational structures that do not sort out minorities for lower-status roles in the social structure; the second view holds that even the affluent are captives of the system in which they usually fare well and are as much victims of the alienative effects of schooling as minorities. For the economically disadvantaged, the alienation appears in the form of guaranteed powerlessness within the prevailing social and economic system. They are at the bottom, to be sure, but still a part of the system, since the values of the poor are very much like those of the rich: both want a share of the pie. For middle-class dissidents, the issue is psychological rather than sociological alienation. Alternatives are conceived by this group as adaptations which remove children and adults from the constraints of bureaucratic powerlessness and the concomitant experience of depersonalization and meaninglessness. One group demands equal opportunities to learn the basic skills for mobility, and the other cries for freedom from the manipulation of adults (parents and school personnel) in order to explore self, interpersonal relations, and cognitive curiosities, whether these lead to status mobility or not.

Within the mainstream of schooling, alternatives must be understood as responses to both kinds of complaints. The call for responsible attention to the historical alienation of poor minorities has been met with a number of alternative adaptations, from busing to experimental programs within ghetto and barrio schools. But many assert that such innovations are tokens at best and that opportunities for minorities are only minimally better than in the past. Claims of psychological alienation have fared better, probably because the complaints emanate from the middle class. Nongraded, nongrading schools spring up regularly in public schooling. Student participation in decision making has made inroads, particularly at the upper levels, and the ecology of many classrooms has been rearranged (for example, circular tables have replaced chairs in rows). In many sections of the country, schools have instituted open classrooms with a learning center focus, in place of the closed situation in which all students learn the same thing in the same way simultaneously. Boards of Education have supported the creation of entirely alternative "free schools" within the main districts. Some have questioned the motivation for such action, suggesting that it is a convenience either to quiet dissent or to localize the dissenters (students, parents, and faculty). Even if this is so, the result is that alternatives emerge as viable structures and—what is more significant for the movement at its ideological base—that the idea of alternatives begins to appear in the consciousness of the mainstream of society. Not that approval is widespread, but that the possibility of things, in this case schools, being other than they are comes into conscious existence.

conclusion

This chapter has attempted to reveal the meaning of alternatives within a comprehensive framework. It has explored a range of ways of conceptualizing alternatives so that the major concepts and structures could be known to those who are either analyzing or doing alternatives in education. It is, I believe, to the credit of those who are interested in the phenomena of educational alternatives that the conventional posture of detached reporting and observation is being replaced by active involvement in doing what they are studying. This step, too, has emerged as an alternative for academics, and if it becomes a viable choice in the sense that they do not suffer the conventional negative sanctions for departing from a detached posture with respect to educational research, the advantages could be considerable. Professional academic education could evolve into a closer, more meaningful association with the real business of schooling, which would improve understanding as well as relationships with school personnel who view academics as removed from the real world of teaching and learning. The methodological advantages should also be apparent. If we are willing to admit, as few academics ever are, that things are not necessarily what we call them, or how we decide to operationalize them, we are well on our way to discovering a new basis for knowing about educational processes.

Reality is indeed difficult to pin down, but it is better to discover it in the meaning systems of those who experience their reality than to label it from our own and believe that we have captured an idea simply because we are willing to give it our own meaning.

references

Allport, G. *Becoming.* New Haven: Yale University Press, 1955.

Coleman, J. S., and others. *Equality of Educational Opportunity.* Washington, D.C.: Government Printing Office, 1966.

Freire, P. *Pedagogy of the Oppressed.* New York: Herder and Herder, 1968.

Georgi, A. *Psychology as a Human Science.* New York: Harper and Row, 1970.

Husserl, E. *Ideas.* London: Collier-Macmillan, 1962.

Illich, I. *De-Schooling Society.* New York: Harper and Row, 1971.

James, W. *The Meaning of Truth.* New York: Longmans, Green, 1909.

Kierkegaard, S. *A Kierkegaard Anthology.* Robert Bretall (Ed.). New York: Modern Library, 1959.

Kozol, J. *Death at an Early Age.* Boston: Houghton-Mifflin, 1967.

Kozol, J. *Free Schools.* Boston: Houghton-Mifflin, 1972.

Laing, R. D. *The Politics of Experience.* New York: Ballantine, 1967.

Maslow, A. *Towards a Psychology of Being.* 2nd ed. New York: Van Nostrand Reinhold, 1968.

Parsons, T. *The Social System.* Glencoe, Ill.: Free Press, 1951.

Pascal, B. *Pensées, the Provincial Letters.* New York: Modern Library, 1941.

Perls, F. *Gestalt Therapy Verbatim.* New York: Bantam Books, 1971.

Polanyi, M. *Personal Knowledge.* New York: Harper, 1958.

Reimer, E. *School Is Dead.* New York: Doubleday, 1971.

Rogers, C. *Freedom to Learn.* Columbus, Ohio: Charles E. Merrill, 1969.

Roszak, T. *The Making of a Counter Culture.* New York: Anchor Books, 1969.

Weber, M. *The Protestant Ethic and the Spirit of Capitalism.* New York: Scribner, 1930.

Willard, E. *Sexism in Education.* Minneapolis: University Station, 1972.

humanistic roots of
alternatives in education

val d. rust

In recent years a social movement has come into being which is beginning to take on revolutionary proportions. It is found almost exclusively in affluent areas of the world and is the main impulse of alternatives in the United States. Some of the labels attached to the educational component of this development are alternatives in education, confluent education, antiauthoritarian education, and humanistic education. (Thomas J. La Belle, in Chapter 2, calls it the thrust toward educational relevance.) The historical roots of the movement are closely tied to the various humanistic expressions which have dominated the minds and actions of men from time to time in the West.

This essay discusses the dominant humanistic movements in Western thought, namely, literary humanism, religious humanism, rational humanism, and scientific humanism. I review certain historical bases in each movement, mention twentieth-century educational points of view which identify with each movement, and discuss their relationship with contemporary humanistic education.

The first three of these movements are derived from Renaissance humanism and concern themselves with the notion of *Humanitas*. Cicero used this term originally to refer to the Greek idea of man, not common man, but the "expression of an absolute and timeless ideal" human character (for a lexicographical discussion of the term see Schneidewin, 1897). The literary, religious, and rational humanists of this century have subsequently sought to illuminate the manner in which the highest revelation of man might be realized, though each group has focused on distinctive elements and therefore must be treated separately.

Of the four, scientific humanists comprise the most distinctive group. Originating mainly from the naturalistic science of the modern world, they challenge the traditional humanist concern for ideal man, as they concentrate on humanitarian aims more than on human perfection. Scientific humanists also form the most direct link with contemporary humanistic education, though manifestations of all movements are clearly identifiable.

literary humanism

Renaissance humanism began in Northern Italy, culminating a revolt against traditional feudal and ecclesiastical authority. Its birth was not sudden or violent, but a gradual social and cultural adjustment to human and institutional tensions that resulted from the rise of urban centers, the emergence of new monarchical states, the development of secular forces which challenged the Church, and the introduction of Eastern influences.

The primary characteristic of the Italian Renaissance in the fourteenth century was its emphasis on man, his senses and feelings, the sense of fulfillment man achieves by reasoning, and the beauties of the earth which man is capable of experiencing. Awakening to a new self-consciousness, scholars and leaders rejected the other-worldly focus of the past and were successful in bringing to fruition a sense of the worth of man as an individual. Although the Italians had become more aware of themselves, they were not yet creatures of the modern world and were unwilling, therefore, to venture alone into an unknown realm of new thought and action. They required a guide to interpret the physical and intellectual world for them, and they found it in the growing collection of newly discovered writings from ancient Greece and Rome. Soon these writings became a new authority, just as binding in many respects and as limiting as the religious authority in the medieval world. With these writings to lead them, the humanists imitated the ancients to such an extent that they soon knew what their predecessors had known; they wrote as they had written and thought as they had thought. They even tried to feel and sense as the ancients (Burckhardt, 1958, p. 211).

The humanistic learnings demanded a new kind of education, and a number of patron princes established new schools to disseminate these ideas. These institutions broke from the stifling scholastic tradition which held sway at the time, and such men as Vittorino da Feltra and Guarino of Verona set about educating the well-rounded man. Unlike humanism at large, their schools had not hardened into rigidity. Da Feltra's boarding school for boys most perfectly embodied the aims of physical, intellectual, and character development that typified the court schools. His "House of Joy" concentrated on the classical writings, ancient history, philosophy, logic, astronomy, mathematics, and music, but it did so in a pleasant, stimulating way. He insisted that his teachers note the different inclinations, interests, and approaches to learning of each pupil. Here was a child-centered environment where games and playthings were incorporated into the curriculum for the young, and discipline of the body for older boys was achieved through rigorous games and exercises (Woodward, 1912).

In a very short time, however, the court schools fell into the sterile literary reproduction tendencies of humanism in general and were characterized by rote learning of Greek and Latin texts and memorization of teachers' commentary on the grammatical, literary, geographical, and biographical aspects of the texts. Their erudite staffs were not unlike what Paul Goodman today describes as "school monks," exhibiting very little creative expression, either verbally or through the written word (Goodman, 1962). Within a few decades those schools, which had enjoyed such a brief life of vitality and progressive reform, became deeply absorbed in classical and religious studies. However, they eventually came to enjoy a preeminence unchallenged for several hundred years, and formed the basis of the elite grammar school, exemplified until this century by the public school in England, the *lycée* in France, and the *Gymnasium* in Germany.

Colonial America carried on the literary tradition in its Latin grammar schools, but frontier conditions soon proved too taxing for these institutions to thrive, and by the time of the American revolution classical literary studies had largely faded from the scene. The early part of the twentieth century in America witnessed a return to literary humanism in the guise of traditional literary criticism. Literary editor Paul Elmer More and Harvard professor Irving Babbitt led an attack on what they considered to be the hopeless destruction of any human, ethical standards, aesthetic tastes, and leadership capacity in the American people. Their revolt was against the wholesale adoption of scientific naturalism, which they claimed had led to complete faith in reason or romantic naturalism and thereby to "unbridled imagination."

Babbitt's and More's call for a revival of standards of taste and a return to the tradition of a liberal education as found in classical literature pertained to only a few individuals, for their focus was on the aristocracy. They maintained that the masses are not equipped to rise to the heights possible in a rhetorical and literary tradition and, consequently, are not equipped to make sound judgments, lead temperate lives, or exercise freedom judiciously. More was fond of quoting Burke, who said: "It is ordained in the eternal constitution of things that men of intemperate minds cannot be free. Their passions forge their fetters" (More, 1915, pp. 26-27).

A disciple of Babbitt, Norman Foerster, a professor of American Literature at the universities of Wisconsin, North Carolina, and Iowa, carried on the tradition of literary humanism to the middle of the twentieth century. Toward the end of his career he moved away from his position that the masses were only capable of being indoctrinated, suggesting that even at the state universities where Jacksonian democracy and the humanitarian movement of scientific humanism had reached full expression, the literary tradition was also possible. He even accepted the equivalency of modern languages as a substitute for the liberal studies of Greek and Latin (Foerster, 1937, p. 39).

This literary humanism is expressed today in the humanities courses of our institutions of higher education. Literary humanists, including such men as Jacques Barzun, Gilbert Highet, and Mark Van Doren, also call for education not only for the few but for the many. These men reiterated the claim that the purpose of teaching is to educate the well-rounded man. To them, teaching is more an art than a science, and similar sentiments can be found among many contemporary humanistic educators.

There are other correlates between the literary humanists and humanistic educators in general. Both have been suffused with a sense of rebellion against the pervasive norms of society. As Renaissance Italy rejected its medieval heritage, humanistic educators are rejecting the externally imposed norms of modern urban, industrial society. As modern literary humanists seek to revive the spirit of balance and well-roundedness in man, humanistic educators are also groping toward a learning environment which encourages a full expression of man beyond that which our schools are now willing or able to provide. However, it must be pointed out that only limited support for the broader directions of humanistic education comes from the humanities since these academicians continue to rely on the ancient classics as the foundation stone of an adequate education. Any claim to a single medium, such as literature, or to a certain age, such as ancient Greece, as the best expression of mankind is too limiting for most contemporary humanistic educators. Even though some prominent spokesmen, such as Paul Goodman and Norman O. Brown, would characterize themselves as "men of letters" in the classical sense, they do not share the narrowness of their counterparts in Renaissance or contemporary literary humanism.

humanism and reason

The one-sidedness of Renaissance Italy was recognized by certain masters of word and form who defended the notion that truth and beauty are evident in all ages, not just in antiquity. Pico della Mirandola eloquently reminded his contemporaries of fourteenth-century Italy: "We shall live for ever, not in the schools of word-catchers, but in the circle of the wise, where they talk not of the mother of Andromache or of the sons of Niobe, but of the deeper causes of things human and divine; he who looks closely will see that even the barbarians had intelligence not of the tongue, but in the breast" (Burckhardt, 1958, p. 210). Although Italian humanists had indeed become word-catchers, the fascination with the writings of the ancients was based not only on their literary style but on their insights into the meaning of being human.

The Christian religion had asserted for centuries that understanding and vision are a product of faith alone and a matter of divine grace. The ancient documents promised a new and wider perspective of man. The Greeks had claimed that man could come to knowledge by intellectual activity as well as by faith. Scholars were inspired to consider the possibility that a fundamental dualism—faith and reason—could be bridged. Though different, they could lead to the same end, illuminating the highest principles of the world and of human life itself. The Italians, Northern Europeans, and, ultimately, modern man were to be captivated by the classical concept that human beings are by nature rational beings.

Though Greek culture took various forms during the period of its greatest achievement several centuries prior to the birth of Christ, from Sparta to Athens, from Pythagoras to Socrates, all reflected a rational approach to establishing standards for the highest expression of man. Of the three grades of citizens distinguished by Plato—artisans, warriors, and guardians or philosopher kings—the philosophers had the most important function: to display wisdom and reason, the function peculiar to man. Aristotle, Plato's student, also maintained that reason was the highest virtue possible in man, for that was what distinguished him from vegetative and animal levels of life, and "the lower always exists for the sake of the higher" (Aristotle, 1962b, p. 317).

In Aristotle's view, education should focus on liberal subjects, those which lead to the cultivation of intelligence or reason; nevertheless he maintained that a liberal education required the balanced development of intellectual, moral, and physical qualities in each person (Aristotle, 1962b, pp. 332-352). He also stated that subjects should neither be taught so intensively that students become professionals, nor be pursued for the sake of gain, nor be presented in such a manner as to encourage competition between students.

The importance of rational thought is still a hallmark of humanism, though the form presently advocated is more utilitarian than Aristotle and Plato would have wished. The rationalists of the seventeenth century, Descartes, Leibnitz, and Spinoza, thought out comprehensive systems of truth based on first principles. The intellectual climate of the eighteenth century witnessed a uniting of reason with the inductive processes of scientific observation, testing relationships and piecing together a global picture of the universe out of systematic research and inquiry.

Twentieth-century America has also produced its proponents

of rational humanism. Men such as Mortimer Adler and Robert M. Hutchins called for a return to a clear understanding of man as a rational animal and a clarification of educational goals that derive from first principles. These men and their followers have for several decades advocated a liberal education designed to liberate man's powers of thinking. They castigate the educational trend toward illiberal vocationalism and fragmented subject matter disciplines; as they reason with syllogistic perfection: "Education implies teaching. Teaching implies knowledge. Knowledge is truth. The truth is everywhere the same. Hence education should be everywhere the same" (Hutchins, 1962, p. 66).

The content of rational humanist education is to be found in the great literary works of the Western world. The student spends the major share of his time reading, discussing, and analyzing the classics. This is not done for antiquarian purposes; rather, "the books are to be read because they are as contemporary today as when they were written, and because the problems they deal with and the ideas they present are not subject to the law of perpetual and interminable progress" (Adler, 1939, p. 144). The rational humanist approach is best exemplified today at St. John's College, whose total curriculum is the *Great Books of the Western World*. Here students spend four years in a systematic, unified, and ordered program of reading and analyzing these works in order to discipline the mind and master the liberal arts.

Absent from the program at St. John's is any concern about educating students for a specific specialty, profession, or business. The leaders of this movement maintain that the purpose of education is to produce a person who would perform whatever functions he or she engages in with justice, magnanimity, and thoughtful skill. In this respect modern humanistic educators are in full sympathy with rational humanists. Both groups maintain we have vulgarized education into a vocational mill which concentrates on the specialist and his skills; we have lost our vision of the ends of education.

At the same time, most contemporary humanistic educators cannot help but feel a measure of discomfort with the singleness of attitude and restrictive intellectual focus of the rationalists. They would claim that all children should be given an opportunity to develop intellectual faculties, but contemplation as an all-consuming and self-fulfilling activity lacks the appeal that it undoubtedly held for Aristotle. The uneasiness with reason goes still deeper, for however much we all wish at times that our lives were bound by reason, there are aspects of life which defy such processes, and meaningful living often transcends our powers of reasoning.

Reason is indeed a primary attribute of man, but much more distinguishes man from brutes. John Martin Rich, in his recent statement on humanistic education, argues that man "has a highly developed cerebral cortex, walks upright, and has an opposable thumb for tool-making. He not only is conscious but is aware that he possesses consciousness. He has a cosmic sense and can laugh at the inscrutability of the world and his fate. He also has complex emotions and feelings that lead frequently to the development of imposing ethical systems" (Rich, 1971, p. 10).

Erasmus, one of the dominant figures of Northern European humanism at the time of the Renaissance, forcefully demonstrated that reason is often subordinate to other factors in his masterful satire *In Praise of Folly,* where folly itself merits in many instances some admiration. Such a claim in no way demeans reason; Erasmus showed that life is overwhelmingly and brutally absurd unless it is guided by reason, but the adventure of life is based in part upon folly in all men, and even the cool calculations of the intellectuals, the critics, and the theologians are a bit foolish when compared with living experiences that move humans and inspire activity. And when these activities are moving, their inspiration is generally from a wider and a deeper source than logic and reason.

humanism and religion

One force that has been of prime interest to humanists has been the spiritual dimension of man. On the one hand, humanists have attempted to destroy the pillars on which religion and spirituality have depended, such as the idea of a creator or otherworldly elements of life (Van Praag, 1969, pp. 14-15). On the other hand, humanists have maintained a commitment and devotion to the religious life. This conflict has found expression in essentially every age of Western history.

Although in classical antiquity manifestations of theocentric humanism can be found in Plato, Aristotle, and a host of other masters of word and thought, a countercurrent of religious skepticism in Greece challenged these notions. Protagoras, the most renowned and respected Sophist in Athens, maintained that the source of human knowledge was the immediate sensual experience of man's natural and social environment. He eloquently argued a subjective viewpoint in philosophy, which demanded that "man is the measure of all things," not some externally imposed supernatural or universal reality. Here was a proclamation that man's sensations, his perceptions, his feelings and intelligence were valid avenues to knowledge. In man himself was to be found the most genuine source of truth, goodness, and beauty (an extensive account of Protagoras is in Schiller, 1907).

Sophists such as Protagoras were concerned less with speculation about the inscrutable than with helping men become the best of man. "Regarding the Gods," Protagoras is known to have said, "I have no way of knowing whether they exist or whether they do not" (Diels, 1956, p. 4). Protagoras, first and foremost an educator, argued that his primary task was neither to discover the truth nor to dwell upon things religious but to teach pupils prudence in private and public affairs, the orderly management of home and family, the art of persuasive speaking, and the ability to act capably in the affairs of state (Plato, 1871, p. 140). Learning for its own sake was not the goal of these philosophers. The democratic form of government of the day put great power in the hands of the orator, and the Sophists, who were itinerant teachers, professed their ability to equip the young to take their place in public life.

Protagoras rejected the surety of religious belief and even questioned that objective truth existed. Later teachers of rhetoric such as Gorgias went even further, questioning whether or not truth existed and maintaining that if it did exist in some form, it probably could not be communicated. Such a relativistic view was largely incorporated by Roman rhetoric masters such as Quintillian and later captivated Italian humanists, who gained inspiration from these arguments as they broke away from the medieval tradition of religious servitude and dogma at the time of the revival of learning.

Although Renaissance Italy was largely irreligious, as humanism crossed the Alps into Northern Europe it took on a devoutly spiritual tone, though this expression stood in marked contrast to that of the medieval period. The humanist leaders in the North were generally serious churchmen who wanted to purify and reform religious life. Through classical studies they pointed out the ignorance and immorality that was rampant in the Church. Their efforts represented a release of mind, a rational humanism, a joining of mind and spirit.

Like the South, Northern Europe was fascinated by the documents of the ancient world, though the North turned to the treasures of Christian antiquity as well as to Greek and Roman manuscripts. Whereas the South was highly concerned with words and language, the North valued morals and education. The theology of Erasmus exemplified the northern focus. Called *Philosophia Christi,* his humanism was illustrated by the example of Christ as a person, the Sermon on the Mount, and a simple ethical life. Erasmus dismissed the abstract, complicated methods of scholastic logic and railed effectively against the theological nit-picking that characterized the universities of the day. Through his use of the language, Erasmus challenged the narrowness, corruption, and error rampant among the clergy and civil administrators.

Erasmus not only was a man of erudition and high standing but devoted much time to establishing learning environments where young minds might best grasp their finest heritage. He suggested that such a process should begin early: mothers were expected to impart habits of health and Christian character. He also wanted mothers to introduce children informally to reading, writing, and drawing by exposing them to familiar objects and by using pictures, stories, and games. When the child was seven, the father would either assume personal responsibility for his education or place the child in school. Under no circumstances were flogging and punishment considered appropriate, and even strong words were thought to be detrimental to the child's learning.

Among Erasmus' writings was a statement of the *Right Method of Instruction.* His curriculum included Latin, Greek, Scripture, Moral Instruction, and History. His method for studying the classics is illustrative. He insisted that rules of syntax were necessary, though recognized that it was a waste of time to teach children rules. "It is not rules that will make children acquire the power of speaking language, but daily reading of the best authors of ancient literature" (Woodward, 1904, p. 81). But for all of Erasmus's stress on classical literature, his activities were inspired by a single aim: "The propagation of Christian humanism, of a purified Catholicism in alliance with the moral wisdom and rational culture of antiquity" (Bush, 1939, p. 63). Education must necessarily carry with it ideals of piety, moral duty, and good manners as well as learning.

And so today we find humanists who identify directly with Christianity as well as with assorted other approaches to spiritual communion. Many of a more temperate bent identify directly with Erasmus, for he was opposed to extremes, advocating "proportionateness through cultivation of the law of measure," a view later echoed by Irving Babbitt (Babbitt, 1930, p. 30). Still others are Catholic scholars such as Gilbert Chesterton, Jacques Maritain, and, more recently, Romano Guardini, who, though they identify in large measure with rational humanists, attach supreme significance to the role of religion and to the study of theology in the educative process. These men have been powerful spokesmen in demanding reassessment of our reckless plunge into a scientific and technological world.

Maritain, a Catholic layman, maintained the optimistic belief that the pervasive naturalism of modern civilization could be harmonized with the supernatural. To him contemporary sociological and psychological explanations of man gave but a partial explanation of his true nature. Christian man is "an animal endowed with reason, whose supreme dignity is in the intellect; and man as a free individual in personal relation with God, whose supreme righteousness consists in voluntarily obeying the law of God" (Maritain, 1943, p. 7). For Maritain, true man harmonizes reason and faith perfectly, and the role of education is to cultivate his natural powers of reason and move him to exercise his faculties for the glory of God. To a religious humanist this is the meaning of a liberal education.

Maritain was writing at a time when technology did not constitute such a threat to mankind as it does today, and he believed that the technical was a part of modern liberal education. He believed, also, that technology could be humanized if it were integrated with other aspects of man's education. More recently, however, important spokesmen have been less optimistic. Jacques Ellul, still another Catholic layman, characterizes modern society as one having a "technique ideology" which gives ultimate value to efficiency, means, and "know-how." Other ends have become superfluous in the process (Ellul, 1964).

Though men such as Maritain and Guardini have made significant contributions in spreading a way of thinking about contemporary social ills, they are still bound in established religious movements, especially in Catholicism. Consequently, they do not express the anti-institutional sentiments of spiritual spokesmen in the mainstream of contemporary humanistic education. These humanists would agree with Erasmus that the personality of Christ should serve as one role model for their own lives, but they go beyond Erasmus's fetish for moderation, restrained harmony, and peace, and follow the lead of contemporary spiritual leaders such as Harvey Cox in demanding direct experience with affirmative life and celebrating the larger "cosmic phenomena open to us through intuition, awe and ecstasy" (Cox, 1970, p. 62).

Contemporary humanistic religious life, according to Theodore Roszak, who has described the counterculture movement of today, is "neither escapist nor ascetic." Religious, humanistic educators are in harmony with Erasmus in their struggle to achieve a more inclusive and humane religious expression, but many move toward a "This Worldly Mysticism," and seek "an ecstasy of the body and of the earth that somehow embraces and transforms mortality" (Cox, 1970, p. 129). They negate or disregard the extraworldly designs which traditional Christianity has imposed on them and scoff at the metaphysical speculation that accompanies so much of theology. But such attitudes should not be construed as a trend toward a totally anthropocentric orientation, for the new humanists are seeking communion with nonmaterial forces. It is they who are turning to Eastern religions as possible avenues to a higher consciousness, to a relationship with the universe which dogmatic religious practices seem to have destroyed.

These yearnings for a higher consciousness are reminiscent of Plato's metaphor of the cave in which the life of experience with all its paradoxes, tragedies, and ugly manifestations is nothing but shadows and distortions of the real and really beautiful. Contemporary humanism is most vulnerable when it rejects the reality of common-sense experience, for the quest for higher consciousness inevitably places one in the Platonic trap: the ultimate source of ideas and virtues is profoundly mysterious, and therefore in the world of experienced reality one is almost forced to be a spectator in a shadow play. Such an admission in no way diminishes the philosophic concern of the religious humanists. Their rejection of contemporary reality is little more than a rejection of the reigning scientific-mechanistic view of reality; they demand that the real world, including the schools, be more than that found in impersonal mathematical formulas. Education must include not only a physical, objective dimension but a subjective, spiritual dimension as well.

We have seen manifestations of literary, rational, and religious humanism in contemporary education, but without question this movement is mainly a child of, and a revolt against, the most pervasive expression of humanism in the twentieth century: naturalistic science and pragmatism.

As has been mentioned, naturalistic humanists concentrated on humanitarian service more than on a quest for ideal man. Such an orientation was an important departure from a fundamental principle of traditional humanism. As long as one focuses on ideal man, one is also compelled to uphold social distinctions in the community. The humanism of the pragmatists challenged the aristocratic thrust in society. Despite their great achievements, even men such as Plato and Aristotle had been unable to rise to the "idea of mankind." They continued to class slaves merely as creatures, suggested that weak children be destroyed, and believed that artisans should not be accorded the privilege of true citizenship (Schweitzer, 1960, p. 129).

In the evolution of social thought after the Hellenistic period such extreme distinctions were broken down, but the humanists until very recently continued to reflect aristocratic tendencies. At the beginning of this century, however, John Dewey, F. C. S. Schiller, and others attempted to find a new humanism, built on achieving the potential of scientific method and modern technology. Here was a call for a universal brotherhood of man whose inspiration was derived from the confidence gained by man in the astounding accomplishments of the physical sciences. For the first time in recorded history, human beings anticipated the real possibility of gaining control of the forces of nature, and the new humanists saw an opportunity to alleviate man from physical and social pain.

The spokesmen for progressivism in the Western world placed their faith in a utilitarian mode of operation. They shunned metaphysical questions and concentrated on method. "If it works it is true" became their adage, and they turned to a glorification of the scientific expert, who would be willing, undoubtedly, to sacrifice himself to contribute his share to progress. Here was a philosophy of humanitarian service, service to mankind, with an optimistic sense that man was by nature good and would therefore devote his skills to the betterment of human beings. This improvement was to be brought about through schooling, the process that was to mold the child's latent powers and set him on the road toward continuous growth. Along the way he would constantly adjust and extend himself in his quest to be a productive member of an industrial, urban society.

The liberal tradition at the root of modern progressivism is an outgrowth of the social and humanitarian liberalism which arose from French political philosophy in the eighteenth century. Jean Jacques Rousseau, who is probably most representative of this spirit in that period, maintained that human nature in its original state is good. "Let us lay down as an incontestable principle," demanded Rousseau in his lengthiest educational treatise, *Émile*, "that the first impulses of nature are always right. There is no original perversity in the human heart" (Rousseau, 1962, p. 40). He claimed that human beings are corrupted by social institutions. If members of a society are immoral, they are victims of an immoral society; and if bad men are to be made good, then society itself must undergo fundamental reform.

Potentially, society might be brought into conformity with nature, and if it were, the moral citizen would find his life totally and naturally immersed in the life of the state. Such a condition might have been possible in an ancient Greek city-state, but Rousseau deemed it impossible in the large, complex modern nation (Rousseau, 1962, p. 170). Since there is an irreconcilable conflict between natural man and social institutions, he admitted that natural man and moral citizen might never be realized, and thus the education of a young man would only be possible outside the influence of society. However, after assessing social development in his day, Rousseau felt it was no longer possible to advocate the "noble savage" notion, and so he considered less adequate but more realistic educational alternatives. One would be to give the child a veneer of civilization sufficient for him to get on in society but not enough to destroy his natural attributes.

A second and more viable alternative is to consider the fact that all institutions are based on certain natural expressions or relationships which are found in man and the family. The state, the city, and other institutions reflect father-child or husband-wife type relationships and would be natural if they were allowed to genuinely retain these relationships. The educational implications of this alternative are easy to see. Rousseau maintained that a single person should have charge of the child throughout his education in order to avoid authority conflicts for the child. The primary purpose of education is to create a fertile environment in which the child may develop his original nature. Such a self-actualizing process should be joyous and spontaneous. Along the way the tutor should help the child make the natural relationships inherent in social institutions personal to himself (Rousseau, 1962, pp. 184-185).

Rousseau challenged many of his contemporaries, taking direct issue with John Locke by maintaining that children are not capable of reasoning. Such a process comes at the end of the child's development. "Childhood," he claimed, "has ways of seeing, thinking, and feeling peculiar to itself" (Rousseau, 1962, pp. 38-39). He advised his readers to view the child as a child, to recognize the fact that childhood has its place in the scheme of life, and to see that the child must be allowed to progress naturally through the various developmental stages in life. Although Rousseau provided his own personal insights into infancy, boyhood, preadolescence, adolescence, and manhood, his most profound admonition was that all tutors should begin by actively studying their own pupils, "for assuredly you do not know them" (Rousseau, 1962, p. 6).

Rousseau's impact on child-rearing patterns, social reform, and more humane educational practice was immediate and profound. The core of his educational ideas was soon incorporated by the Swiss reformer Johann Pestalozzi, who argued for natural educational methods and incorporated the tutorial ideas of Rousseau in a school setting. Pestalozzi intended his school to reflect the whole of social life, not restricting itself, therefore, to intellectual pursuits, but engaging the children in activities that would help them grow naturally and fully into manhood. Pestalozzi argued that a teacher could only accomplish such a task by participating in a relationship of mutual respect and by ceasing to impose himself on an environment that required the unfolding of spontaneous self-activity.

The naturalism of Rousseau continued in Europe through the work of men such as Friedrich Froebel, the father of the kindergarten, and culminated in the New Education Movement around the turn of this century. That movement began as isolated educational reform projects in various countries. There was no unity in the early stages; in fact, many critics of certain activities were leaders of other reform undertakings. For example, in Germany, four primary

educational trends emerged prior to World War I: the Country
Home Schools (*Landerziehungsheime*), the Art Education Move-
ment, the Movement for Self-Directive Character Training, and the
Activity School Movement (*Arbeitsschule*).

The first Country Home School in Germany was founded by
Hermann Lietz, who responded negatively to the inhuman technical
advances of his day and who was disturbed with the trends toward
urban life. He had spent a year at Abbotsholme, a progressive
school in England, and wanted all youth to have an opportunity to
participate in the native culture and customs of the Germanic people in a rural, forested setting where they would be immersed in the
ideals of nature, health, and simplicity.

The Art Education Movement in Germany began in Hamburg
under the leadership of Alfred Lichtward. It represented a revolt
against the dominance of intellectualism in the schools and revealed
a new will and form of expression. Art was to be the central focus
of all schooling. Lichtward's curriculum focused mainly on modern
art and *Volk* art, but also on movement through sport, plays, and
dancing. Young people were encouraged to express themselves and
come to know the rhythm and creativity of their own bodies and
souls.

Still another trend of the New Education in Germany was
character education, a reaction against the bureaucratized, teacher-
centered school of the past in which the teacher was expected to
uphold the dictates of state and school tradition. Educators recognized that schools had been developing "yes-men and dependent
people," and though order and discipline suffered in the process,
they began advocating Deweyian-type educational environments in
which an "embryonic community life" would equip the young for
civic life (Nohl, 1928, p. 53). Men such as Friedrich Wilhelm Foerster demanded that such character development required a specific
type of education, one which proceeded from the child. The role of
the teacher was to detect the child's needs, interests, attitudes, and
mental capabilities, and then to provide the surroundings which
would allow him to grow and develop into the person divinity had
intended him to be (Foerster, 1908).

The final New Education Movement was created mainly by
the Munich superintendent of schools, who recognized that spontaneous free expression and social interaction were important aspects of the educational process, but who also claimed that real

learning depended on concrete and actual life experiences, especially manipulative experiences. The manual work and activity ideas of Froebel were developed into one of the most extensive technical education programs in the world at that time. Georg Kerschensteiner's industrial schools were intended to help the child learn by doing so that he could build up a means of becoming "a useful citizen endowed with the maximum of skill, ability, and joy in work" (Kerschensteiner, 1913, p. 78). This aspect of the New Education Movement united the romantic naturalism that had typified the programs of Rousseau, Pestalozzi, and Froebel with the twentieth-century faith that occupational training and technical skills development are potentially "truly liberalizing in quality" (Dewey, 1916, p. 235).

Stories similar to those of Germany could be told of Switzerland, Italy, Belgium, England, and other countries in Europe. The reciprocal impact of European reform and American developments at that time was significant. A steady stream of American progressives visited Europe and brought back ideas to the United States, which was undergoing its own version of social and educational reform. As in Europe, American educational reformers concentrated on the social conditions in which children were being placed and railed against the unfavorable aspects of urban, industrial life, but they protested especially about the failure of schools to reorient themselves to serve the needs of the modern child.

John Dewey emerged as the foremost spokesman for progressive education in America, and his laboratory school at the University of Chicago, founded in 1896, became a model for the school of the future. Dewey pointed out that the modern child lives in a world of manufactured products and is separated from the processes through which these products come into being. In the premodern world "the entire industrial process stood revealed, from the production on the farm of the raw materials, till the finished article was put to use" (Dewey, 1970, p. 10).

As a matter of course, children in this earlier society came to understand the means through which society survived and flourished. Since participation of the entire community was a matter of "immediate and personal concern," discipline, habits of order, responsibility, and the duty to help contribute to the welfare of all were learned by the young. Modern society, however, had destroyed this integrative force. Dewey insisted that modern man cannot return to a prior period even if he wished to, and the task of schooling must be to help the child begin to integrate the social, economic, and political processes which his natural community could no longer teach him. The school was to swell beyond its walls and "secure an organic connection with social life" (Dewey, 1970, p. 79).

Dewey's laboratory school consisted of three main learning centers: shop work with wood and tools, cooking work, and work with textiles. There was free interaction between these parts, but more important, the learning centers were connected with the gardens, parks, homes, businesses, and university of the broader community so that children could understand the social life without. Dewey was not content that children might learn narrow technical skills or modes of routine employment, and he maintained that these occupations "were points of departure whence children shall be led out into a realization of the historic development of man" (Dewey, 1970, p. 79). His new school was to have a dual effect. It would help the child regain his sense of identity with and commitment to an expanded cooperative community, and it would help overcome the appalling conditions of urban living and the conformity, boredom, and arbitrary division of labor of the factory system by helping the worker to see the human significance of his task.

Dewey was but one of several outstanding spokesmen for reform at the turn of the century. Progressive education developed from a number of isolated reform projects, each of whose leaders resorted to his own mode of expression. Following World War I, these forces jelled into a movement with a common identity which flourished through the twenties and thirties. In the forties a moratorium on progressivism was called while the nation was enveloped in war, and the movement never fully recovered. Lawrence Cremin, in his classic historical statement on progressive education (1964), even gave its death a date. Its demise was complete when the journal *Progressive Education* ceased publication in 1957, two years after the Progressive Education Association had formally disbanded.

The most striking phenomenon of the late fifties and early sixties was the pervasive feeling that education was finally under control, that with the application of modern technology and a reversion to the academic disciplines, our schools would redress their sins and once again get on with the business of giving children a fundamental grounding in the basics. The few critics such as Paul

Goodman and Edgar Friedenberg who spoke out during that period were "as voices in the wind." Then, journalistic statements by such writers as John Holt, Jonathan Kozol, Herbert Kohl, and George Dennison began to appear describing in a personal way their own experiences with an oppressive authoritarianism that pervaded every element of the classroom environment as well as the entire school system.

Control itself became the central concern of a growing segment of public criticism about the school. Existing patterns of control were seen as destructive of both human personality and intelligence. The first course of action taken by some parents was to withdraw their children from the public schools. They then placed them in free schools, several hundred of which sprang up around the country. More recently, the free school movement has begun to penetrate the public schools themselves in the form of "schools in a school," "open-structure classrooms," or publicly financed "mini-schools." The backbone of contemporary humanistic education is evidenced in this trend.

A direct link exists between progressive education and the present humanistic education movement, but it is not often recognized either by those who identify with progressivism or by those who call themselves humanistic educators. Students often exclaim their amazement after reading A. S. Neill's *Summerhill* that a man of such prophetic foresight could have written this book as early as the 1950s. In actual fact, *Summerhill* is nothing other than a last vestige of the New Education Movement in Europe which, for all intents and purposes, died at the beginning of World War II.

The postulates of the new schools and those of progressive schools are much the same: the child learns best when involved in self-selected activity; learning is best when it is experiential and activity oriented; the "whole child" (not just the intellect) is necessarily involved in learning; schools are social environments requiring the development of productive, communal relationships; the child is an individual in his own right and requires environmental support appropriate to his particular developmental stage. There are subtle differences between them but the overarching principles of the two movements are very similar. How can we explain such a lack of mutual identification?

For one thing, most of the progressive schools that are still around are well-established private schools. They resemble suburban public schools which incorporated certain humanitarian elements of progressivism. In other words, progressive education has been assimilated into our educational tradition. It has accommodated itself through "life adjustment" and "social usefulness" to the point that it is no longer capable of resolving the problems which caused its birth—industrialization, advances in technology, urbanization, mass consumption, and mass production.

A major reason for the lack of mutual identification is certainly generational. Scholars who identify themselves with progressivism are often no longer in touch with the youth culture and tend all too often to relate problems of the present with solutions of the 1920s and 1930s. Like the progressive scholar the professional educator is separated from the contemporary youth culture. From its inception, progressive education theorists were at the forefront of that movement. Laboratory schools were located at universities, where leading educational scholars attempted to coordinate theory with sound educational practice. In contrast, although humanistic education has had its scholarly spokesmen, they have rarely been located at schools of education, and free school practices have been suspect and certainly less than respectable in many parts of the education profession.

One striking difference between present developments and progressive education has been the lack of complementary pedagogical and social theory in humanistic education. One reason for this situation is undoubtedly its estrangement from the education profession. This condition is beginning to change, but the process will probably be slow and painful. Some schools of education have overcome certain barriers and have established centers for the academic study of humanistic education. For example, the University of Massachusetts created the Center for the Study of Humanistic Education in 1969; the University of California at Santa Barbara has an advanced degree program in Confluent Education; and U.C.L.A. has developed a field of specialization in philosophic and humanistic education studies.

Present-day humanistic educators also share the burden of the failure to relate themselves to progressivism. To begin with, humanistic educators often express disdain for inspiration that comes from beyond the present collective self. They tend to interpret the dictum of Frederick Perls that "maturing is the transcendence from environmental support to self-support" in such a way that they reject historical meanings as foreign sources of direction and definition. All forms of the past are victims of this attitude, including the immediate progressive education past.

This rejection is also a product of contemporary arrogance, which insists that contemporary man is indeed unique and that history is a bad teacher for coming to grips with our emerging postmodern life. Humanists are correct in claiming that historical perspective has the potential for locking us into solutions and may not extend our vision to creative, new possibilities. They are justified in their assertion that historical ways of handling drug problems, decisions as to birth, abortion, and death, as well as group relations, rarely hold for contemporary conditions, let alone the historically unprecedented problems related to atomic power, pollution, and the growing worldwide ecological imbalance.

In the context of these crises can be found a key to the revolt of humanistic education against our immediate past. It is a revolt against the optimistic progressive ideology of technique. The scientists and technicians of our world have led us as often as not down a cul de sac in which their solutions have led to other problems more severe and dehumanizing. The sobering awareness that we are caught up in a technological society which concentrates on the specialist, whose main concern is his craft rather than the humanitarian outcomes envisioned by Dewey, has caused us all to reassess the contributions of progressive ideology. But Dewey and all the other humanists of Western tradition would surely respond differently to the world were they living in today's society. The value of historical roots might well be for us to know human beings, to locate them within their social and historical contexts, and thereby become more human and humane ourselves.

references

Adler, M., "The Crisis in Contemporary Education." *The Social Frontier*, 1939, *5*, 114.

Aristotle. *Nicomachean Ethics*. Translated by J. A. K. Thomson. Baltimore: Penguin, 1962a.

Aristotle. *The Politics of Aristotle*. Edited and translated by E. Barker. New York: Oxford University Press, 1962b.

Babbitt, I. "Humanism: An Essay at Definition." In N. Foerster (Ed.), *Humanism and America*. New York: Farrar and Rinehart, 1930.

Burckhardt, J. *The Civilization of the Renaissance in Italy*. Vol. 1. New York: Harper, 1958.

Bush, D. *The Renaissance and English Humanism.* Toronto: University of Toronto Press, 1939.

Cox, H. "A Conversation with Harvey Cox." *Psychology Today,* April 1970.

Cremin, L. *The Transformation of the School.* New York: Vintage, 1964.

Dewey, J. *Democracy and Education.* New York: Macmillan, 1916.

Dewey, J. *School and Society.* Chicago: University of Chicago Press, 1970.

Diels, H. *Die Fragmente der Vorsokratiker.* Vol. 2. Berlin: Weidmannsche Buchhandlung, 1956.

Ellul, J. *The Technological Society.* New York: Vintage, 1964.

Foerster, F. W. *Schule und Character.* Zurich: Schulhess u. Co., 1908.

Foerster, N. *The American State University.* Chapel Hill: University of North Carolina Press, 1937.

Goodman, P. *Compulsory Mis-Education.* New York: Vintage, 1962.

Hutchins, R. M. *The Higher Learning in America.* New Haven: Yale University Press, 1962.

Kerschensteiner, G. *The Idea of the Industrial School.* Translated by R. Pinter. New York: Macmillan, 1913.

Maritain, J. *Education at the Crossroads.* New Haven: Yale University Press, 1943.

More, P. E. *Shelbourne Essays.* Boston: Houghton Mifflin, 1915, ninth series.

Nohl, H. *Die Paedagogische Bewegung in Deutschland und ihre Theorie.* Frankfurt: G. Schulte-Bulmke, 1928.

Plato. *The Dialogues of Plato,* edited and translated by B. Jowett. Vol. 1. London: Oxford University Press, 1871.

Plato. *The Republic of Plato.* Translated by F. M. Cornford. London: Oxford University Press, 1968.

Rich, J. M. *Humanistic Foundations of Education.* Worthington, Ohio: C. A. Jones, 1971.

Rousseau, J. J. *The Émile of Jean Jacques Rousseau.* Edited and translated by William Boyd. New York: Teachers College Press, 1962.

Schiller, F. C. S. *Studies in Humanism.* London: Macmillan, 1907.

Schneidewin, M. *Die Antike Humanität.* Berlin: Weidmannsche Buchhandlung, 1897.

Schweitzer, A. *Philosophy of Civilization.* New York: Macmillan, 1960.

Scot, I. *Controversies over the Imitation of Cicero as a Model for Style and Some Phases of Their Influence on Schools of the Renaissance.* New York: Columbia University Press, 1910.

Van Praag, J. P. "The Humanistic Outlook." *International Humanism,* 1969, *3,* 14-15.

Woodward, W. H. *Disiderius Erasmus Concerning the Aim and Method of Education.* Cambridge: Cambridge University Press, 1904.

Woodward, W. H. *Vittorino da Feltra and Other Humanist Educators.* Cambridge: Cambridge University Press, 1912.

evaluating educational alternatives

rodney skager

The practice of evaluation as we know it today has grown and prospered within a complex social context that seems almost inevitable to those who live within it. Like Shaw's ancient Briton, socially conditioned to believe that respectable people painted their bodies blue, most of us involved in evaluation have not yet gotten around to wondering whether there might be another way. Given reasonably common public perceptions about the nature and purpose of schooling, there has perhaps been little impetus for reexamining evaluation practice.

So the growing reality of alternatives to traditional schooling has caught the evaluation field somewhat by surprise. Many of us have already been confronted by people who view our most objective and rigorous evaluation strategies and instruments as either irrelevant or dangerous. Moreover, these same people often want us to attend to phenomena that we have previously ignored. The incompatibilities are at times so fundamental that one is forced to approach the question of evaluating educational alternatives by thoroughly examining the assumptions with which contemporary evaluation practice is anchored.

Occasional exceptions to the contrary, evaluators and their clients have implicitly accepted the notion that evaluation is concerned primarily with the *outcomes* of schooling and that it is sufficient to define those outcomes in terms of concrete and immediately measurable knowledge, skills, and attitudes. The mass of evaluation reports we have read (and written) over the years, the evaluation guidelines published by state and federal funding agencies, and the expectations of school administrators, board members, and legislators all reveal the dominant "product" emphasis of evaluation practice. The forces that have shaped that practice need to be understood.

the social context

One often senses that schooling is assumed to be a special type of "industry." Matriculating students are often viewed as analogous to "products" and schools as institutions that produce those products. In industry there is a clearly recognized relationship between standardization, productivity, and profit. This sort of concrete materialism has been extended to schools and school programs, which are also expected to survive in the competition for resources by achieving favorable cost-benefit ratios. The accountability movement in education is the latest and most spectacular manifestation of such thinking. According to Lessinger (1971, p. 73) public agencies are demanding that "school personnel must answer for the performance of students in relation to dollars expended." He defines accountability as "a regular public report by independent reviewers of demonstrated student accomplishment promised for the expenditure of resources." Business and industrial terminology is extensively utilized in Lessinger's arguments for accountability. "Independent reviewers" are described as "auditors," education is a "labor-intensive industry," and so on.

While offensive to those with a humanistic perspective, the industrial model doubtless has its uses. It is, however, a narrow way of looking at the role of schooling in society, consistent with the belief that concrete, objective criteria are sufficient for determining how well schools produce students with standardized behavior, knowledge, and attitudes. Education's potential for helping individuals gain unique perceptions and sensitivities is ignored as too intangible to be assigned a value in the marketplace.

The tendency to focus on immediate outcomes also neglects the long-term personal and social consequences of schooling. Admittedly some of these consequences are directly predictable from characteristics of the student-product once all of the terminal objectives have been mastered or failed. The car with a defective steering system is more likely to generate business for undertakers. The man or woman who cannot read will probably contribute less in taxes and absorb more in welfare. But many of the most important consequences are more complex and far less predictable. Highly perfected internal combustion engines and superbly engineered freeways in combination threaten to destroy the cities they were supposed to serve. If performance contracting proves successful in increasing students' achievement, what kinds of citizens will ultimately result from the hidden curriculum built into its payoff system, from its emphasis on immediate gratification, its degradation of the learning-teaching process, and its potential for rewarding successful cheating?

The observation that contemporary evaluation practice tends to neglect long-term consequences for immediate outcomes is hardly original. Simplistic conceptions which limit the evaluator's role to that of a staff member serving up information in short-term decision-making situations have been criticized recently (Pace, 1972). Pace sees such a role as restricted to a relatively limited variety of situations where the "unit" to be evaluated is not complex, where behavioral objectives and hypothesis-testing experiments are feasible, and where interest is legitimately confined to the intended effects of whatever is being evaluated.

psychological learning theory

Coupled with this social context, perhaps also springing from it, is the influence of contemporary psychological learning theory. Such theory has been criticized as applicable to "training" rather than "education" (Cronbach, 1971). It is primarily a psychology of standardized conditions associated with stereotyped responses or behaviors. Training, as Cronbach uses the term, is an important, even major, function of the schools. But training is "closed": it has definite end-points in terms of capacities that can be precisely defined and measured. In contrast, Cronbach argues that "intelligent analysis, problem-solving, and creative self-expression" are open-ended and multidimensional. Whatever an educational environment can do to foster such learning usually cannot be specified as concrete outcomes, nor is it necessarily manifested at a fixed time.

The notion of the behavioral objective connects the industrial-product model of education and behavioristic conceptions of the learning process. Using terms similar to Cronbach's, Combs (1973) describes "behavioral-objectives approaches as closed systems of thinking" which define the outcomes of instruction as immediately observable and ideally the same for everyone. This mode of thought is obviously ill adapted to humanistic alternatives which are "open systems [that] do not call for specific ends determined in advance [and] are problems-oriented with ultimate goals established only in very general terms if at all" (Combs, 1973, p. 20).

Evaluation practice is thus visibly influenced by the view of man inherent in behavioristic learning theory and by educators' zeal for specifying outcomes in terms of concrete behaviors. While devices such as behavioral objectives are certainly useful, they reinforce the tendency to focus solely on standardized, immediately measurable outcomes.

the experiment

Still another, and probably the most important, influence on assessment processes is the experimentalist tradition. Its dominance of education research and evaluation is awesome. At all levels, from local education officials to the federal bureaucracy, obsession with this particular form of inquiry at times appears to exclude interest in substance.

A problem in doing field studies is that they are not often funded by government agencies who give money for research in education. A strong educational psychology bias demands that only certain research strategies be used to ensure presumed "rigorous" controls, sampling conditions, and "objective" measurements of the activities studies. Most of these "rigorous" studies miss their intended goal because they are so inflexible vis-a-vis what is to be called data and how these data are to be collected [Cicourel, 1974, Introduction].

Experimentalist views on the procedures that may be used to legitimate data inevitably reinforce popular notions about the proper business of evaluation. A skeptical, taxpaying public is interested in "results," and experimental research methods focus on results rather than on processes. In laboratory research process variables, ordinarily referred to as "treatments," are under the control of the experimenter and can, in a sense, be taken for granted. Potentially influential factors other than the treatment are either held constant or varied systematically to test for possible interactions with the treatment. Different treatments are compared on the same output dimensions.

This tunnel vision unfortunately often associated with the dominant experimentalist tradition obviously simplifies the evaluator's task. Not only may many subtleties and complexities of the learning environment be safely ignored, but so can the panoply of legitimate scientific methods available to assess the nature of that environment. All this in the face of the practical evaluation situation in which it is rarely possible to define control groups in any scientifically acceptable sense, in which factors other than the treatment of interest cannot ordinarily be separated out, and in which the attempt to distinguish between treatments and outcomes is often artificial.

An Urban Institute survey of federal evaluation policy displays several fine examples of this kind of thinking. We learn that "evaluation (1) assesses the *effectiveness* of an *on-going* program in achieving its objectives, (2) relies on the principles of research design to distinguish a program's effects from those of other forces working in a situation, and (3) aims at program improvement through a modification of current operations" (Wholey and others, 1970, p. 23). The definition of evaluation is straightforward and businesslike. But what do the terms really imply? As it investigates "program effectiveness," evaluation is "goal oriented, focusing on output rather than input" (p. 23). Just how it is possible to improve an educational program while ignoring its operational characteristics remains a mystery, but this is not the main issue here.

We are particularly concerned with the term "research design." In this regard we learn that "program impact evaluation . . . depends on the definition and measurement of important *output variables* and on the use of appropriate comparison groups" (p. 25, italics in original). "Program strategy evaluation" turns out to be an analogue of the multifactor research design, where outputs of different educational strategies are compared to one another, presumably on the same dimensions, and in spite of the fact that genuinely different variations in "strategy" might well have thoroughly different goals and consequences. Finally, " 'project evaluation' requires measurement of the important *output* variables as well as the use of appropriate *comparison groups*" (italics in original), although "a more feasible form of project evaluation simply compares project results with performance objectives or baseline conditions, omitting the possibility of attributing effects to the treatments provided" (p. 25).

It is also relevant for the discussion that follows to note that the experimentalist tends to have a highly analytical conception of the things he studies. "Variables" are viewed more or less as knobs or dials that can be turned up or down independently of one another. Thus, "The 'ideal' evaluation will tell not only whether a program produces effects, but also what strategies or components of the program are most important to production of the effects" (Wholey and others, 1970, p. 97).

Whether this analytical approach can be realistically applied to any but relatively trivial and standardized training situations is doubtful. An environment organized under a coherent and comprehensive model of the learning process might best be pictured holistically as a kind of integrated control panel, rather than as a set of independently operating variables. The question is not which one of the dials produces the most spectacular results, but whether the panel itself is (a) fully operating and (b) capable of carrying out its intended functions. Perhaps a better analogy would be art criticism. One ordinarily reacts to a painting by dealing with the whole as an organized entity, not by suggesting that a little more red is needed in the lower right corner.

formative evaluation and process goals

Much has been written about the importance of "formative" or "program-improvement" evaluation. As originally proposed, this concept stressed the long-run utility of evaluation practices which focused on improving program components through ongoing feedback of information to developers and staff at all levels (Cronbach,

1963). While Scriven continued to maintain that "summative" or outcome evaluation was both useful and necessary, he did not deny the importance of the formative role for evaluation (Scriven, 1967).

As the term is ordinarily used and understood, formative evaluation means to examine the way the bits and pieces of the instructional process can be best designed and arranged to achieve desired outcomes. The evaluator presumably monitors the achievement of partial or en route outcomes and compares alternative strategies or techniques. This is a constructive and pragmatic approach to product engineering. It attends to aspects of process in order to enhance the probability that intended outcomes will be achieved, not to emphasize process for its own sake.

Concern with educational process variables merely for instrumental or engineering purposes is in no way inconsistent with the widespread preoccupation with outcomes noted above. Only recently have there been signs that the pendulum might begin to swing in the other direction. One writer argues that accountability should be defined in terms of the "quality of teaching and learning opportunities" provided by the school rather than solely in relation to the quality of student performance (Stake, 1973). This suggestion is so radical that many, if not most, professionals associated with evaluation will probably react more with incomprehension than with serious counterargument. We are so accustomed to the comfortable circularity implied in defining the quality of teaching and learning opportunities in terms of the quality of student performance that it is very difficult indeed to see the two as potentially separate and distinct.

Almost forgotten amid the clamor for a better educational product is the fact that many people have always viewed various modes of education as having legitimate independent goals. The long-term consequences of humanistic alternatives can be described only in the most general way and may well differ from individual to individual (Combs, 1973). If humanistic teachers and schools are to be held accountable, then accountability should be defined in terms of discrepancies between intended and actual processes. Humanists are obviously not the only group believing that processes built into the learning environment have their own results, independent of and in addition to those of the substantive curriculum. At the opposite pole from humanism we have the military academy with its discipline, recitation, standardized learning conditions, rigid status system, and verification by authority. Surely these disparate educational processes were developed over the years because their proponents believed them to have instructive qualities of their own, qualities that might ultimately have a broader influence on the student's behavior and self-image than the academic curriculum itself.

The means and ends debate is, of course, perennially with us and ultimately unresolvable. In times such as the present, when one side so resoundingly dominates the field, it is inevitable that countermoves in the form of alternative educational structures will be made. That the educational process itself is often—perhaps always— a separate and independent curriculum with its own outcomes and consequences is a point that seems self-evident. But from the perspective of evaluation, there is another reason why the neglect of process for outcome has in many ways rendered the contributions of evaluators trivial and superficial. Stake's distinction is important. Not only is it possible conceptually to separate quality of process and quality of outcome, but the widely assumed one-to-one empirical relationship between the two is frequently a distortion of the real state of affairs.

This distinction is critical to the point of view I am developing here. Evaluation, after all, ought to be looking primarily at the *quality* of educational products, practices, and institutions. If this is not the proper business of evaluation, one wonders what its function actually might be? Evaluation has to be guided by pragmatic concerns. We are interested in outcomes and consequences not so much for their own sake, but for what they tell us about material, instructional, and institutional alternatives.

quality of process versus quality of outcome

If it is true that quality of process and quality of outcome can be separated, it is logically possible that high quality processes might be accompanied by unsatisfactory outcomes and vice versa. Improbable as such a state of affairs might seem, its very possibility ought to make us uneasy about the validity of a standard evaluation practice that makes inferences about process indirectly from output. The uneasiness is justified. There are at least three reasons for believing that output considered in isolation frequently gives a misleading impression about process.

Evaluation findings are often based on measures that only

partially reflect the possible outcomes and consequences of the educational phenomena being evaluated.

Many, if not most, of the "output" data considered in evaluations today actually tell us very little that is important about teachers, schools, programs, and students. A recent summary of the history of Swedish studies of modern comprehensive schooling provides a classic demonstration of this proposition (Dahllof, 1973). After World War II Sweden began to introduce comprehensive schools as an alternative to the traditional European system which juxtaposed parallel but unequal streams for elite and ordinary students. The new schools were assigned an important role in Swedish society. They were not simply an organizational device for accomplishing curriculum objectives more effectively, but rather were viewed as a direct means for promoting social equality. Children were to be grouped in the new schools on a heterogeneous basis. Instruction was to be individualized, with cooperative work and group learning activities receiving emphasis. The schools were to address all facets of the child's development, not just the academic.

An early evaluation study comparing students' achievement in the older selective system with that in the new schools revealed that the two groups achieved at the same level. This result was considered a plus for the modern schools which, while attempting to do more, appeared to be accomplishing just as much in terms of traditional goals. Later work by Dahllof and his associates changed the picture radically. First of all, the achievement tests used in the initial study covered only very basic skills that had already been at least partially learned by the students before entering either type of school. Secondly, process data revealed that both institutions were using traditional, whole-group instruction. The comprehensive school model emphasizing individualization had not been implemented. Most important, in spite of the similar patterns of test scores, students in the selective schools spent far less time on basic curriculum objectives than did students in comprehensive schools and therefore were able to devote significantly more time to advanced units. Thus, process information suggested that instruction in the comprehensive schools was of lower quality, particularly in light of the teachers' failure to implement individualized instruction and cooperative patterns of learning. The comprehensive schools were expected to do so for egalitarian purposes. But such instructional techniques were also intended to give teachers a way to avoid delaying the progress of brighter students and to provide alternative learning strategies for slower learners. Quality of instruction was thus not inferable from quality of output.

Perhaps a better job could have been done in selecting output measures in the first study. For example, tests measuring achievement of the more advanced units might have revealed that students in the selective schools were learning things that students in comprehensive schools were not. This is certainly true. Had such measures been included a different deduction about the quality of process might have been made. However, even with better and more relevant achievement data it still would not have been possible to infer that the comprehensive schools had failed to implement the instructional model they had been created to utilize.

In the United States hundreds of evaluation studies are conducted annually, most depending primarily on the same kinds of basic achievement measures used in the initial Swedish study. One wonders what proportion of them is misleading in the same sense. More fundamentally, however, one cannot help but ask how outcome measures can legitimately be selected without direct knowledge of the educational processes being assessed. If we do not really know what we are evaluating, how can we feel qualified to select criterion measures? The notion that it is sufficient to have a list of the goals of a program or school is frequently unrealistic. The goals themselves can often be so unrelated to what is actually happening that at least one writer suggests that evaluation might be more effective if it were goal-free (Scriven, 1972b). This general point is reminiscent of a report on problems encountered in evaluating broad-aim social programs (Weiss and Rein, 1969). These authors documented a study in which the criterion measures, selected in advance without knowledge of what the program really was, turned out to be irrelevant to its eventual accomplishments.

The quality of teaching and learning opportunities provided in an educational setting cannot be inferred directly from achievement data when it is likely that other factors have a significant impact on those outcomes.

Efforts to improve the effectiveness of schooling tend to "focus on specific pedagogical procedures and the measurement of pupil outcomes" (Goodlad, 1972, p. 207). Yet, factors other than pedagogy per se also bear on learning, and they may account for more of the variance in achievement than teaching itself. (This is one reason why current notions about the benefits to be derived from teacher accountability programs are unrealistic.)

Goodlad emphasizes the "culture of the school" as a whole, particularly "decision-making authority and responsibility, relations between principal and teachers and between teachers and children, processes of human interaction, and the like" (p. 208). Undoubtedly, one might also consider influences other than the school, such as the family, the peer culture, and the community, all of which can enhance or detract from the effects of instruction. In the face of these forces, given instructional devices and procedures may be found to make little difference, not because they are invariably ineffectual, but because other elements prevent them from having any impact.

In this connection, Dahllof stresses the influence of "frame factors" on the teaching process (Dahllof, 1973). These are conditions of the learning environment not really susceptible to change over a short period of time: (a) physical facilities and resources of the schools, (b) factors such as administrative organization, class size, patterns of grouping students, time allowed for instruction, and (c) skills and tactics available to a given teacher. Frame factors operate as borders in which the teaching-learning process is confined. The success or failure of educational practices may be attributable in small or large part to such limitations rather than to their own relative quality.

It is thus not surprising that Dahllof and his associates emphasize the relevance of data bearing on frame and process factors for the interpretation of students' achievement patterns. Detailed studies of the interaction between frame factors and the teaching process have helped to verify and elaborate the original model (Lundgren, 1972). Interestingly, research on teaching is seen by Dahllof as moving away from "avoidance behavior in the laboratory ... [and] experimental designs, refined procedures of measurement and analysis which ... do not represent conditions for real advancement" (p. 22). It is significant that Dahllof's approach to evaluation is "curriculum-related and process-centered."

Carroll's model of schooling suggests that the quality of teaching and learning opportunities cannot be inferred directly from outcome data because of an independent relationship between the latter and "time allowed for learning."

Carroll's model and the concept of "mastery learning" later

derived from it stress the relationship between individual differences in the learners and factors that are potentially under the
control of the school (Carroll, 1963, and Bloom, 1968 and 1973).
Characteristics of the learners are classified into three broad categories, beginning with *aptitude for learning a given task*. This very
broad category includes both relevant or transferable prior learning
and possible genetically based individual characteristics. Aptitude is
ordinarily thought of as a powerful limiting characteristic. Children
who do not learn may be said to have insufficient "aptitude" for
the successful completion of a given task. Carroll's conception is
sharply different. Aptitude is defined in terms of the time required
to learn something under "ideal" conditions (Carroll, 1963, p. 725).
Clearly implied here is the idea that, given sufficient time, virtually
"all students can conceivably attain mastery of a learning task"
(Bloom, 1968, p. 2). This deduction provided a jumping-off point
for the mastery learning concept.

The second individual-difference variable in Carroll's model,
ability to understand instruction, is roughly equated with a combination of general intelligence and verbal ability. The third is *perseverance,* or the amount of time the learner is willing to spend on a
given task. Reflecting motivation for learning, degree of perseverance in the learner can be inferred from such statements as "the
student was unwilling to work on the task for even a short period of
time" or "the student got so involved in the project that he wanted
to work on it at home."

Two equally broad classes of variables are open to direct
manipulation by the school. The first is *time allowed for learning.*
Earlier I noted that Dahllof classified this same variable as a "frame
factor." Carroll's use of the concept is obviously different. Within
the frame factor of absolute amount of time available, the teacher,
or learners themselves, for that matter, can choose to allocate more
or less time to the accomplishment of a given activity. Mastery
occurs when the time allowed for learning is equal to the time
needed, the latter being a function of the other variables in the
model.

Finally, we have *quality of instruction,* cited earlier as the
central concern of evaluation. In this chapter, instruction is viewed in
perhaps a broadened way, as it includes all the forces or materials
that can potentially be utilized to facilitate learning. However, this
definition does not detract from the relevance of the model.

Obviously there are a number of potential interactions. Teaching practices and learning environments of high quality for a given learner are likely to enhance that student's level of perseverance. The learner who easily understands instruction will be less handicapped by teaching of low quality than will the learner whose ability to understand instruction is relatively low, and so forth.

The Carroll model makes it abundantly clear that quality of outcome can be high (for example, achievement of mastery), because sufficient time was allowed for learning, rather than because the quality of teaching and learning opportunities was optimal. Suppose the reading attainment of children in inner-city, minority schools in Los Angeles rises after a new reading program is installed. Can we legitimately attribute the gain to the effects of the program if we do not know whether a greater proportion of the school day is being spent on reading instruction? If this turned out to be the case, the only possible conclusion would be that reading scores go up if more time is spent teaching reading. The interpretation of such a finding would of course depend on the extent to which other aspects of the curriculum are defaulted. Moreover, it is evident from this example that more information is needed to draw an inference about the quality of instruction, unless the new program clearly devotes an equal or lesser proportion of the school day to reading.

Unfortunately, overall judgments about the quality of complex, contextually embedded instructional programs are hard to come by, even given process information on such basic factors as time allowed for instruction, number of units accomplished, and the like. The best we can ordinarily hope for is to make reasonably definitive statements about the conditions under which a given form of an instructional model, program, organizational structure are likely to be successful. To do so we require more information. Assume that a prescriptive, diagnostic approach to reading is installed in forty or fifty schools in a large, urban district. The program incorporates new materials and objectives, requires teachers to develop new management skills, imposes its own set of logistical procedures, and, when used as intended, results in a reorganization of the classroom. To think of it as a "reading program," except in the most generic, administrative sense, is fatuous. The program originally intended will differentially grow and adapt, or wither and die, in various schools and classrooms. The program might be effectively utilized in some contexts and forms and disastrously misused in others.

Under these real-life circumstances the experimental, laboratory model, which would deliberately vary aspects of the program in order to find out "what works," is ordinarily irrelevant, contemporary biases notwithstanding. It is not relevant because the "treatments" are out of the experimenter-evaluator's control and in fact *should,* in most cases, be out of his control. Evaluators typically have professional competences in various facets of educational research, particularly educational psychology, measurement, and research design. As a group we are not intimately knowledgeable about curriculum theory, school organizational structures, the teaching process, or alternative theoretical and philosophical concepts of education. We should not, in other words, be calling the shots, but rather ought to concentrate on finding out what is actually occurring. The need for information-gathering strategies in evaluation which are less intrusive and more naturalistic has been anticipated by others (see, for example, Wittrock, 1969).

Carroll's model and the related concept of mastery learning apply fairly well to aspects of schooling that can be roughly described as training, but are not so applicable to the development of higher functions such as "intelligent analysis and problem solving" and "creative, self-expressive production" (Cronbach, 1971, p. 55). Here the kinds of outcomes one hopes for usually cannot be snared and confined within a performance objective, nor can "mastery" be readily defined. This point is important. Proponents of many current alternative educational philosophies are giving more than lip service to the importance of such higher human functions and the alternative learning environments that may facilitate their development.

In this regard, an extremely significant problem confronting the evaluation of humanistic alternatives is the prevailing obsession with the output-product of schools, as I mentioned earlier. It is reasonable for the larger society to expect that children will not leave a humanistic alternative school as functional illiterates, especially where such schools are supported by public funds. The development of basic skills can and should be assessed objectively at certain key points. But it is both foolish and potentially destructive to demand that a test for creativity or self-awareness or even independent, critical thinking be given at the end of the school year and to expect that students in a humanistic alternative school will score higher than a putatively equivalent group of students in a traditional school. "Outcomes" at these higher levels of functioning do not necessarily occur at fixed times. As they also can be manifested in different ways in different individuals, overall scores might be meaningless. Finally, these higher levels of functioning are difficult or impossible to measure by traditional objective means such as tests or other standardized situations. Far more relevant would be methods analogous to the case study, the biography, the life-history. But these techniques are ill suited to serving up information annually to administrative "decision-makers."

Nevertheless, public expectations about schooling emphasize training in the basic skills and, more recently, the development of "salable" job skills. Much of the curriculum is devoted to teaching the three R's and other kinds of basic skills that can be specified in terms of objectives and thus are objectively measurable. Thus there are extensive regions in which the Carroll model applies, even though its author is the first to admit that it is often artificial to assume that the functioning of the school can invariably be broken down into a series of "discrete learning tasks" (Carroll, 1963, p. 724). Whatever is being learned, though, it seems reasonable that individual learners will require differing amounts of time, depending on their own personal characteristics, the overall quality of the instruction, and the appropriateness of that instruction for them personally. Surely these variations must affect the learning even of higher types of functions, even those whose mastery cannot be defined. Whenever this is the case, and one suspects that it commonly is, then outcomes taken alone are not reliable indicators of the quality of teaching and learning opportunities.

evaluation and instructional theory

Contemporary theories or conceptualizations of evaluation tend to concentrate on the process of evaluation itself. For example, a model with which I have been associated proposes an ideal evaluation having five stages, each of which defines certain activities or concerns of the evaluator and results in the delivery of a particular kind of information to a "decision-maker" (Skager, 1969, and Alkin, 1971). Thus, the first step is to assess needs in a given educational situation, the next is to evaluate plans for meeting those needs, and so on. The last stage is the kind of final evaluation of an operating program that in reality has been and still is the typical function of evaluation.

The CSE model (developed by the Center for the Study of

Evaluation at U.C.L.A.), as well as other models, has been and hopefully will continue to be a useful guide for evaluation practice. However, like many others, it does not incorporate any aspects of instructional *theory*. It tells the evaluator about qualitatively different evaluation functions and duties, but it does not tell him what to look at, what information to collect, what are the ideal forms with which the reality he observes might be compared. These essentials appear to be taken completely for granted, as if by nature an evaluator with expertise in measurement and research design naturally knows what data ought to be gathered. Evaluators dutifully measure accomplishment of the goals or objectives of the program or school, most often simply by applying the standardized tests which come closest to addressing those ends.

Without abandoning contemporary evaluation models, it is useful to consider the use of theories or models of instruction and learning as a means of conceptually structuring the evaluation process—particularly what is looked at in the evaluation and how whatever is observed is *valued*. I have argued that outcomes are an insufficient basis for determining the quality of instruction and the learning environment. Moreover, in important areas of higher mental functioning (not to mention knowledge of self, emotional development, and the like) the very idea that standardized, objectively measurable results can be identified and measured at the end of the school year seems naively simplistic. But so far I have not even touched on how we know what value to attach to our observations. We have too often been content to take the valuing process for granted. Our sophistication has rarely extended beyond the notion that the higher the achievement scores the better things are. But now such data do not appear to be so easily interpretable nor so broadly relevant (particularly to the more visible contemporary approaches to alternative education, especially those classifiable in Goodlad's "alternative ends-alternative means" category). We need additional criteria for assigning value to data, as well as for helping us decide what data to collect to begin with.

values and models

This is not the place, nor am I a suitable authority, to deal with the value question in any profound manner. But for practical purposes in evaluation we can assign values to events in at least two ways.

First, we can cite pragmatic considerations such as efficiency and effectiveness, as does La Belle in Chapter 2. For example, the alternative means implied in an individualized, open-structured learning environment may help children to learn more, to learn it faster, and to have more positive experiences in the process. This cost-effectiveness criterion is conveniently objective on the surface, although it rests ultimately on the conviction that it is good for all children to learn whatever comprises the curriculum. (The fact that doomsday weaponry and ecological disaster go hand in hand with a highly literate and technologically sophisticated citizenry conceivably could bring one to question even this apparent "given.")

Recognizing the underlying value status even of the efficiency criterion should make the second criterion, *goodness* or *rightness,* easier for self-styled objective thinkers to swallow. (See, for example, arguments for the objectivity of "moral real-value claims" in Scriven, 1972a, p. 131.) That is, we can assign values to events on the basis of moral and philosophical principles quite apart from considerations of efficiency and effectiveness. La Belle's categories of "relevance" and "equality" have such a basis. Admittedly, one could argue for the pragmatic value of equality of educational opportunity, yet surely no one would maintain that this ideal does not also have a moral foundation. The parallel Weinberg establishes between the goals of liberation movements and alternative educational forms suggests just how significant such criteria are for evaluating alternative education, whether one is confronted with alternative means, alternative ends, or both.

It appears, then, that relevant educational theories or models provide us with a basis for deciding what to look for in an evaluation as well as how to assign values to what we observe. It is hard to conceive of a model worthy of the name that is not based on findings or assumptions relating to efficiency as well as considerations of goodness or rightness, although the latter are more likely to be explicitly defined in many contemporary approaches to alternative education.

But what is an educational model? For present purposes we can define it as any sort of formal conceptualization which provides a guide for the educational process. Existing models vary widely in generality, ranging from Carroll's almost generic model to considerably more specific and detailed ones described in *Models of Teaching* (Joyce and Weil, 1972). But whatever the model, from "non-directive teaching" to "operant conditioning," one can identify assumptions about appropriate processes and outcomes that in turn can be utilized to focus the evaluation on certain critical events and to assign values to whatever is observed.

There are two reasons why the use of an explicit educational model inevitably should lead the evaluator to look at the educational process in addition to learning outcomes. First, an evaluation structured around an educational model has the potential for drawing conclusions about the model itself, or at least about the particular way it was implemented. But such deductions cannot be made without monitoring the process. Second, considerations of goodness or rightness ordinarily enter into the processes defined by various educational models. That a certain kind of learning environment should exist for moral and philosophical reasons is a legitimate basis for any educational endeavor.

> Educational procedures are generated from general views about human nature and about the kinds of goals and environments that enhance human beings. . . . [B]ecause of their frames of reference . . . educators are likely to focus on specific kinds of learning outcomes and to favor certain ways of creating educational environments [Joyce and Weil, 1972, p. 5].

Clearly, then, evaluation must look at process in order to interpret outcomes as well as to determine whether what actually occurs coincides with what was intended. The most useful vehicle for organizing this type of evaluation appears to be the model of teaching and learning.

an example

Recently I had the opportunity to participate in the evaluation of a publicly supported alternative school during its first year of operation (Skager, Morehouse, Russock, and Schumacher, 1973). This experience was the basis for a number of the ideas discussed above. The Los Angeles Alternative School (LAAS) was established by the Board of Education in response to a proposal developed by a group of parents, teachers, and community members. The school during its first year of operation had certain distinguishing characteristics, among which the following were salient: (1) Decision making was extensively democratized; individual students, teachers, and parents were expected to take the initiative in assuming and carrying out learning, teaching, and organizational responsibilities. (2) Deliberate attempts were made to create a learning environment in which warm and direct personal relationships existed between participants of different ages and roles, including teachers and students, and older and younger students. Thus, instructional staff attempted to function as "advisors" rather than "teachers" and were so described. (3) Learning was individualized, with great stress placed on personal choice of the time, content, and place of learning, and with equivalent emphasis on using the outside community as a source of experience. The school was nongraded, except for purposes of record keeping.

Our team was confronted with an unusual task. We were asked by the Los Angeles Board of Education and the staff of the school to evaluate a *school,* not simply an instructional program, a set of reading materials, or an approach to teaching. Naturally we eventually had to look at a number of aspects of the functioning of the school, including organization and planning, communication among participants, acceptance by parents and students, and, of course, the nature of the learning opportunities provided within the school. Here I will elaborate only on the last category.

First we had to decide what we ought to look at. Scores on state-mandated achievement tests would be available at the end of the year, but we knew for reasons stated above that such data would (a) reflect relatively little of what the school was trying to accomplish (although Caesar, in the person of the taxpaying public, deserved his due), and (b) be relatively meaningless without interpretive data relating to process. We clearly needed a structure that went beyond any contemporary evaluation models to help us select what to observe as well as interpret what we saw.

Since the school focused on individualized learning, the Carroll model appeared to be relevant. It is clear from the model, as well as from Carroll's own analysis of its characteristics, that quality of instruction can only be optimal for a given learner if it is adapted to his or her particular characteristics (Carroll, 1963, p. 726). The question of the degree to which the learning environment was oriented to the needs of individual students thus appeared to provide us with a way to assess the quality of instruction independently of outcome as measured by achievement tests. Specifically, we could assess whether or not the learning environment was organized so as to take into account differences among students on at least one of the three variables in the model.

Given the time and resources available, we could not observe all the three hundred plus students during the learning process. However, we were able to do repeated, independent observations on a relatively small number of students selected because they and their relationship with the school and its programs were of particular interest to the evaluation. Specifically, we reasoned that an individualized learning environment would treat high- and low-persevering students differently. We expected, for example, that students with short attention span, who tended not to initiate or complete tasks on their own, would receive more individual attention, participate in more structured learning experiences, and the like. By observing a sample of these students we would be able to determine how the school responded differentially to students with these characteristics, and thus arrive at at least a rough judgment about the quality of teaching and learning opportunities.

With the teachers' help we were able to identify groups of students at the high and low end of the perseverance dimension. We proceeded to observe these students individually over the period of about one month, each time recording what the student was doing and how he or she came to be involved in a particular activity. The latter was sometimes evident from our observation. At other times we interviewed the student, advisor, or both. In the end we were able to establish patterns of activity for the two groups of students and to assess the way the school approached their differing needs. These observations told us something very important about quality of instruction from the standpoint of individualization. Conclusions drawn from the observations were later confirmed by interviews of teachers and through formal interviews of two groups of parents, the first of students who had withdrawn from the school and the second of students still enrolled. All of this, again, without referring to scores on achievement tests.

Earlier in this discussion, I expressed considerable skepticism about the general relevance to evaluation of laboratory research procedures and the frame of mind that accompanies their use. In the LAAS evaluation our team was able to learn a great deal about the school. We did so without randomization, control groups, or the manipulation of "treatments." Our methods were direct and experiential. We observed systematically and interviewed many students, teachers, and parents. Our primary tools were the tape recorder, the telephone, and the interview schedule.

We utilized such social science field research methods because they were the most appropriate means for exploring the educational environment we had agreed to evaluate. Just as there are educational alternatives, so too are there alternative methods of inquiry. Tools and methods have to be compatible with the phenomena being evaluated. If they are not, the information resulting from their use will be at best trivial and at worst misleading. The utility of naturalistic research methods in the evaluation of alternative educational forms has already been cited (Moore, Johnson, Wilson, and Wilson, 1972). The apparently prevailing belief that such procedures should be used only when more "objective" methods cannot be applied also needs to be challenged.

choosing a model

Thus, even as generic a model as Carroll's turned out to be quite useful in telling us what to observe and how to interpret our observations. Of course it can be countered that the choice of a given model for a given situation is arbitrary and in itself implies a value judgment about the appropriateness of the particular notion of quality instruction incorporated in the model. This is certainly true. However, one wonders whether it is not better to have an *explicit* value base, related to an educational or instructional model, than to proceed—as most evaluations do now—with *implicit*, unexamined values.

Surely the nature of the school, program, or whatever is being evaluated has very much to do with selecting the model. One would not apply Rogers's nondirective model of teaching to a military school (Rogers, 1969). All the variables observed would have a value of zero, or perhaps minus infinity. Likewise, Skinner's operant conditioning model would not be of much use in evaluating a humanistic free school (Skinner, 1957). Thus the manner of selecting the model (or models, since in the evaluation of the Los Angeles Alternative School it would have been useful to use Rogers's model as well) need not be as arbitrary as it might seem.

Finally, it should be apparent by now that we cannot validly approach the evaluation of alternative educational forms without accepting the idea that in small or large part they may be derived from alternative value systems. Achieving certain kinds of educational processes in and of themselves will often be a goal under those value systems. Educational models provide tools for articulating such value assumptions and at the same time guide the evaluation toward the production of meaningful and relevant information.

conclusion

We may be at the end of the pendulum's period of swing toward the industrial-product analogue for education. Certainly this way of viewing the function of the schools and the educational process has not greatly facilitated the usefulness of evaluation. It has, in addition, frequently encouraged the use of seriously inappropriate methodology, the unsophisticated equation of quality ends with quality means, and a conception of the function of education too often chained to the common denominator of standardized outcomes. Goodlad's admonition that accountability through performance-based teacher evaluation will flounder in the sea of ignorance about what methods work best significantly reflects the failure of educational evaluation to produce useful information. What is it we need, then—more of the same?

Conceptualization and practice in evaluation and the corresponding expectations of administrators, board members, and legislators represent a formidable force inadvertently working to limit the emergence and persistence of alternatives in education. At the fulcrum of the struggle is the question of the kinds of information generally accepted as relevant to evaluation. If we are to go on ignoring process while seeking information on only a limited set of standardized outcomes, selected on the basis of an unexamined and unarticulated core of values, then movements toward alternatives are doomed to have little significant public support and impact. Genuine alternatives cannot be expected to dance to tradition's tune. They require the atmosphere of freedom that has been recommended elsewhere in this issue. An evaluation practice that works against such freedom is worse than useless.

It will be suggested that the arguments presented in this chapter for the use of educational models as conceptual devices for structuring what is observed, how it is observed, and how it is valued, threaten the field of evaluation with rampant relativism.

It is true that what is observed in one assessment may in part differ fundamentally from what is seen elsewhere, and the value one places on a given event is affected by the context in which that event is embedded. Still, without reasonable flexibility in this regard we cannot generate meaningful and relevant information about truly alternative ends and means. A reasonably well-defined and comprehensive model of education is likely to have considerable generality within broad classes of alternatives. This characteristic, combined with the usefulness of models for making values explicit and for directing the evaluation process to relevant information, suggests that we have more to gain by opening our conceptual doors than by leaving them shut.

references

Alkin, M. C. "A Theory of Evaluation." Working Paper No. 18. Los Angeles: Center for the Study of Evaluation, U.C.L.A., August, 1971.

Bloom, B. S. "Learning for Mastery." *Evaluation Comment*, 1968, 2(1).

Bloom, B. S. "Time and Learning." Address to the Annual Convention of the American Psychological Association, Montreal, 1973.

Carroll, J. B. "A Model of School Learning." *Teachers College Record*, 1963, 64, 723-733.

Cicourel, A. "Introduction." In Cicourel, A., Jennings, K. H., Jennings, S. H. M., Leiter, K. C. W., MacKay, R., Mehan, H., Roth, D. P., *Language Use and School Performance*. New York: Academic Press, 1974.

Combs, A. W. "Educational Accountability from a Humanistic Perspective." *Educational Researcher*, 1973, 2, 19-21.

Cronbach, L. J. "Course Improvement through Evaluation." *Teachers College Record*, 1963, 64, 672-683.

Cronbach, L. J. "Mastery Learning and Its Implications for Curriculum Development." In E. Eisner (Ed.), *Confronting Curriculum Reform*. Boston: Little, Brown, 1971.

Dahllof, U. *Data on Curriculum and Teaching Process: Do They Make Any Difference to Non-Significant Test Differences—and Under What Conditions?* Institute of Education, Publication No. 30. Goteborg, Sweden: University of Goteborg, 1973.

Goodlad, J. I. "Staff Development: The League Model." *Theory Into Practice*, 1972, 11(4), 207-214.

Joyce, B., and Weil, M. *Models of Teaching*. Englewood Cliffs, New Jersey: Prentice-Hall, 1972.

Lessinger, L. M. "Accountability: Its Implications for the Teacher." In D. W. Allen and F. Seifman (Eds.), *The Teacher's Handbook*. Glenview, Ill.: Scott-Foresman, 1971.

Lundgren, U. P. *Frame Factors and the Teaching Process*. Stockholm: Almqvist & Wiksell, 1972.

Moore, D. R., Johnson, R., Wilson, S. H., and Wilson, T. A. "Strengthening Alternative High Schools." *Harvard Educational Review*, 1972, 42, 313-350.

Pace, C. R. *Thoughts on Evaluation in Higher Education*. Essays on Education, No. 1. Iowa City, Ia.: The American College Testing Program, 1972.

Rogers, C. W. *Freedom to Learn.* Columbus, Ohio: Charles E. Merrill, 1969.

Scriven, M. "The Methodology of Evaluation." In R. E. Stake (Ed.), *Perspectives on Curriculum Evaluation.* AERA Monograph Series on Curriculum Evaluation, Vol. 1. Chicago: Rand-McNally, 1967.

Scriven, M. "Objectivity and Subjectivity in Educational Research." In L. G. Thomas (Ed.), *Philosophical Redirection of Educational Research.* Seventy-First Yearbook of the National Society for the Study of Education, Part I. Chicago: University of Chicago Press, 1972a.

Scriven, M. "Prose and Cons About Goal-Free Evaluation." *Evaluation Comment.* Center for the Study of Evaluation, 1972b, *3*(4), 1-4.

Skager, R. W. "Evaluation and the Improvement of Compensatory Educational Programs." In J. C. Ferver (Ed.), *Compensatory Education: From Theory to Political Strategy.* Madison: University of Wisconsin Extension, 1969.

Skager, R., Morehouse, K., Russock, R., and Schumacher, E. *Evaluation of the Los Angeles Alternative School: A Report to the Board of Education of the Los Angeles Unified School District.* Los Angeles: Center for the Study of Evaluation, U.C.L.A., 1973.

Skinner, B. F. *Verbal Behavior.* New York: Appleton-Century-Crofts, 1957.

Stake, R. E. "School Accountability Laws." *Evaluation Comment.* Center for the Study of Evaluation, 1973, *4*(1), 1-3.

Weiss, R., and Rein, M. "The Evaluation of Broad-Aim Programs: A Cautionary Case and a Moral." *Annals of the American Academy of Political and Social Science,* 1969, *385*, 133-142.

Wholey, J. S., Scanlon, J. W., Duffy, H. G., Fukamoto, J. S., and Vogt, L. M. "Federal Evaluation Policy." Washington, D.C.: The Urban Institute, 1970.

Wittrock, M. C. "The Evaluation of Instruction: Cause and Effect Relations in Naturalistic Data." *Evaluation Comment,* 1969, *1*(4).

to what is alternative education an alternative?

gary d. fenstermacher

This chapter, like the others that have preceded it in this volume, is an attempt to understand the notion of alternative education. My approach is somewhat different from that of my colleagues, however, because I try to place the concept of alternative education within a philosophical framework. Perhaps this explains why my title is a question rather than a glimpse of my answer. But if this chapter were to have a declarative title, it would be: Sometimes Alternative Education Is Not an Alternative to Anything.

everyday definitions

One way to begin a philosophical inquiry is to try to understand more fully the meaning of key words or ideas within a particular topic. The word "alternative" is certainly a crucial one in this investigation. It may prove profitable to look at the way we use the word in ordinary, everyday language.

Not long ago I was faced with patching a crack in the living room wall of my house. I knew that I could do the job with plaster patch, but the stuff was messy, and I seldom mixed the water and powder with success. A neighbor told me I should try spackle, the kind that comes in cans. I did, and was pleased with the results.

I now know that spackle is an alternative to plaster patch. From other experiences, I also know that a credit card is an alternative to cash, a table knife is an alternative to a screwdriver, and U. S. Highway 1 is an alternative to Interstate 405. What makes these examples of alternatives? In each case, it seems that the alternative is a different way of reaching the same goal, a substitute which takes us to the same place we would get to if we used the original thing. We employ the alternative or substitute when we believe it is a better or more feasible way of attaining our objective. Thus, before we can choose the transportation we have to know where we are going. If we want to purchase something, a credit card or a bank check is an alternative to cash. But if we want to add to our collection of Federal Reserve Notes, then neither credit cards nor checks can substitute for cash.

If we carry this interpretation into the realm of education, it seems that the phenomenon called "alternative education" is a substitute for some other kind of education. That is, there exist some ways of educating persons for which the practices embodied by Alternative Education are some kind of substitute. But what is this thing for which Alternative Education is a substitute? An overview of the Alternative Education literature indicates that its proponents are reacting to (for lack of any better way to say it) "what typically goes on in organized, formal education, particularly public schools." Since we seem to lack a brief, catchy label for identifying what typically goes on in formal education, I need to make up one. Conventional Education is as good a label as any, although I might just as easily use Regular Education, Standard Education, or Traditional Education.

If Alternative Education (AE) is indeed an alternative to or substitute for Conventional Education (CE), then its implementation should attain the same goals as that of Conventional Education. Thus, the first step in determining whether AE is an alternative to CE is to identify the purpose of education. But here we encounter a genuine obstacle. It has always been difficult to state the goals of education, and particularly to describe with agreement and precision the goals of Conventional Education. Yet in the absence of some clear goal statements, how are we to find out whether AE is truly an alternative to CE? If as citizens, parents, or professionals we are to make decisions about adopting or dispelling AE, we ought at least to be aware of whether the effects of our decisions will be to alter CE so that it is better than before or to destroy its form as we now know it.

Because of the lack of clearly defined and commonly held goals, I need to stipulate a few so that we can proceed with the discussion. Two manifest goals which I believe to be central to what typically goes on in organized, formal education are "to know" and "to value." By "to know" I mean having moved from a state of relative ignorance to a state of relative understanding. To know is to comprehend the meaning of such concepts as truth, falsity, fact, belief, opinion, hypothesis, and theory. By "to value" I mean having moved from a state of being unable to choose, judge, prescribe, and evaluate to a state of being able to engage in continual choosing, judging, prescribing, and evaluating. To value is to be aware of one's own values and their relationships to the values held by others. It is also to be able to make decisions about what one's values should be and how they should relate to the values of others. For those familiar with the Bloom and Krathwohl taxonomies, these two goals could be crudely described as follows: to know is to be cognitively well equipped and to value is to be affectively well equipped.

The assumption that AE and CE hold these two goals in common seems safe enough, as I know of no educator espousing AE who denies that AE strives for the ends of knowing and valuing. Given their joint sponsorship of these aims, AE can now be understood as an alternative means to the same goals sought by CE (at least in the everyday sense of the word "alternative"). But we have yet to learn *how* AE can substitute for CE. We know that if AE and CE strive for the same ends, then AE may be an alternative to CE; but merely because AE *may* be an alternative does not mean that it actually is. Here we encounter a second impediment to understanding the notion of Alternative Education (the first, you will recall, is the general lack of clearly defined and commonly held educational goals, whose existence would allow us to determine whether AE strives for the same goals as CE). The second difficulty is the absence of any categories that sharply differentiate the educational means proposed by AE from those employed by CE. Without these categories, it is hard to say whether AE is truly *different* from CE in the way goals are attained.

Under the heading "Common Ends, Alternative Means," Goodlad has already described many of the different methods and structures with which Conventional Education has experimented in the last decade. My intention here is to elaborate on Goodlad's discussion by grouping these various means. I am headed toward showing that one way to understand Alternative Education is as a means of adapting CE by assimilating practices which are currently considered alternatives.

AE and CE: do they get there differently?

In at least three categories the means employed by AE can be seen to be different from those used by CE. They are instruction (AE_i), environment (AE_e), and time (AE_t). Alternative Education may employ different instructional strategies, techniques, or devices; it may occur in different environmental settings; or it may have different time frames for the attainment of educational goals.

Looking back at the two educational goals stipulated earlier, it is easy to see how AE_i, AE_e, and AE_t can be applied to them. For example, textbook and lecture are fairly typical instructional means for attaining the goal of knowing in Conventional Education. In contrast, discovery methods may be considered an instance of AE_i as highly structured and challenging questions are partially substituted for text and lecture. Large group instruction is often encountered in CE, to which learning centers and individualized instruction are proposed as alternatives. Conventional Education frequently utilizes the learner's ability to memorize subject field content as the basis for assessing achievement, but specified performance competencies may constitute an alternative means for evaluating the effects of instruction. In Conventional Education adults usually decide what is to be learned, while one form of AE_i calls for delegating this decision-making power to the learner.

A second way to generate alternatives is to vary the environment in which knowing and valuing take place. Alternatives in the AE_e category range from redesigning existing CE classrooms, to creating new learning environments which parallel existing CE classrooms, to eliminating existing CE classrooms in favor of nonschool

types of learning environments. The move toward the open classroom is an example of AE_e which attempts to place the alternative
within the context of the existing classroom. Community-based
education intends to generate new learning environments to stand
alongside the conventional settings. Carl Bereiter (1971) is an advocate of these parallel environments, arguing that a portion of formal
education should take place outside the CE classroom. The deschooling proposals of Ivan Illich and Everett Reimer represent the
extreme AE_e position, as both these educators believe that conventional schooling should be eliminated.

Time can also be manipulated to create alternatives. This AE_t
category may involve not only rearranging time frames for education, but also altering the importance of time as a controlling factor
in the learning situation. Nongrading, continuous progress, open
access, continuing education, and lifelong learning may all be considered forms of AE_t. In Conventional Education the goals of
knowing and valuing are usually strongly influenced by such temporal factors as chronological age, grade levels, class schedules,
school calendars, and legal age requirements governing entry to and
exit from CE. Within the AE_t category, time frames become a
function of the learner's readiness and need and his or her desire to
engage the available educational resources.

value bases

If one looks back over the pedagogical examples given under
each of the categories of AE_i, AE_e, and AE_t, it will be clear that I
have not used any particular value orientation as the basis for selecting examples of alternatives in each category. Rather, several different value positions are represented, including behaviorist, humanist,
and rationalist (often referred to as the cognitivist position). I cited
performance objectives as an example of AE_i, and this example
clearly falls within the value base of the behaviorist. The humanist's
values were represented in the case of learner readiness and need,
which was cited as a form of AE_t. The parallel environments proposal of Bereiter is a part of the rationalist's value scheme.

My failure to adopt one specific value orientation as the basis
for understanding AE is intentional. In order to be consistent with
the definition of "alternative" which I developed from the way we
use this word in everyday discourse, it is necessary to admit that

any different way of attaining a common goal is an alternative. Thus the instructional, environmental, and temporal means advocated by behaviorists, rationalists, and humanists are alternatives to the means employed in CE, provided that each of these means is a different way to reach the ends of CE.

In rejecting the view that a single value orientation is built into the meaning of AE, I am taking exception to a contention by Weinberg in Chapter 3 and accepting a position developed by La Belle in Chapter 2. Weinberg states that the movement toward alternatives in education should be thought of as a counterpart to similar liberation struggles on the part of alienated members of our society. Weinberg goes on to propose five goals for Alternative Education which, taken together, form a fairly consistent value orientation. The five goals are equality, autonomy, opportunity, openness, and integration. While I do not personally dissent from the worth of these goals, I am contending that the meaning of Alternative Education cannot be legislated by a claim that these five goals *define* the notion of Alternative Education. It is acceptable for Weinberg to stipulate that these goals make up part of what he means by the notion of AE, but I believe it would be an error to limit the meaning of AE to these goals.

La Belle, on the other hand, views alternatives as departures from conventional educational practices which are aimed at three major societal concerns: relevance, efficiency, and equality. He would, I believe, place the educational program arising out of the value orientation represented by Weinberg within the category of relevance. But, in addition, his categories of efficiency and equality permit many other value orientations to be included within the meaning of Alternative Education. The moves toward behavioral objectives, accountability, and program planning and budgeting systems can be viewed as alternatives directed at efficiency. Decentralized decision making, racial integration, statewide school tax bases, and career education can be considered alternatives generated in partial satisfaction of the concern for equality.

In short, the meaning of Alternative Education is not exhausted by Maslow, Rogers, Holt, Kozol, and Postman and Weingartner. Their value orientation is but one among many, although the educational values of these writers seem to consume most contemporary discussions of Alternative Education. To many, Alternative Education is synonymous with humanism, client-centered education, the counterculture, Consciousness III, and free schools.

If the contention that AE is made up of many different value orientations is accepted, we are confronted with a third difficulty in grasping the full import of the notion of Alternative Education. Some alternatives are based on value positions which seem consistent with the value base of CE, while other alternatives rest on value orientations which appear quite foreign to CE. For some reason, performance-based instruction seems not to disrupt the value premises of CE, while learner control over curricula and schedules causes a violent wrenching in the system. Although value conflicts between conventional and alternative practices are often easy to explain post hoc, they are often difficult to predict.

Assimilating an alternative means into CE has, in the context of values, all the characteristics of a tissue match between donor and recipient. As educators, our understanding of how to match the value base of an alternative practice with the value base of the conventional system stands about where transplant physiology stood fifty years ago. If we are to modify successfully CE by selectively incorporating alternative means, we must understand the value bases of both the alternative and the conventional and be able to assess the extent to which a match will engender conflict or consistency. It is depressing to see many of today's teachers, learners, and schools fighting to get halfway to five different places, with each of them wondering how they are going to get everywhere at the same time.

Just as many retail products come without consumer information tags attached to them, many recommended alternatives come without their value bases clearly labeled. From the standpoint of values, saying that pliers are an alternative to a box wrench for loosening a nut is quite a different thing from saying that learner-controlled environments are an alternative to teacher-controlled environments for achieving knowing and valuing.

expanding the definition

So far, Alternative Education has been analyzed solely as sets of different means for attaining ends commonly held by CE and AE. There is another possible interpretation: Alternative Education consists of sets of educational goals different from the goals sought by Conventional Education. At first glance, this new interpretation of AE appears to contradict the definition of "alternative" which was developed earlier. If an "alternative" is defined as a different means of reaching a common goal, how then can an alternative be understood as a different goal?

The answer lies in understanding that goals can be stated at different levels of abstraction and generalization. For example, if my goal is to get from Beverly Hills to San Clemente, U. S. Highway 1 is an alternative to Interstate 405, but U. S. 101 is not (it does not go to either Beverly Hills or San Clemente). But if my goal is to visit the Spanish missions in Southern California, U. S. 101 becomes an alternative to both U. S. 1 and I. S. 405. If my goal is to charge the battery in my car, then many other highways become alternatives to these three. In the case of education, a conventional goal might be to develop the learner's mastery of language arts skills but not to develop his sensitivity to his own feelings and emotions. But this latter goal might be proposed as an alternative. In this case, the conventional goal and the alternative goal are different, but at the general level of goals for the education of mankind both the conventional and the alternative goal can be considered shared or common.

Thus, I am not abandoning the original definition of "alternative," but simply expanding it to include goals as well as means. An alternative still must share some features of the thing to which it is an alternative in order to deserve the name. But now the shared characteristics are the primary or ultimate goals of education; the secondary or tertiary goals of the two categories of education may differ. This expanded version of Alternative Education will be identified as AE_g, indicating that the reference is to the goals of Alternative Education rather than to the three means of Alternative Education (instruction, environment, and time).

alternative goals and Tinker Toys

The argument is becoming complicated enough to warrant the introduction of a metaphor which would allow us to form a mental picture of the discussion as it proceeds. Imagine a giant set of Tinker Toys. On the left is a huge structure built out of these Tinker Toys. On the right is a pile of unassembled Tinker Toys. The structure on the left represents Conventional Education. The pile of pieces on the right represents Alternative Education in the means forms of AE_i, AE_e, and AE_t. In order to take advantage of an alternative means, we would remove a Tinker Toy piece from the

CE structure on the left and replace it with an AE piece from the unassembled pile on the right. We go through a similar process when we take cash out of our wallet, put it in the cookie jar, and then put credit cards in the wallet. Or dig the unsightly plaster patch out of the crack, throw it away and refill the crack with spackle.

This Tinker Toy metaphor may make it a little easier to comprehend the three previously discussed difficulties related to alternative means. Each of these difficulties can be framed as a question which must be answered before a CE piece is removed and an AE piece takes its place:

Will the AE piece help to effect attainment of the goals already embodied in the CE structure?

How is the AE piece different from the piece it is replacing?

Is the value orientation out of which the AE piece has been formed consistent or in conflict with the overall value orientation of the structure into which it is being incorporated?

assimilation, separation, and replacement

The process of replacing CE means with AE means is one of adaptation and assimilation. The CE structure is altered by assimilating alternative means, in the forms of instruction, environment, and time. But with alternative goals rather than means, the process can change radically. Suppose, for example, that someone sat down in front of the pile of unassembled AE pieces and built something. The proposals for special schools, such as alternative or free schools, seem to be doing just that: building new structures to stand alongside existing conventional structures.

The demand for alternatives is frequently justified by the claim that if education is to take place in formal institutional settings, then learners and their parents should have more freedom to choose the kind of education they wish to have. This freedom of choice would be provided by giving learners optional settings in which to undertake their education. On the more-freedom-through-options position, AE_g takes the form of a separate educational structure, somewhat reminiscent of the separate-but-equal schools brought into existence by policies of racial segregation. Peaceful coexistence is yet another way to view the multiple options approach.

However, much of the writing emerging from advocates of a

particular value strain in AE is a strong reaction against Conventional Education. Proponents of the counterculture, certain forms of
humanistic education, and Consciousness III appear to favor very
little of the contemporary state of formal education. It is not difficult to presume that these writers want to see AE structures replace
CE structures altogether. This replacement position differs markedly from the separation position in that it eliminates the existence of
options. Without options, the claim that alternative environments
would provide freedom of choice for educational consumers is vacu-
ous. A "separatist" uses the pile of AE Tinker Toys to build a new
structure beside the conventional edifice, whereas an advocate of
replacement destroys the conventional structure when he has completed the new one.

Before I delineate too strictly the differences between the
separation and replacement positions, I should note that they might
not be as far apart as initially supposed. In the separation position,
the CE and AE structures are standing side by side, but their relationship to one another is not necessarily static. Tension arising
between them may place them in a dialectical relationship.* The CE
structure may serve as thesis, and the AE structure as antithesis.
The synthesis of this relationship may be a single new structure
which we are at this moment hard pressed to describe. Thus, over
time, the effects of the separation and replacement positions may
be the same.

While it may be legitimate for the separatists to argue that
alternative structures multiply educational options (which over time
may produce the opposite effect), it is patently immoral for the
replacement advocates to assert that their program yields increased
freedom of choice for the consumers of education. In so saying, I
am not contending that the replacement position is in any way
inherently immoral. Rather, I am arguing that it is improper for
anyone to justify a program on the basis of benefits which cannot
be obtained should the program be realized. A severe critic of Conventional Education, who seeks its elimination by advancing alternative structures, destroys his integrity if he claims that the alternative structures will provide greater freedom through the creation of
options.

---

*I owe this Hegelian insight into the separation position to Dr. Thomas
Robischon.

This discussion of the differences between the separation and replacement positions has some interesting implications for the meaning of "alternative." Up to this point in the chapter an alternative has been defined as a different means to a common goal or as a different secondary goal which leads to the attainment of a common primary goal. Both definitions implied that conventions and alternatives were things we could choose among, making our decisions in whatever ways we saw fit. But the replacement form of AE_g calls this implication into question. It turns out that in some cases the effect of choosing an alternative is that we are left with no alternatives; that is, the selection of certain alternatives may require the elimination of all other options, leaving us with something which may quickly become a monolithic constraint. Thus, that education which is today an alternative to CE may tomorrow be Conventional Education itself. Alternatives, it seems, can be understood as either options or replacements.

So far I have described three possible conceptions of Alternative Education. Adaptation describes what happens when CE assimilates alternative means. Separation takes place when structures with alternative goals are built alongside structures with conventional goals. Replacement occurs when alternative goals entirely displace conventional goals. There is a fourth way to view Alternative Education.

annexation

There are some types of alternatives that appear to be additions rather than substitutions or replacements. Some educators have said that formal education must do more than promote communication and computation skills; it must also engage in more study of the person as a human being and member of mankind. Schools must attend more to values, helping the learner to become an autonomous individual. Schools must expand their curricula, preparing learners not only for citizenship and adulthood, but for a vocation, for leisure, and for the revolutions of knowledge which now take place several times within a single lifetime. What seems to be called for here is not adaptation, separation, or replacement, but annexation. Here alternative structures do not coexist with traditional ones, nor do they replace them. Rather the new structures are simply attached to the existing one. The alternative program is, in effect, annexed in order that the extra goals can be attempted by whatever institutional form education takes as a result of the annexation.

In annexation as in replacement, the alternatives are not truly options. They are single courses of action to be accepted or rejected outright, but not on the basis that there are other equally plausible means or ends which might have been chosen in their place. Only in the cases of adaptation and separation are we actually permitted to choose from a range of different opportunities, all aimed at the attainment of shared primary goals. Replacement and annexation exist as forms of alternatives only until they are chosen. The decision to adopt them is a decision to foreclose the options by either eliminating the conventional or making it bigger than it was before.

processes and products: more on knowing and valuing

Throughout this discussion of Alternative Education, the notion of goals has figured almost as prominently as the concept of alternatives. In a sense, goals are a source of alternatives, for as we devise new and different objectives for education we create options which can serve as alternatives. A great number of the goals which currently fall under the heading of alternatives can be identified as process as opposed to product goals. In Chapter 5, Rodney Skager called attention to this goal distinction, and demonstrated the need for evaluators to undertake the study of educational effectiveness in terms of process goals. While I concur with Skager's position, I think it important not to lose sight of the fact that all processes eventually lead to products; to improve consciously the educational enterprise we must describe the products we desire, be able to recognize them when they appear, and have the criteria necessary to judge their worth. But as alternative educators turn their attention to process goals, they may neglect the significant potential available for generating alternative product goals. To lend credence to this point, I want to discuss in somewhat greater detail the goals of knowing and valuing.

While lip service is almost always given to the view that knowledge is among the primary commodities of education, professional educators tend to know pitifully little about knowledge itself. One does not often hear practicing educators ask questions like: What is it to know something? How does one know when he knows something? What is involved in teaching someone else to know something? But front-line educators are not the only ones who pay little attention to these questions. The advocates of nearly any form of Alternative Education also are strangely quiet on such matters. Yet further development of the concept of knowledge within the context of education may be worth as much or more than many of the alternatives with which we are more familiar from reading the popular critics of Conventional Education.

An alternative way to attain the product goal of a knowledge-able human being is to ask the kinds of questions that place the learner within the midst of the process of coming to know. In Conventional Education, texts and teachers usually ask learners three questions about the phenomenon being studied: What is its purpose? What is it made of? What are its properties? The answers to these questions are known in advance and are nearly always in the possession of the teacher or the text. It is assuredly the case that if a person can answer these three questions, he knows some-thing. But it is a very limited kind of knowledge. It is someone else's knowledge. It is often knowledge for which the learner has no use. It is not the kind of knowledge which entices the learner into becoming a self-perpetuating knower. Other questions can be asked, but they are not asked very often. For example:

How can I change it?

What does it feel like to change it?

What else could it be?

How would my life be different if it were not part of my world?

In what ways can it be useful to me?

Where is it coming from, and where is it going?

These questions shift the learner from outside an established body of knowledge, where he stands as little more than spectator, to within the interior of knowing. It is not difficult to speculate on how the concept of knowledge would change were these six ques-tions asked in addition to the first three. Think of the way common table salt is discussed in chemistry classes, the way birth is studied in health and hygiene classes, the way orchestras are examined in music classes. Perhaps in our haste to rehabilitate the school trou-blemaker, we lose sight of the fact that in turning his chemistry lessons into Molotov cocktails, or his physics lessons into a zip gun, he may be asking himself the last six questions while his teacher and his peers have stopped at the first three. Whitehead (1949, p. 16) said that "education is the acquisition of the art of the utilization of knowledge." That is a long way from saying that education is merely the acquisition of knowledge.

Behaviorist and humanist orientations toward education do not provide very much assistance in the formulation of product goals involving knowledge. Yet unless educators generate alternative means for attaining the goal of knowing, many of the process goals which now make up the repertoire of Alternative Education may do nothing to change the learner's skill at and mastery of knowing. We may be in somewhat the same position in relation to valuing, although AE seems to have much more to say about the nature of values than it does about the nature of knowledge. Nevertheless, an example of a different way to achieve valuing might help to establish further the need for attending to alternative products as well as processes.

It is generally assumed that one function of Conventional Education is to teach values. While there is no longer much emphasis on religious values, a great deal of attention is given to political, economic, and social values. Values instruction in CE goes on as if the mind of the learner were empty of any values and the task of CE is to fill it with values, or as if the mind of the learner were ethically corrupt and CE's job is to wipe out the bad values and replenish with good ones. Seldom does anyone consider that the mind of the learner is already laden with values, but they are imperfectly understood by their possessor, or he is only subliminally aware of them. This state of affairs is a natural one because the young learner usually does not come by his values through a rational process. Rather they are the result of conditioning, habituation, and the need to conform. That the young learner initially obtains his values through these means is not necessarily bad. But one would be morally bankrupt to expect the learner to go on obtaining his values in this manner.

It is possible to teach values by helping the learner understand the values he holds as he comes to school, by showing the learner how he can make decisions about the worth of the values he already holds, and by explaining to the learner how he can justify the values he chooses to retain. The alternative goal, then, is to teach the learner to understand what he already values, and teach him how to go about acting on values he already holds. Raths

(1966) and Simon (1972) have developed a way to accomplish this alternative value goal.

In examining more closely the goals of knowing and valuing, I have provided two illustrations of how many proffered alternatives, especially of the process variety, may not alter or affect the status of two goals which most of us would consider absolutely essential to the nature and purpose of education. There are as yet no guarantees that alternative or free schools, team teaching, behavioral objectives, open classrooms, lifelong learning, and many other alternatives arising out of the several different value orientations will substantively affect two very central product goals: the development of human beings capable of knowing and valuing. The attainment of these goals requires that we attend to considerations of rationality as much as we attend to behavior and experience.

This extended discussion of knowing and valuing poses another possible way to understand the relationships between Alternative and Conventional Education. Previously I described the replacement form of AE in such a way that it amounted to a wholesale substitution of AE for CE. But this need not be the case. It is possible to replace selectively CE goals with AE goals. To return to the Tinker Toy analogy, one would simply remove a goal from the CE structure on the left and replace it with a goal from the AE pile on the right. Thus the CE structure can be adapted by assimilating either alternative means or alternative goals.

answering the first question

What about the question with which this chapter began: To what is Alternative Education an alternative? The quick and simple answer, of course, is that Alternative Education is an alternative to Conventional Education. But because Alternative Education is made up of different sets of means, different sets of goals, and different value programs, the quick and simple answer is of little value to the scholar or decision maker. If we are referring to alternative means, then AE is an alternative to the instructional, environmental, and temporal means employed in CE. The decision to adopt these means does not necessarily generate options, as the means are assimilated by the conventional structure, where they become the new conventions. If we are speaking of alternative goals, then AE may assume several different forms. They may be replacement goals to be inserted within CE, where, like means, they become the conventions. Or they may be goals out of which a new structure is built. The new structure may stand beside the old one and provide the learner with choices about what he shall learn and how he shall learn it, or it may replace the old structure, leaving the learner with no choices about what and how to learn. Finally, the alternative goals may be very new and very different from the conventional goals, and may come to be considered so important that they are annexed to the conventional structure. If AE takes the form of complete replacement or of annexation, then it would not be an alternative to anything. It would simply be a new form, the way things are, without options, choices, or further alternatives.

final thoughts

One of the most intriguing thoughts about Alternative Education is that it may not be with us for very long. No matter which conception of AE one chooses, time and the dynamic nature of social institutions seem to force us into convention. Both alternative means and goals can be incorporated by the conventional structure. A complete alternative structure can replace the conventional structure, but then the alternative itself becomes the conventional. Alternative and conventional structures standing side by side may relate dialectically with one another, producing a single entity with shared elements. Or CE can simply gobble up the alternative by annexation.

Realizing that these may be the eventual outcomes, the educational decision maker's task is to understand the possible forms of change so that he can plan results by controlling the change process. Should CE foster schools within schools? Should it construct its own separate alternative schools? Should alternatives be left to the private schools? Should classrooms be opened? Should learners be given decision authority? The answers to these questions depend on how the decision maker wishes change to take place.

I have tried to identify the possibilities for Alternative Education. Some of them yield genuine alternatives in the short run; others do not. In the long run, today's alternatives will most likely be tomorrow's conventions. It is the educational decision maker who must determine what form change shall take and which alternatives shall be selected to become the conventions.

The educational historian Henry J. Perkinson has examined the response of the schools to three great societal movements in the past one hundred years: nationalization, urbanization, and integration. Perkinson (1968, p. 220) contends that in aiding nationalization, the schools "completely reversed themselves, moving from the original role of preventing governmental tyranny to become a primary agency of the state in its pursuit of national purpose." In seeking to assist the nation with its problems of industrialization, the schools "polarized the society by identifying, indeed creating, the winners and the losers." By accepting responsibility for racial integration, "the schools reinforced segregation; rather than educate people to cope with life in the city, they accelerated the flight from the city and aided in the spread of urban blight." As educators, perhaps we should not let formal education get close to any of those parts of Alternative Education with which we find ourselves in sympathy.

references

Bereiter, C. "A Time for Experiment with Alternatives in Education." In D. U. Levine and R. J. Havighurst (Eds.), *Farewell to Schools???* Belmont, California: Wadsworth, 1971.

Perkinson, H. J. *The Imperfect Panacea: American Faith in Education, 1865-1965.* New York: Random House, 1968.

Raths, L. E., Harmin, M., and Simon, S. B. *Values and Teaching.* Columbus, Ohio: Charles E. Merrill, 1966.

Simon, S. B., Howe, L. W., and Kirschenbaum, H. *Values Clarification.* New York: Hart, 1972.

Whitehead, A. N. *The Aims of Education.* New York: New American Library, 1949.

part ii
prospects

The future in education is not likely to be simply more of the same. Nor is it likely to represent such an abrupt break with the past that there will be no familiar forms. The thrust to use technology more effectively will still be there, as will the thrust to create more intimate, personal settings for learning. The tension between long-standing tendencies and antagonisms will remain and, indeed, will be productive of innovation and successive cycles of reform. On one thing we all seem to be agreed: there will be a continued opening up of the system to admit and even support alternatives, many of them outside the formal system of schooling, increasingly with public funds.

Schools contribute differentially to the goals set for them. They are generally less influential than the home in the teaching of language skills, for example, but more influential in teaching mathematics and science. The implication is that a multiple intervention strategy is required to enhance the probability of achieving individual, institutional, and societal goals. Consequently, collaboration among institutions and groups is called for in providing a range of educational alternatives, especially when some learning is of a direct kind and some is more secondary or abstract. Successful change strategies of the future necessarily will embrace a comprehensive array of these institutions and groups, all of which must be viewed in a systemic fashion.

Conventional indicators of the success of alternative educational ventures simply will not suffice. This means much more than alternative measuring devices, more than criterion-referenced or norm-referenced tests. It means new criteria for judging success, such as satisfaction, and new ways of working out whose criteria will prevail. In much of its determination and conduct, education is a sociopolitical process within which there will be confrontation and conflict among groups with differing interests, however large or

141

small the settings and whether or not the process is bureaucratized. To repeat what is said many times in these chapters, education simply cannot be separated from the larger systems and problems of which it is a part and to which it contributes.

We continue in Part II to be very interested in the what and how questions of education because the operational answers to them convey the values to which those conducting the process subscribe, perhaps more than any other aspect of education. Evaluative criteria and processes attached to yesterday's educational ways simply will not suffice for the alternatives we envision. As those who would oppose changing them well know, holding to conventional ways of evaluation is one of the most potent inhibitors of change.

And it is to change that most of what follows is directed. Some educational futurists paint a rosy picture of an idealized learning society lying just beyond present problems and crises. They are not at all clear on how we get there from where we are. Extrapolation from the present does not carry us unequivocally to widespread implementation of open classrooms, alternative schools, and a range of educational options well suited to the lifelong learning interests and needs of all our citizens. There are trends and forces conspiring to suggest quite the opposite. At the center of these is the problem of whether the self-interests of the organized teaching profession, organized lay groups, and politicians are likely to be turned toward the commonweal. There is the problem, too, of whether our existing educational institutions can become adequately responsive to the fundamental changes now taking place in the world community. One can have, at best, only rather restrained optimism in the face of such problems.

Part I attempted to place the so-called alternatives movement in broad perspective. Part II places future possibilities, issues arising from these possibilities, and prospects for attaining them within the framework of understanding developed in preceding chapters.

alternative futures
in education

val d. rust

The term "alternatives in education" denotes both criticism of the prevailing order of things and the need for a look into the future to suggest new paths, new structures, new patterns. A major objective of this chapter is to project the future, with projections evolving from extrapolations from the past. The discussion is based on a social-historical theory of change that maintains that the forces bringing about evolutionary social processes are dialectical in nature. That is, we recognize in all phenomena the existence of contradictory, mutually exclusive, opposite tendencies. The tension between these tendencies, the struggle of the old and new, the positive and negative, the past and future, is seen to constitute the content of any process of development. Change is not completely continuous, but is, rather, characterized by intermittent, sudden changes in states; it is analogous to the phenomenon of biological mutation.

The dialectical process can be observed in all social phenomena. The world is in a state of constant evolution, each social condition coming into existence out of contradictions inherent in the immediately preceding condition. It is possible to discern in struggles of social life an epochal development that places our immediate problems in a less momentous perspective than we are prone to attribute to them and provides firmer footing in our quest to move intelligently into the future. The last major epoch of Western countries is that of the modern age, which emerged out of traditional societies through the industrial revolution, which began in England, and the political revolution, which began in France and the United States. The institutions and life-styles of the modern age stand in stark contrast to the traditional ones that existed in premodern countries and that continue to exist in much of the underdeveloped world.

From all indications we are moving rapidly into a new epoch in the stream of history, the modern age having run its course. In the highly developed areas of the world, economic, social, political, and intellectual processes have set in motion a life orientation that has led to modernity in the extreme. There have emerged, consequently, countervailing forces that have come to challenge the very core of modernity. These challenges are now so pervasive as to suggest that the modern age has come to an end and will soon be replaced by a new age termed by some a technotronic age and by others the postindustrial or postmodern age. Kenneth Boulding has coined the term "post-civilization" to characterize the emerging era (Boulding, 1964).

Already a vast futuristic literature has accumulated, though the most comprehensive single work remains a volume published during the last decade and put together by the American Academy of Arts and Sciences Commission on the Year 2000, chaired by Daniel Bell (1967). Education has also produced its share of futurists, though most of them are reluctant to identify their speculations with anything as radical as a postmodern era.*

As we leave the modern world and enter into a new era of postmodernity, we should not expect an extension into a supermodern state, but the dialectical process dictates that we should expect a synthesis of the contradictions between the traditional and the modern. We should enter into a condition qualitatively distinct from traditional as well as modern societies but closer to both of these extremes than they are to each other.

If a new era is a possibility, almost every aspect of modern

---

*One of the better bibliographical compilations is found in Harold G. Shane, "Looking to the Future: Reassessment of Educational Issues of the 1970's," *Phi Delta Kappan*, 1973 (January), 326-337.

society will be changed, including the functions and structures of educational institutions, as well as the minds and values of man. Within the confines of this statement, it is difficult to cover the entire panorama of changes that might be anticipated. I have chosen to concentrate on structural analysis as a focus of inquiry, and I have selected spheres of concern that allow me to go all the way from the structure of political units such as the nation-state to local learning environments. First, I discuss the impact of the nation-state on education and anticipate that impact in a world in which the nation-state will have lost its autonomy. Second, I raise the issue of bureaucratic structures as they relate to school systems as whole units and anticipate emerging administrative arrangements for education. Finally, I concentrate on modern schools and anticipate some characteristics of learning environments that will emerge during the postmodern era.

the nation-state modified

That social body which came to dominate the modern world and which rationalized and centralized all authority within itself was the nation-state. Authority is probably the most crucial variable in social organization, for both the type of authority and the degree of legitimacy determine in large measure the viability of any social activity. We define authority, first, as that power to which the voluntarily obedient defer and thereby legitimize compliance to dictates or directives and, second, that power which leaders or functionaries call on to bring about voluntary accommodation.

In spite of the fact that modern authority has been consolidated into single bodies in the form of nation-states, other bodies have not ceased to exist. They function and exercise authority, however, only if the state allows them to function, or if authority is delegated to some nonstate unit. Thus, a church may exercise certain sanctions on its members or a labor union may act against industrial firms only to the degree that they are permitted to do so by the state. Even the authority of the father over his son is to a considerable degree circumscribed and prescribed by the authority of the modern state.

As in other spheres, not only has education come under the jurisdiction of the state, but most of its functions are performed in specially designated institutions. In other words, schooling has become an integral part of the infrastructure of the nation-state. This is not to suggest that attendance occurs exclusively in state schools. Almost every nation in the world provides for private schooling; such schooling is, however, approved or accredited by authorized agents in order to satisfy the requirements of the state. The preceding two centuries have witnessed the thrust toward a growing percentage of young people in school for more and more years with longer school terms and decreasing absentee rates. Relative figures for American children well illustrate this trend. In 1870 less than 60 percent of school-age children were enrolled in school, whereas by 1970 over 98 percent were. The average length of the term during this interval has increased from 132 to approximately 180 days. Children enrolled in school in 1870 failed to appear two days a week whereas today the average absenteeism rate is approximately one day every two weeks (U.S. Bureau of the Census, 1960).

Compulsory education laws are the most common means by which universal schooling has been achieved in the developed areas of the world. As nation-states began to engage in modernization efforts, compulsory schooling became an integral element in the process. We have reached the point where it is almost axiomatic that to be modern is to be schooled. Modern nations usually maintain from 15 to 30 percent of their population in school at any given time (Easterline, 1965).

Even though school attendance is not completely universal in modern countries, its virtues have been largely unquestioned, and heroic efforts have been undertaken to achieve it, especially in the developed areas of those countries. The few remaining pockets of people who fall outside the grasp of state control are slowly being incorporated. In France, for example, legislation was passed in 1966 to bring children of Nomads finally under the schooling umbrella even though each child now attends, on the average, more than thirty different schools a year (Fohr, 1969).

The question arises as to why nation-states have invested such enormous efforts and resources in universal schooling. In the first place, the state assumed many educational functions that were performed by other spheres in traditional societies. They included basic skills in reading, writing, and computation; catechetical instruction; and some form of higher cultural or enlightenment learning in the vernacular. Though these tasks might well have been allowed to remain the responsibility of disparate groups in modern society, one objective was exclusively an element of modern times and could only be achieved through state institutions: education in the realm of patriotism and loyal identity with the folk or nation-state. There have been variations in the degree of indoctrination in patriotism. Countries such as Prussia, France, Russia, and Japan devoted themselves unabashedly to national pride, loyalty, and obedience to the state, whereas England and the United States have been more subtle, stressing what might be considered universal virtues such as freedom and democracy. The objective peculiar to modern state schools in all lands has, nonetheless, been to instill a sense of devotion to the nation.

As the modern age draws to an end, the situation appears to be that the highly developed areas of the world have almost completed the goal of bringing everyone under the jurisdiction of state-dominated education, and the developing areas are making gallant efforts to do the same. The nation-state has embodied the values guiding this schooling, the schools inculcating a sense of allegiance and devotion to the state and providing the training necessary for human adaptation. Though private schooling has existed and conflicting views have been tolerated, both have survived only so long as they did not seriously threaten the fundamental authority of the state.

This state of affairs is now being seriously challenged. In Chapter 2 La Belle outlined the major categories of protest challenging state domination and control of the educational enterprise. These include critics who claim the modern school represents aims designed for institutional preservation, goals that are claimed to be detrimental to the maintenance of human growth and cultural continuity. Advocates of efficiency maintain that formal schooling on a worldwide basis is so expensive and so time consuming that it represents a luxury which, if provided, will benefit only a select few in most societies. Those who advocate equality of education claim that formal schooling has come to represent oppression, that it is used as an instrument of power designed to instill subservience and committed obedience to the ruling class of the state. I add a fourth category to this list: revolutionaries who claim that the message of both the formal and the hidden curriculum is that of the mainstream thought of the particular ruling powers of the state; this must be overthrown for a new ideology.

The message here is clear. State-controlled mass schooling, charged with instilling in the general public the values that the state has deemed appropriate, is being seriously challenged. The individual, the community, and the larger human culture with which people identify are assuming increased importance in the eyes of more and more people. Such a challenge is obviously more than a problem of education; it strikes at the core of the dominance and sovereignty of the nation-state. It is inappropriate to discuss in detail the larger social issue, whereby languages, religions, races, and cultures were integrated, often with force, into unitary wholes as nation-states emerged. Almost every country opted for some form of unity, though great variance was tolerated in some states. This concept is now under siege. In Canada the French maintain injustice exists in terms of their voice in the affairs of state. Ireland is at war, with religion being at the heart of the clash. The Basques are rebelling in Spain, the blacks and Mexican-Americans in the United States. New forms of government already are emerging. At the same time economic and ideological forces are breaking down certain national boundaries and are moving groups toward greater international union. Belgium, for example, already has declared the nation-state dead, opting for greater regionalization as well as international ties (Tindemans, 1972).

These forces of protest have coalesced during the past decade to challenge state authority and also have contributed to the movement toward alternative futures in education. Formal schooling, at least in the form patterned after the typical state school model, is viewed more and more by these groups as dysfunctional in terms of the interests many groups would like schooling and education to serve.

We can anticipate, therefore, a distinct shift in authority as we move into the postmodern era. The transitional period will be filled with enormous problems, and, in fact, writers such as Heilbroner are probably correct in claiming that this period will require a further consolidation of power in the nation-state (Heilbroner, 1974). Ultimately, however, even though the state will continue to exist, its autonomy will be destroyed. Authority will be shared in a manner that resembles in many ways traditional authority, which was highly pluralistic in nature, with legitimate powers being dispensed through empire, universal church, tribal duchies representing a multitude of feudal states, and other lesser units of authority such as village or clan, as well as through authority of custom and belief.

As was the case with traditional authority, the legitimate

powers that are emerging will not be separate powers or have authority restricted to specific functions or activities, but different authorities will overlap each other. Within the dialectical process we should not expect a complete reversion to traditional forms. The state will, in fact, continue to exercise enormous power, and when pluralistic authority joins hands in supporting the state in its quest to deal with such problems as war, energy conservation, and population control, power will be consolidated in such a manner as to appear to generate superstate status even though authority itself will remain diffused.

With the diffusion of authority, unitary schooling programs, which were characteristic of the modern age, will break down. We can anticipate the emergence of organic power sources deriving from family, culture, spiritual community, and workplace that will move to fuse skills, discipline, and the development of values with the life-styles characteristic of a given group. Like traditional education—where considerable blurring existed between schooling and other institutions because instruction went on in households, churches, and workshops—postmodern educational institutions will blur with other institutions to the point where schooling as a separate, isolated enterprise will largely disappear.

Education will be linked to organic units as in traditional environments, but, for the most part, the educational function will not be in the hands of immediate and local authority units as was the case in traditional environments simply because communications systems will connect large as well as small authority units with the life experience of the child. One main function of broader authority structures will be to force the more local organic units to function with far greater tolerance for divergent languages, cultures, and ideologies. They will, however, also provide a positive thrust in that local concepts related to ultimate values and truth will continually be challenged by broader concepts. Such a commentary is alien to modern educational imperialism which forced itself onto the nonmodern world, certain that its mode of inquiry provided the only legitimate source of objective truth to the point where other systems of knowing were dismissed as myths.

The educative process can function productively in a state of diffused authority only when the concepts and operations of an authority entity are perceived by that entity as existing in the context of its own historical time and social conditions. The reality of each person's universe must be put in a historical context, which will not dispute the fact of past and potential contributions of other authority entities with regard to legitimate knowledge. This reality also must demonstrate the absurdity of a monopoly on legitimate access to truth and reality as usually was practiced by the modern nation-state. The role of acupuncture as an alternative medical technique with its unique assumptions and world view illustrates the possibility of systems functioning simultaneously and legitimately in a multireality universe.

The contribution of the nation-state in this interplay of authorities will be significant. Though the autonomy of the nation-state will have been diminished, its viability will be retained. It will function as a mediator and arbiter of interests in the postmodern world rather than as a social determiner, which is a major part of its present role.

The arbitration function of the state is well illustrated in compulsory education. During the modern age the state mandated school attendance for specific years. As schools blur with other institutions, such mandates will become meaningless. The state will serve as a mediator of basic standards; these standards will be subject to a wide variety of peculiar cultural determinants as the length and kind of schooling deemed appropriate must become differentiated, its form and substance being colored by the particular forces at play among particular groups in the pluralistic world. Perhaps the most popular phrases used to characterize emerging education are that of "lifelong learning" or, as termed by the Faure report, "towards a learning society" (Faure and others, 1972, part 3), but these terms simply imply that education will cease to be defined as schooling in the conventional sense, especially as learning in a special institution for a certain number of years, and will once again become integrated into the total life activities, be they local or worldwide. The manner in which this can be accomplished operationally is largely technical in nature, and we turn now to the administrative adjustments that will become necessary.

administrative arrangements

As nationalism wrenched education from diffused educational authority and placed it directly under state control, two main tasks emerged for modern states. On the one hand, it was necessary to establish and maintain a state system of schools. On the other hand, it was necessary to ensure that certain standards and conformity were maintained in those schools which continued to be run outside direct state administrative jurisdiction. Nation-states come to maintain a variety of different administrative schemes for school systems. These have ranged from highly centralized to highly dispersed authority structures, though it is important to note that this issue remains secondary in that, ultimately, modern schools were all interlinked into a rationalized system containing a proliferating number of specialized personnel who would make greater and more varied demands on the people and on the resources of the state.

The highly centralized system in France following the revolution largely set the tone for the rest of Europe as feudalistic, ecclesiastical, and aristocratic powers were made subject to the sovereign state, and the schools existing within that sovereign territory were run by a central ministry that dictated every vital element of the school program throughout the country.

The system that emerged in America was more decentralized than most of the other modern nations, probably because indoctrination in loyalty to the state was not emphasized to the same degree as in areas with a feudal heritage. Even in this country schooling came under the control of separate state central boards though these boards delegated many of their powers to individual districts as long as they reflected a willingness and ability to meet minimal state requirements. Katz has pointed out that America opted for an incipient bureaucratic school model which eventually replaced various traditional modes of school administration. This model came to typify all modern systems of education (Katz, 1971), and incipient bureaucracy probably functioned as adequately as any system during the early stages of modernity. It is only when bureaucracy reaches the state of a full-fledged, large-scale organization that, with justification, it becomes a perjorative term as the "system" becomes so self-serving that it stifles any change, fails to respond to human needs, and becomes an alienating force.

Presthus has outlined the basic structure of full bureaucracies as being so large as to prevent face-to-face relations; developing a growing division of labor, resulting in narrower specialization by participants that destroys almost all integrative appreciation; providing a definite status system that produces differentiated rights, income, and privileges; developing an oligarchical rule that determines that vital decisions are made by a ruling few who are often out of touch with broader interests and demands; developing a system of co-optation or a process where those in power determine succession and thereby ensure perpetuation of status quo standards and order; and, finally, defending the bureaucracy on the basis of a supposed rationality and efficiency, which usually only acts as a cover to irresponsibility and substandard performance (Presthus, 1962, pp. 27-58).

As school districts and state systems have grown in the modern age, they have taken on the bureaucratic mode in the extreme and in the process have become a focus of protest. At the close of the modern age we are able to sense some signs of new arrangements that might be more successful in coping with problems of the emerging age.

As we move into the postmodern age components of the state system of schooling will remain, but these will be synthesized with traditional modes in such a manner as to cope with authority arrangements that were discussed in the previous section. It appears certain that centralization will continue in terms of educational finances. Advocates of equality of educational opportunity will demand that such a process come to fruition. No longer will unequal distribution of public resources for educational purposes be tolerated. Recent court decisions and commission reports suggest that such a course of action is inevitable. On the other hand, questions concerning peculiar learning styles, emphasis on cultural variations, and satisfaction of the needs of individual children are making it necessary that more and more administrative decisions be made at local levels. Such a move challenges the modern version of "He who pays the piper calls the tune," in that the payer, who has posed as the sovereign government in the past, will represent diffused authority in which centralized autonomy will cease to exist.

Even in the modern world some nations, such as Switzerland, Yugoslavia, Denmark, and Holland, have been able to foster diversity effectively within a unitary system. In Holland, for example, as a result of constitutional law, if a group of parents, a religious body, political group, or some other collection of people who share beliefs as to the kind of education that is appropriate for a minimal number of children (for example, fifty children per primary school) can raise but 15 percent of the estimated cost of building a school, the government and municipality are compelled to provide the remainder of the capital outlay and all the costs of running the school. As a consequence of this law, almost 80 percent of the nursery schools, 70 percent of the primary, and 60 percent of the education beyond primary schooling are run by independent bodies. Such enormous diversity has not resulted in a breakdown of cohesion in the country; it is, in fact, viewed by many as a contributory factor in bridging what often amount to superficial religious differences. This suggests that life-style, temperament, and concern for the centrality of the child in the educational process are other basic areas where cohesion is possible.

Even systems such as that of Holland must adjust, however, as we move beyond the era in which single institutions assume the responsibility of the entire formal education of a child. It is more likely that the child will engage in several systems simultaneously, each providing some form of education related to the general role that the institution serves in the society at large.

In the United States our peculiar constitutional tradition has worked against the natural evolution of schooling for a pluralistic society. Creative political and scholarly proposals are, however, bringing to light possible new administrative arrangements. The Fleischmann report on school reform in New York State, community advisory council activities, and voucher proposals are but a few examples of transitional efforts paving the way to new roles. New York State recently recommended the abolition of all local financing and the centralization of it at the state level. Funds are to be redistributed throughout the state, bypassing local district officials and going directly to individual schools which would have extensive discretionary powers as to their use. District boards in other states are being compelled to share their authority in fundamentally new ways. Community advisory councils, now mandated in districts such as Los Angeles, mean that each school has an elected board which, at this point, advises the principal on school priorities, programs, curriculum, and overall policies. The above instances are reminiscent of the paternalistic voluntarism of traditional institutions that emerged at the time of Luther: local pastors and sextons were able to conduct Protestant schools financed by local princes.

Among the most innovative endeavors of recent times are the so-called voucher proposals; a number of different ones have been suggested by men such as Milton Friedman, Henry Levin, James S.

Coleman, and Christopher Jencks. The one common element in these proposals is a type of free market system in which public officials would get out of the business of environmental and programmatic policies and remain in the realm of service agent for the clients who make the decisions concerning the type of education they feel is appropriate for their children. In a voucher plan a parent would receive a certificate, often called an edu-credit card, which can be traded in for a certain amount of schooling at an approved school. Approved schools would be those adhering to minimal obligations such as open financial accounts, accurate publicity as to staff and program, and assurance of no racial discrimination. Under this system the parents, rather than the state, determine the appropriate type of education for their children. Since the parent can withdraw the child at any time, decisions concerning standards or quality of instruction are taken from the control of public officials and revert to the parents.

One of the major insights emerging from the voucher system, at least in the United States, is the fallacy of the distinction between public and private education. We can anticipate that one day we will cease defending the existence of some "public" institutions whose tuition excludes many potential learners, while rejecting the right of some "private" schools to receive public funds in spite of the fact that they may provide free openings to those unable to pay. We may one day cease defending the "neighborhood" school, which appeals to certain publics that may wish to take advantage of the kind of learning experience some schools offer but that are excluded because they cannot afford the houses in the neighborhood. We may one day cease to support the existence of school boards that conceal how they use certain public funds while denying the right of private enterprises to receive funds even though there is a willingness to provide full disclosure of the manner in which resources are being used.

In the coming age, learning environments will cease to be classified exclusively on the basis of who runs them, for that is most misleading. A more appropriate classification would be the assumptions, activities, and aims of any program and the degree to which admissions are open to diverse groups. Parents and youth will be confronted with options across a range of publicly run and privately sponsored learning environments, all at the expense of the general resource pool.

In spite of the radical nature of voucher proposals, they appear destined to serve as models for administrative arrangements to come simply because they are finding sympathy from every spectrum of society except those advocates of expanding state control. As authority becomes diffused, advocates of an outdated modernity will no longer be able to withhold power from diverse segments of society. Some administrative form of the voucher system seems inevitable since it allows for equal financial distribution while providing for individual choice as to styles of educational participation.

Even though the voucher notion provides conceptually for the most flexible operational system of options, in its present forms it remains school based. We can anticipate even more flexibility as provisions become available for simultaneous learning affiliations. That is, a child might attend more than one educational institution at a time. The accounting of these experiences, at least for the purpose of resource distribution, might be similar to the credit system that pervades higher education in the United States, with a given institution receiving payment for specific services rendered. We can anticipate that whatever arrangement emerges it will not be completely "school" oriented and will provide resources for learning to take place in forms we can only vaguely perceive at this point.

Thus, the broad social forces as well as internal adjustments of schooling will force the modern bureaucratic model, which characterizes the way modern schooling is run, to give way to alternative forms of administration because bureaucracy is unable to tolerate diverse standards and overlapping lines of authority. Some form of central bureaucracy will be retained to ensure universal and uniform financial provisions as well as to monitor minimal standards having to do with such factors as disclosure regulations, but we can anticipate diminished roles on the part of administrative bodies in policy making related to actual programs.

learning environments

The modern age developed its characteristic and, in many respects, unique structures to educate its youth. In spite of the fact that the aims of modern education have been aligned with the aims of the nation-state, the model for the actual schooling process is drawn from industry. Such a model suggests the compatibility of modern patriotic attitudes and industrial imperatives. Both need participants who function smoothly in mass settings. Both require participants willing to flow with the political and industrial process without friction. Marcuse has described, in negative terms, this condition with regard to industry: "In the Society, the productive apparatus . . . obliterates the opposition between public and private existence, between individual and social needs. Technology serves to institute new, more effective, and more pleasant forms of social control and social cohesion" (Marcuse, 1964, p. xv). In like manner, the state requires willing subjects with standardized behaviors reflecting not only a willingness to conform but a devotion to the mandates of the political process.

Modern schooling broke with the system of the past, which connected learning with informal and participatory conditions, a procedure that at the dawn of the modern age would have demanded conformity to traditional values and beliefs. The new schooling process conformed to the imperatives of the modern age as youth were sent to school to acquire the more vital aspects of industrial organization as exemplified by the factory.

The genius of industrialization seems to have been organizational in nature in that the factory was conceived as a system whereby a multitude of fairly simple mechanical processes could be joined into a coherent whole. The system was labor intensive as it provided a mechanism in which great numbers of people would perform simple but specialized functions as appendages to the overall mechanical processes. Even as technology reached high levels of sophistication the same notion persisted.

As Galbraith has observed, the accomplishment of science and technology in the modern world "consists in taking ordinary men, informing them narrowly and deeply and then, through appropriate organization, arranging to have their knowledge combined with that of other specialized but equally ordinary men" (Galbraith, 1967, p. 73). Dramatic consequences have followed such organization; perhaps the most impressive example is that of space travel where thousands of specialists have combined their expertise in the single enterprise of putting a man on the moon.

Toffler reminds us that the factory came to serve as a model structure for modern learning as the school isolated itself from the organic life of the broader society, functioned with the precision of a calibrated clock, utilized the physical plant as effectively as possible by work shifts, and defined a specific and integrated division of labor. ". . . the whole idea of assembling masses of students (raw material) to be processed by teachers (workers) in a centrally located school (factory) was a stroke of industrial genius. The whole administrative hierarchy of education, as it grew up, followed the model of industrial bureaucracy. The very organization of knowledge into permanent disciplines was grounded in industrial assumptions. Children marched from place to place and sat in assigned stations, bells rang to announce time changes" (Toffler, 1970, p. 400). Toffler maintains that those features of the school which were most instrumental in preparing young people for industrial society were "regimentation, lack of individualization, the rigid systems of seating, grouping, grading and marking."

Modern industrial work, by its very nature, is admitted to be mechanical, uninteresting, and alienating, and when so much human power is involved in highly complex processes it is destined to experience continual breakdowns. The technological solution to these deficiencies has been to automate as much of the process as possible. As we emerge into the postindustrial age, that dream appears to be on the brink of extensive fulfillment as some manufacturing processes have already been almost totally automated.

The dream of automation has captured the imagination of large numbers of futuristic educational technologists who in the past have conceptualized systems as complete and complex as the modern factory only to find that teachers are as uninterested and alienated in the system as factory workers, and they also fail to perform their specialized functions to the point where the learning process usually breaks down. Some educational scholars have predicted that postmodern education will eliminate this problem as people-staffed schools will be replaced by machine-based instruction and thereby optimize the learning process.

As we emerge from the modern age, some mechanism must be found to retain an optimum contribution of technology, which every thoughtful person both recognizes and appreciates. We can expect the continuation of technological development into the new era. Goodlad predicts, for example, that a large portion of the schooling process will be replaced by machine instruction, and, in keeping with our earlier discussion of the demise of schooling in a factory-like setting, he maintains that through electronic instruments such as television and the computer this instruction will take place on a totally individual basis drawing on the resources of all knowledge and having the capacity to bring that knowledge within the grasp of the clients in whatever physical setting they so choose. Whatever schools remain will be devoted primarily to serving functions of personal orientation and integration (Goodlad, 1968).

Video equipment, holography, and mobile units will become a part of this effort as schooling moves beyond the lockstep structure of the modern era into a future where students are not only freed from the drudgery of doing the same tasks unadjusted and untailored to their individual needs, but they are able to set priorities in a way that modern life could not tolerate.

These technical advances might eliminate their alienating qualities from the teacher, but the learners, as participants in the system, would find themselves in a sterile nonhuman environment that mitigates against those qualities of life which are essentially human. The technical elements of the postmodern age must be complemented by traditional qualities which are largely interpersonal in nature. We can barely perceive what forms may emerge, but challenges to contemporary formal schooling provide some clues. We shall comment on three of these challenges.

The first of the challenges is regression to smallness. Numerous empirical findings indicate that people find it difficult to identify with large masses of people who are joined in large organizations. The sheer size of such institutions brings about a feeling of alienation, anonymity, and lack of personal power. Schools are no exception as students have come to drop out mentally, emotionally, and physically from large institutions in increasing numbers. In spite of the evidence of social science, the mythology of social evolution remained pervasive as "bigger and better" schools were being built throughout the modern world. The most grotesque idea emerged with the concept of "educational parks" which were conceived as the ultimate solution to the problems of urban schooling. In this scheme all the schoolchildren of an entire city would be brought to a single campus that was fed by rapid transit systems. The campus might contain tens of thousands of students ranging from the lowest grades through high school. They would be placed in appropriate slots throughout the day, thus ensuring the satisfaction of educational and social needs of the city and the children. This dinosaur of modern schooling was never realized, however, for a variety of reasons. With the challenge of the humanistic education movement in the sixties the concept of small, intimate environments was revived. Free private schools that sprang up rarely had more than sixty students. Moboc, which is a school on wheels, maintains an adult-pupil ratio of eight to one. When one school is full, another is organized, rather than expanding the old. It was inevitable that the alternative schools would eventually penetrate the public domain, and the most vulnerable systems were those of the large cities where bigness reigns supreme. In 1969 New York, for example, launched the pilot school for a large number of minischools. A year later similar projects were begun, including the breakup of the all-male Haaren High School in Manhattan and the subsequent division of its 2,500 ghetto students into no less than fourteen "subject and theme oriented minischools" (Divoky, 1971, p. 61).

There is no question that these initial inroads into "thinking small and intimate" are little more than calls of desperation on the part of parents, teachers, and administrators who admit only that the system has broken down. There is every indication that large numbers will fail and will revert to a system of alienating control and structure in large prison-like institutions, but the signs of a breakthrough to something other than continual growth in size are apparent.

The second challenge is nongradedness. The demand to eliminate the graded tradition, which has become almost axiomatic in most modern countries, originates from two main sources. On the one hand are the educational technologists who maintain that the factory model of grading is obsolete and must be replaced by more sophisticated technology. That technology concentrates on individual differences that disallow wholesale group instruction and encourage the establishment of learning continua in which the child can progress along an established learning path at his own pace. Gross grouping practices based on such factors as age serve to interfere with the technology involved and have necessitated inquiries into alternative modes of operation. Goodlad and Anderson point out that the early challenges to grading in the United States were almost entirely in the direction of achievement grouping in an attempt to homogenize achievement levels and allow for more flexible movement of the child along a learning continuum (Goodlad and Anderson, 1963).

The child-centered advocates view the evils of grading from quite a different vantage point than the technologists. This movement is most strongly reflected in the British infant schools where "family grouping" (also known as "vertical grouping") has been practiced since the end of World War II. Its focus is not so much on achievement or progress in basic skills, though it is often argued that these are in no way diminished and often enhanced, as it is on the emotional and mental health of the child. It is more compatible with social arrangements, especially the family, where the older children interact with the younger to the benefit of both.

In spite of the fact that vertical grouping now dominates the learning environments of the English infant school, other modern countries have been reluctant to change. In West Germany a few schools have adopted the English model. Signs of breakthroughs in the United States are also evident. California, for example, is moving toward a statewide program of early childhood education that includes a "family type age mix" in its recommendations. The major thrust for vertical grouping in the United States has come in the free school, which not only demands that schools be small but that the groups in them include a wide range of ages. It is argued that the mixing of ages gives children a broader choice of relationships as well as other advantages.

Since vertical grouping is a creation not only of the most advanced forms of modern technology but of those who are advocating that humane considerations prevail over achievement and competition, it bodes well for the continued expansion of family grouping, though its final form is yet in question.

Integrated programs are the third challenge. Advocates of integrated programs are child centered and maintain that young people learn through self-oriented activity, including play, as well as through externally imposed learning activities. The integrated day represents the clearest break from the industrial school of modern society. As we have already noted, the clock and timetable were paramount in such a school. Specific subjects were studied by all children in serial order through the day; as one subject was concluded, all children would put their materials away and begin the study of another subject. At the higher levels the young people would shift in blocks from one classroom to another, each environment representing its own subject matter domain. All this disappears in an integrated day, as fixed points are held at a minimum, and subject matter distinctions are blurred.

The English have moved more actively than any country of the modern world toward integrated programs. This concept is closely tied to vertical grouping and team teaching and, paradoxically, is usually characterized by children working in a highly organized and much-utilized environment, where teachers often have created alcoves and centers where different kinds of activities may take place simultaneously. Children move from activity to activity as their interests dictate, though some may be directed by an adult. Under this arrangement it is unusual to find all children working on any one activity at one time, and the activities they engage in rarely correspond completely to the traditional disciplines, since these spheres are now recognized as artificial creations of the modern mind and are not a part of the child's mode of viewing and dealing with the universe. The main tasks of the teachers change from instruction and giving directions to managing the environment and monitoring children to assure that each one has a balanced program throughout the week.

The challenges mentioned above are within the framework of formal schooling; it is anticipated that schools will largely disappear as learning and living become integrated into the ongoing life of communities. The regression to smallness is now represented by smaller schools, but it will eventuate in clusters of learners who will establish intense interpersonal relationships in environments that are intimately connected with the life processes of communities. Family grouping in school now rarely extends over an age range of more than three or four years. It is likely that family grouping in postmodern education will involve interpersonal learning experiences over a spectrum including all ages, with technology satisfying those needs for skills which led to the creation of age-level grouping in the first place. Integrated programs as I have described them above conceive of learning centers in small, confined environments within a building or even a classroom. We can anticipate that learning centers will become vital components of every facet of community life in such a way as to allow the environment for learning to become the community rather than an isolated institution called school that continues to simulate some embryonic form of community life. Technology provides the capability for developing skills so that community learning can remain oriented to the personal.

Within the framework of the forces pushing us to a new era, the focus is once again on the human condition and life-enhancing experiences rather than on a linear rush for an imagined technological utopia characterized by efficiency of machines and technical expertise. Technology will not be lost, but it will serve to enhance cultural differences rather than homogenize societies as if they were built of interchangeable parts. Technological ideals will be utilized to assist in the recognition of the individuality of each human being and the uniqueness of his development within specific groups and cultures rather than to process youths as if they were on an assembly line.

The complaints of modern efficiency experts that "there is too much slippage in our flexible schools" will rarely be heard for that attitude negates the focus of young people at various stages of development on values and activities that may be more human and more humane than proficiency on standardized reading tests. The advanced electronic technology will not be used to tie more tightly the life of the child to its technical demands, as was the case in the modern age, but will be used by intelligent inquirers who will employ computers to provide the flexibility of a private electronic tutor to each child, and thereby allow the time and conditions necessary for qualitative interpersonal and personal explorations.

We have explored possible structural changes that will emerge as we enter the postmodern era. Since education is largely dependent on broad social conditions, it was necessary to devote most of the discussion to political and social issues, particularly with respect to the nation-state and its stake in education, as well as to the consequences of diffused authority within the nation-state. As authority is divided among a variety of groups, a unitary bureaucracy will probably cease to be a viable mechanism for running schools. Some other arrangements must be made for centralizing certain elements, such as resource collection and distribution, while decentralizing those elements which relate directly to growing cultural diversity. The learning environments characteristic of modern schooling will also be altered as the industrial model gives way to synthesized technical and human growth environments that are connected with social institutions of the community and that accommodate themselves to the pluralism of value, knowledge, and reality. Given these few structural changes, we are forced to open ourselves to the possibilities of learning environments that have little relationship to the modern age.

references

Bell, D. (Ed.). *Toward the Year 2000: Work in Progress.* Boston: Beacon Press, 1967.

Boulding, K. *The Meaning of the 20th Century.* New York: Harper and Row, 1964.

Divoky, D. "New York's Mini-Schools." *Saturday Review,* 1971 (December 18), 60-61.

Easterline, R. A. "A Note on the Evidence of History." In C. Arnold Anderson and Mary Jean Bowman (Eds.), *Education and Economic Development.* Chicago: Aldine, 1965.

Eisenstadt, S. N. *Modernization: Protest and Change.* Englewood Cliffs, N.J.: Prentice-Hall, 1966.

Ellul, J. *The Technological Society.* New York: Vintage, 1964.

Faure, E., and others. *Learning to Be.* Paris: UNESCO, 1972.

Fohr, P. "Compulsory Schooling for Nomads." *West European Education,* 1969, *1,* 32-40.

Galbraith, J. K. *The New Industrial State.* New York: Signet, 1967.

Goodlad, J. I. "Learning and Teaching in the Future." *Today's Education: NEA Journal,* 1968 (February), 49-51.

Goodlad, J. I., and Anderson, R. H. *The Nongraded Elementary School.* New York: Harcourt, Brace and World, 1963.

Heilbroner, R. L. *An Inquiry into the Human Prospect.* New York: W. W. Norton, 1974.

James, W. *Pragmatism.* New York: Meridian Books, 1963.

Katz, M. B. *Class, Bureaucracy and Schools.* New York: Praeger, 1971.

Kerr, C., and others. *Industrialism and Industrial Man.* New York: Oxford University Press, 1964.

Marcuse, H. *One Dimensional Man.* Boston: Beacon Press, 1964.

Polanyi, M. "On the Nature of Science." In William R. Coulson and Carl R. Rogers (Eds.), *Man and the Science of Man.* Columbus, Ohio: Charles E. Merrill, 1968.

Presthus, R. *The Organizational Society.* New York: Knopf, 1962.

Roszak, T. *The Making of a Counter Culture.* Garden City, N.Y.: Anchor Books, 1969.

Servan-Schreiber, J. J. *The American Challenge.* New York: Atheneum, 1968.

Tindemans, L. "Regionalised Belgium: Transition from the Nation-State to the Multinational State." *Chronicles,* published by the Ministry of Foreign Affairs, 1972, No. 151-152 (August-September).

Toffler, A. *Future Shock.* New York: Bantam, 1970.

U.S. Bureau of the Census. *Historical Statistics of the United States; Colonial Times to 1957.* Washington, D.C.: Government Printing Office, 1960.

chapter eight

alternative educational strategies: the integration of learning systems in the community

thomas j. la belle

In recent years educators have increased their recognition and respect for the importance of out-of-school experience in shaping the
behavior of youth. We have learned, for example, of the ways that
early childhood experience in the family can be used to predict
later cognitive and affective behavior, of the impact of social and
cultural background on school achievement, and of the importance
of the peer group in channeling interests and activities. We have also
seen a growing concern for cooperation and collaboration between
the local community and the school. Local parent advisory boards,
teacher aids drawn from the community, and an increased concern
for career education involving apprenticeship and on-the-job training in a local commercial or industrial workplace are now prevalent.
While schools retain a captive audience of young people on a day-
to-day basis, educators must increasingly compete with television,
opportunities for travel, and the influence of the wider community

for the attention of youth. Although many alternative educational programs are designed to take advantage of these out-of-school influences as educators come to understand how they can act either to sustain or inhibit the goals of the school, such programs often do so without a guiding analytic and applied framework.

This chapter addresses the integration of in-school and out-of-school educational processes in collaboration with community structures and seeks to provide a method for analyzing and planning alternative educational strategies. It begins by assessing some of the relationships among formal, nonformal, and informal education and expressing the need for greater collaboration between the school and its referent community. Turning to an analytic and applied framework, I draw upon a sociocultural model of learning and outline some of the environmental inducements that motivate and reinforce behavior. Using these more abstract discussions as a base, I then suggest a multiple intervention approach for educational programs in order to increase the probabilities that individual, institutional, and societal goals can be achieved.

formal, nonformal, and informal education

For my purposes, reference to educational or learning activities encompasses three separate yet overlapping concepts: formal, nonformal, and informal learning. Formal education is represented by the school system with its hierarchy of grades or levels from preschool to graduate and professional school. Nonformal education concerns systematic and organized learning activities that take place outside the formal school and are directed toward specific goals and a specific population. It might include apprentice and on-the-job training, educational television, music and artistic instruction, and religious and youth group programs (such as Bible classes, YMCA, scouting, and sports). Informal education is usually unorganized and unsystematic. It includes the "lifelong process by which every person acquires and accumulates knowledge, skills, attitudes, and insights from daily experiences and exposure to the environment— at home, at work, at play; from the example and attitudes of family and friends; from travel, reading newspapers and books; or by listening to the radio or viewing films or television" (Coombs and Ahmed, 1974, p. 8).

It is assumed that these patterns differentially affect individuals in accord with, among other things, the importance placed on each within distinct cultural settings and the extent to which they are integrated or mutually supportive for the achievement of stated goals. Anthropologists have demonstrated that the integration of learning modes is a greater problem in urban industrial societies than in societies with simpler technologies. One of the major reasons is that teaching and learning in more traditional societies often are carried out at the place or site where new knowledge and skills are to be applied rather than in schools removed from everyday life. In traditional contexts there is considerable reliance on demonstration and practice. Young people often spend the major part of their period of maturation at the side of adults or siblings who guide their behavior by offering appropriate instruction, demonstration, and practice in the learning of new information and behavior. The emergence of modern technological societies, integrated politically and economically at the national level, accompanied by schools, alters considerably this rather practical and applied orientation. The nation often supplants community identity in order to pass on the wider cultural heritage, and the school becomes a major institution for the transmission of national and often international perspectives and goals (Cohen, 1971). The local community's social organization, ideology, and technology undergo considerable transformation as the population begins to identify and to relate to wider behavior patterns. The emphasis on learning may shift to teaching, the practical and applied may be supplanted by the theoretical and abstract, what is taught becomes more important than who does the teaching, and the site of the process is shifted from the family and workplace to the school and similar institutional settings (see, for example, Mead, 1943). Thus, in the nonschool, or more "traditional" societal context, learning focuses directly upon specific behaviors; in the school, or more "modern" societal context, the behavioral application of largely abstract learning is often left to each child on an individual basis.

There appears to be a new, worldwide, recognition of the importance of the relationship between education and concrete approaches to practical problem solving at the local community level. In many of the so-called underdeveloped nations of Latin America, Asia, and Africa, for example, attention recently has been focused on the role of nonformal education as a supplement to or substitute for formal schools. It is argued that nonformal education is potentially less expensive, may provide for greater equality of access to education, may be a catalyst for innovation in the formal school system, tends to emphasize skills rather than certificates, and is more flexible, less bureaucratic, and can meet specific needs of populations in particular contexts (Brembeck, 1973). Although these benefits have yet to be convincingly demonstrated, there is great hope that nonformal education will aid in providing some relief to countries where the demand for education generally exceeds the number of schools available. While educators in the United States are not confronted by an inability to meet the demand for formal education, there is a need for greater integration and coordination of the various institutional and noninstitutional forms of education to achieve many of the same objectives of cost-effectiveness, innovation, flexibility, achievement of members of ethnic minorities, and so on. In order to achieve such objectives, however, we must be prepared to look beyond the school as society's only mode of transmitting knowledge and introducing new behaviors. In other words, personnel associated with educational alternatives may see a need to create a greater interface between their educational program and the people and institutions to which it responds and refers. One might assume that when goals of the educational program, whether they be concerned with basic skills, citizenship, or most other topics, clearly transcend the immediate locus of the program, there would be a need to view education as more than that which transpires in institutions generally isolated from the everyday life of the population served.

education and the community

Should the educational institution become more involved with the everyday life of the child outside the institution? There are many who feel that forging a stronger link between the educational program and the family and community is inevitable if the goals set for education are ever to be met. It can be argued that charging the educational institution with the resolution of social problems or the achievement of individual goals is folly unless a coordinated effort by mutually supporting agencies and processes can be made manifest. The need perhaps is for a more integrated community-based program of innovation and change to which various forms of education can contribute rather than the placement of responsibility for such changes on the educational program alone. It is not uncommon to hear these and other such arguments from school personnel when such problems as desegregation, drug abuse, the reduction of violence, and sex education are discussed. The argument is likewise compelling in terms of relating the educational program to the background of children from differing ethnic and social groups. In order to learn the skills demanded by the wider society, the individual must build on the skills learned in his own community. There is growing evidence that what such youngsters know is not only functional for their environment but influences to a considerable extent the ways in which they approach formal, school-oriented learning. As Scribner and Cole assert, "school represents a specialized set of educational experiences which are discontinuous from those encountered in everyday life . . . it requires and promotes ways of learning and thinking which often run counter to those nurtured in practical daily activities" (1973, p. 553).

Thus, in both the areas of the resolution of social problems and of individual educational success, it can be argued that greater recognition of the supporting role of other agencies, especially family and community structures, is a prerequisite to achieving the goals of the individual, the educational institution, and the society.

The other side of the issue might provide equally compelling arguments for narrowing rather than extending the role of an educational institution. It might be posited that an educational program is designed primarily to transmit the cultural heritage or to act as society's selecting mechanism permitting only individuals who have backgrounds and skills in common with the academic tradition to succeed. Thus, one might argue that the school need not concern itself with a child's background, his family, or his goals and need not become enmeshed in social problem solving because there exist other institutions better equipped to assist in these areas.

The relationship between a school and its referent community can be conceived in accord with the amount of "social distance" that is maintained between the various institutions or structures. The nature and extent of this distance depend on the importance attributed to mutual collaboration for the achievement of the school's and the community's goals. For example, Litwak and Meyer (1974) discuss three points on a school-community social distance continuum. The "closed door" position represents those educators who view community involvement as extraneous and who

believe that the school can handle all the major problems of education. The effect here is to maximize the social distance between the
school and the community. The "open door" position is, of course,
the opposite of that taken above. Educators who hold this view
suggest that many important educational activities take place in the
family and the community, and these processes influence and interact with the methods and goals of the school. Adherence to this
point of view would thus produce a close relationship between the
community and the school. The third, or midpoint, on the continuum of social distance is described by Litwak and Meyer as one that
fosters both the "closed" and "open" positions, depending on the
circumstances and objectives present. This final approach enables the
school to collaborate with the community while retaining sufficient
distance so as not to impair the functioning of either set of structures.

The need for some collaboration between the school and the
community is based, therefore, on the view that both professional
and nonprofessional expertise is needed in order to maximize the
learning process. While the school embodies the technical expertise
in terms of subject matter, facilities, and methods, the community
offers other facilities, knowledge, and resources that can sustain or
inhibit the school's program and objectives. The analytic separation
of schools from the community on the basis of the expertise manifested by the respective personnel is only appropriate, however, if
one recognizes that this principle is dependent on the objectives
being sought. In terms of training, for example, the community's
cultural, commercial, political, and industrial resources and expertise may match or exceed those offered by the schools. Further,
the contribution of siblings, parents, and peers as important role
models in the everyday life of the child is likely to overshadow that
of teachers in terms of personality development and general socialization of the child for adult roles.

Educational institutions must link their efforts with those of
other institutions in the community when such collaboration is
necessary to achieve the multiple goals of individuals, institutions,
and society. In other words, often the isolated classroom and school
are insufficient and ineffective mechanisms for solving complex
problems and achieving complex goals; other modes of education in
collaboration with community structures may be required. Furthermore, transmitting information and designing educational experiences should be viewed as only partial inputs into the processes of

innovation and change. The problem is, therefore, to conceptualize such change processes in the context of the community in order to identify and guide the role of education as one crucial, yet partial, contributor to that process.

It is recognized that the learning of basic skills like reading and writing, or basic values like citizenship and the respect for the rights of others, or the nurturing of a positive self-concept can be fostered in the school. The assumption is that when such learning is also fostered outside of school in the everyday environment of the child the probabilities that the learning will be manifested as a characteristic part of the child's behavior are substantially increased. As suggested above, learning to become an adult citizen in most cultures depends solely upon the educational experiences that occur in the everyday activities of the family and the community. With the advent of more advanced technology and the consequent political and economic organization characteristic of the nation or the state, the school emerges as the major surrogate institution for the teaching and learning that occurred at a prior period in the family and the community. Institutions such as the family are then asked to assume supporting roles as the cultural heritage to be transmitted to the new generation through the school transcends particular community settings. In such a context, education becomes synonymous with school. Jobs and status are conferred on those who have achieved more schooling, and what is valued becomes the more universal and abstract knowledge that can be demonstrated inside classrooms. The transition between family-centered education and school centered education is never complete, however, as the school, representing the larger society, and the family, representing basic survival in the community environment, vie for attention from and influence on the child. This struggle between school and family is intentional at times as basic dissatisfactions with the relevance, efficiency, or equality of the surrogate institution are voiced. There exist at other times basic misunderstandings between the two institutions as to what each demands for successful adjustment to its structure, process, and goals. Whatever the points of dissatisfaction or misunderstanding, it is clear that the relatively poor record of schools with children who do not share a basic academic tradition, coupled with the demands on the school for a more active role in social problem solving, suggests the need for a greater interface between educational programs and the variety of subgroups in our society.

This does not mean that schools must be abandoned in favor of some unknown out-of-school programs. Instead, the achievement of many educational objectives depends on coordinated and collaborative approaches that serve the needs of a particular population in terms of particular objectives and goals. The school should play a central, but not exclusive, role in such programs. The current concern with career education may provide an example. It is assumed that youth today are seeking opportunities for access to positions of responsibility in the cultural, political, and economic institutions of our society. It is further assumed that youth are rather isolated from such opportunities because of age-grading, which results in considerable alienation and frustration. The traditional solution to such a problem is the training of youngsters in schools in order that they emerge with marketable vocational or technical skills. Alternative strategies include apprenticeship and on-the-job training or work-study programs that involve the cooperation of business and industry and often come closer to providing an individual with job skills.

Another example of an educational objective that transcends the boundaries of the school is the teaching and learning of basic reading and mathematics skills. Although many innovative and worthwhile strategies have been employed in this area, apparently most rely upon the input of the schoolteacher alone. One might question whether greater coordination among peers, siblings, parents, and teachers might not increase somewhat the probabilities of children achieving what appear to be important family and community goals. Finally, we can use the example of a drug education program. Traditional education methods in schools might include a concerted attempt in natural science and health education courses to point out the dangers of drug usage. Alternative strategies might rely on the use of peers, community centers, drug substitutes, medical doctors, and so on in a coordinated effort to reduce the intake of drugs. In each of the examples above, to which I shall return later in the chapter, it is clear that the school, along with nonformal educational programs and community and family structures, may function potentially for the enhancement of achieving stated objectives. It is assumed that in order to achieve the behavioral changes stated or implied in these examples, however, such coordinated efforts would need to foster strategies based upon common understandings of how learning occurs.

theoretical aspects of a sociocultural model of learning

The argument for a structured education-society interface can be supported by propositions of basic learning theory. At this point I shall turn my attention to some assumptions underlying a sociocultural model of learning that provides such support. The first assumption is that individuals behave in certain ways because they have learned particular actions in a particular environment. Through their interaction with other individuals in that environment, behavior that is reinforced is repeated over time while that which is not reinforced is less likely to be sustained. Thus, underlying the establishment and maintenance of behavior are the consequences of an individual's activities. These consequences or contingencies are found primarily in the actions of other individuals and may be reinforcing or aversive in nature. The contingencies, at a primary level, may be physiological, such as food, and thus universal in nature; they may be secondary contingencies or stimuli that emanate primarily from a social or cultural base and therefore learned; or they may be generalized contingencies, such as money or prestige, that are exchanged for a wide variety of other more specific primary or secondary reinforcers. Kunkel (1970, p. 29) summarizes these interactions as follows: "Most contingent stimuli are basically the actions of men—simple acts such as smiles, complex sets such as 'deference,' or intermediaries leading to primary reinforcers such as the serving of food or the payment of wages that can be exchanged for basic necessities."

Although the debate goes on as to whether continuous reinforcement or intermittent reinforcement over time is more effective in the maintenance of behavior, the ultimate impact of either of these types of reinforcers is assumed to depend on the needs and wants of individuals. As indicated above, such needs and wants are both physiological and learned; the extent to which individuals value them is assumed to be positively related to the potential impact of reinforcers. Because reinforcers are multiple and complex, maximizing contingencies for one individual is likely to be distinct in degree if not in kind for another individual. In other words, the needs and wants of individuals will vary, and only certain stimuli in a person's context may affect his day-to-day activities. Thus, a change in ideology, technology, or social organization will not necessarily lead to a change in behavior. Likewise, learning may

occur without an individual actually experiencing the consequences of his action. In accord with his own knowledge of the
consequences of behavior, he may learn new behavior by observing other people and the subsequent consequences of their behavior. As Kunkel (1970, p. 56) suggests, "an individual acts in terms
of his perceptions of the norms and values which operate in the
social environments, including the reference groups, that are relevant to him."

It is important to note that when one's social and cultural
context forms a stable and continuous system, the maintenance of
behavior patterns is rather easily sustained. When the context is
lacking in stability and is inconsistent, however, uniform behavior
patterns are difficult to maintain. In addition to the application of
consistent and continuous reinforcement to perceived needs and
wants, there is a need to provide opportunities for learning to
occur. For example, in the learning of a foreign language or of technical skills, an opportunity is often provided for exposure to models
and for occasions to perform the new behaviors successfully. The
need for such opportunities brings us back to the issue of fostering
an interface between structured education and society.

As was suggested earlier, there often exists an almost built-in
inconsistency between ideal national values as embodied in the curricula of schools and the actual norms and variations derived from
the personal experiences of individuals at the local level. In accord
with the assumptions underlying the sociocultural learning model
presented here, the existence of such inconsistencies is not likely to
aid the intended process of behavioral change. If educational institutions were to begin by questioning the utility of educational
experiences for the individual in his successful manipulation of the
environment, granting different criteria for success, there would
occur a more efficacious integration of education with the daily life
of the individual. It is clear that the passing on of information and
skills is not sufficient; potential benefits must be effectively demonstrated to students and parents rather than to educational personnel. The reduction of inconsistencies assumes considerable knowledge on the part of teachers with regard to the sociocultural system
with which the learner identifies. This knowledge must include an
analysis of the social determinants of behavior as well as the resultant *characteristics of individuals* as they interact in a teaching-learning context. Before turning to a discussion of these two sets of
variables, however, I shall briefly summarize my orientation.

I have suggested that in attempting to create a greater interface between various educational programs and the community, it is

necessary to consider the inducements that motivate and reinforce behavior. Such inducements, it is assumed, are related differentially to the basic activities that constitute daily life for an individual and are to be found in his environment. In order to create greater continuity and consistency for the individual between his life inside and outside educational programs, the family, the community, and the program itself must, as much as possible, adopt similar reinforcers. I have also said that the learner must have opportunities over time, inside and outside the educational program, to apply or manifest the new behavior he is acquiring. Finally, I have suggested that one must look to the social determinants of behavior in order to create an appropriate interface between education and the family and community. I shall now turn to the proposition that the inducements for motivating and reinforcing behavior are related differentially to the basic activities that constitute daily life for the individual and are to be found in his environment. I shall begin by looking at one way in which that environment can be analyzed and then turn to a discussion of the characteristics of learners.

social determinants of behavior

Honigmann suggests that any given social situation is affected by three overlapping cultural components: ideology, technology, and social organization (Honigmann, 1959).* Honigmann does not, nor do I, see such a tripartite model as including all concepts or activities that one would necessarily include in the analysis of culture. Most such concepts left out of the model involve process variables and include, for example, communication, ritual, and the life cycle; they all fall outside the model while at the same time cut across all three of the major components. My configuration of the three cultural components is presented in Figure 3.† Behavior, at the center of the model, is a result of the interacting impact of the three components of technology, social organization, and ideology. These three components or branches are assumed to be interdependent as any one may be viewed as the independent variable in order to note how it affects the others.

*Other social scientists have used similar configurations to express this structural-functional view of culture. Thomas Rhys Williams, for example, includes language as a fourth component of the culture model. See his *Introduction to Socialization, Human Culture Transmitted*. St. Louis, Mo.: C. V. Mosby Co., 1972.

†I am indebted to my colleague, Johannes Wilbert, for the basic skeleton of the model.

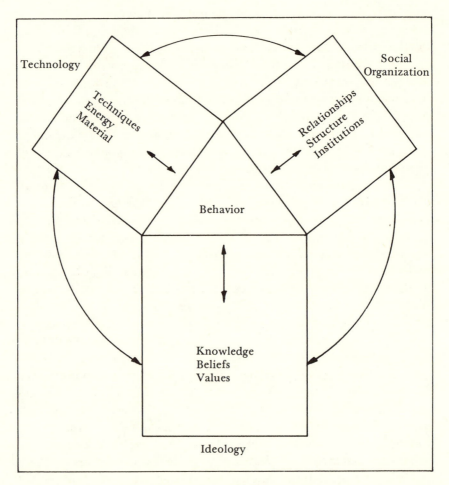

Figure 3. Heuristic Model of Culture

Ideology refers to the beliefs, knowledge, and values by which man lives; technology refers to both activities and the material objects by which man manipulates his material world; and social organization refers to the activities and structures used by man to interact with other men. Thus, through these three perspectives, it is assumed that one is able to analyze more effectively a sociocultural system in process.

It is worthwhile to comment briefly on each of these components. Honigmann views ideology as including "socially standardized beliefs about the universe and man's place in it; conceptions about the sources of illness and other sorts of danger; attitudes of belonging, allegiance, and identification; sentiments about persons, objects, places, and times; . . . values concerning what to do and what not to do; . . . [and] . . . the material embodiments of ideas, like printed books and pictures" (p. 590). As is apparent, Honigmann views this category as having heavy cognitive and affective connotations. One might argue that ideology is the area in which schools make a major contribution to a sociocultural system. They, along with other institutions like the family and the church, pass on the cultural heritage in terms of knowledge, beliefs, and values.

Technology, the second cultural component, is described by Honigmann as the techniques of a community. Thus, "technology covers any act by which man handles, gathers from, or modifies his geographical environment as well as the practices by which he modifies his own or another human body . . ." (p. 290). Whereas the component of ideology encompasses the motives for action in a social situation, technology is the manifestation of the available energy sources that condition other factors in a way of life. For our purposes, technology is also a point where schools make a contribution. Here, however, the concentration is on the techniques taught to individuals enabling them to manipulate the material world. I am thinking, for example, of cultivation, animal husbandry, and hunting and fishing techniques in simple societies and of technical-vocational skills or techniques related to manufacturing, commerce, and industry in more complex societies.

Honigmann defines social organization, the third component of culture, as including "everything that transpires in a web of established relationships [i.e., in the social structure]" (p. 342). While Honigmann includes kin groups, instrumental groups, and associations as major examples, I prefer to view this component as the ways in which individuals organize their relationships and interactions with others, placing emphasis on the structural and institutional aspects of culture. Thus, I include, for example, kinship, economic, legal, religious, political, and educational institutions as well as vertical and horizontal relationships embodied in a social structure. Although the school as an organized unit is found here, traditionally the contribution of the school to the ways in which man organizes his interactions institutionally and structurally is assumed to be limited to the reinforcement of norms emanating from other components and subsystems.

It is assumed that the cultural components and the subsystems of each component as presented here will not be equally emphasized by all sociocultural systems. Because the components are in a state of disequilibrium with each mutually supportive of the other two and thus interdependent, the emphasis placed on any one of the components or subsystems in any given sociocultural system may vary from one such system to the next. Although the use of one component over another as a predictor of potential change in a given sociocultural system may vary, one can assume that because of the interdependence of the system, an alteration in any one component will result in some adaptation to be reflected in the other two.

The heuristic model presented here offers both an analytic and applied framework. The analytic use is primarily that of assessing the interdependence of the components of sociocultural systems and describing the impact of any one component on the total system or on the other components. In the applied framework the model provides a perspective on planning interventions for behavioral change in a particular sociocultural context. It is assumed that there are three major points in the model where interventions can be fostered; these are the three components of the system: ideology, technology, and social organization. The primary input of schools is traditionally through the ideological component in terms of the transmission of information. If, however, as the model suggests, the behavior of a population results from the interaction of the three components, this single intervention is often not sufficient to produce desired changes. If this is true, additional attention must be given to both technology and social organization through alternative educational strategies. For example, it is one thing to provide reading skills (technology) to a child with the hope that he will utilize those skills to acquire new knowledge, but is something else to expect that his family or community is structured (social organization) in a way to permit him to read and that the values of his family and peer group (ideology) will reinforce such reading behavior. Instead of assuming that providing new skills or knowledge will ensure that the learner will employ new behaviors to achieve desired ends, it should be assumed that interventions must be made simultaneously in the other components of the sociocultural system in order to increase the probability that the learner will be able to take action in and on his environment in new ways.

Before turning to a further analysis of the applicability of the model to the problem of creating a more efficacious interface between educational programs and behavior change, I shall summarize briefly the preceding argument. I began by suggesting that increasing the integration of learning modes in association with community structures would enhance the probabilities of achieving the educational goals of school and community. It was then argued that learning theory provides certain basic propositions to support our contention that alternative educational programs must demonstrate consistent, stable, and continuous reinforcement for learners if new behaviors are to be sustained. Such reinforcers were declared to be differentially related to the basic activities that constitute daily life for an individual and are to be found in his environment. I suggested that the effects of the reinforcers on behavior would be directly related to the perceived needs and wants of the learner. My attention was then directed to the analysis of the environment where ideology, technology, and social organization as cultural components were discussed, and I suggested that all social situations are influenced by these three components. I indicated that the alteration of a single component might produce changes in other components, resulting in a modification of the social situation. It was argued, however, that the probabilities of altering behavior depend to a considerable extent on the constraining elements found in each cultural component. Increasing the likelihood of behavior change would, therefore, be closely related to making simultaneous and reinforcing interventions in each of the cultural components.

learner characteristics

The social determinants of behavior found in one's environment not only give rise to the stimuli important for shaping behavior; they also give rise to the behavior itself. Three aspects of the resultant behavior have been discussed thus far: the individual's knowledge, values, and predispositions; the individual's skills with which he manipulates his environment; and the individual's way of coping with other individuals and of organizing for the achievement of objectives. In addition to the model of cultural components from which the three learner characteristics are derived, there exist two additional characteristics—language and conceptual style—which have been shown to interact strongly with the learning process.

These two characteristics are omitted from the model because they are not directly linked to the major cultural components impinging on behavior; they are, instead, linked to the communication process, that is, to how the culture is perceived and transmitted. Thus, although they are learner characteristics shaped by the environment, conceptual style and language together form a constant factor that cuts across all three components of the culture model. Like values and knowledge, skills, and the organization and structure of interpersonal relations, they emerge as learner characteristics determined by the sociocultural system. Language involves standards for the use of words in everyday speech. A vocabulary becomes a cultural storehouse of what is believed important in a particular environment; it also reflects the ways in which material objects and social concepts are described and communicated. Because the individual may vary his language usage in accord with the principles derived from particular contexts, he often uses distinct vocabularies when in church, in school, with peers, or when giving a speech. Thus, for the individual, language reflects a unique perception of the world and a set of standards for speech behavior. Conceptual style, the other characteristic added to the model, concerns learning style or the methods by which a person comes to know something. Rather than what is known, conceptual style concerns the nature of the organization of sense data; it is the way in which an individual interprets reality and makes it meaningful.

Because the learning theory adopted here demands consistency in the reinforcers used for shaping and maintaining new behavior, my concern has been with the ways in which formal or nonformal educational programs relate to the learner's sociocultural environment (ideology, technology, and social organization) as well as with the learner's characteristics that emerge from the environment (knowledge and values; skills; the organization and structure of interpersonal relations; language; and conceptual style). The need is to create educational programs that build upon and extend the individual's environment while providing compatibility with the characteristics he brings with him to the educational setting. Thus, at the environmental, or the sociocultural, level we must design and plan appropriate educational interventions while at the same time identifying where and how other institutions and agencies can make appropriate inputs. At the individual, or the level of learner characteristics, we must be concerned with the compatibility between current behavior and desired behavior. The applicability of such an approach to actual educational programs should become clear as examples of its use are discussed.

multiple interventions for introducing and sustaining new behavior

Through alternative educational programs, multiple intervention approaches for children often require a minimal coordination between the community and the "school" and may involve other institutions or groups like the church, family, or peer group. For example, educational institutions are likely to emphasize subject matter areas such as mathematics, history, biology, English grammar, and so on. In some cases, such knowledge is transmitted for its own intrinsic value without there being any intent of applying or utilizing it. In other cases, the expectation is that the child will utilize the new knowledge to act on his environment in new ways. Because the child's reinforcement for learning the material is derived in part from the wider environment and because the ultimate application of such knowledge will be his everyday life outside educational institutions, planning for the reinforcement of behavior in his environment will likely increase the probability that the educational objective will be met. Does the individual have access to appropriate materials and supplies (technology) in order to practice and apply what he has acquired? Are his parents and siblings apprised of the objectives of the education program, and are they supportive (ideology)? Do opportunities exist in the individual's environment where he can apply what has been learned (social organization)? Positive answers to these and other similar questions indicate that there are inducements, both material and sociocultural, in the environment, and these may be utilized to reinforce appropriate behavior. Thus, the child's environment inside and outside the confines of the educational program potentially becomes a stable one where reinforcement is applied consistently and systematically by individuals important to him.

The same types of questions could be posed with regard to the role of the educational program as social problem solver. Drug education programs are an example. If the individual's environment reinforces the use of drugs, the education program's intervention in terms of transmitting information may have relatively little impact. This may be a case where the out-of-school environment swamps or wipes out the impact of the educational program. The individual may associate with a peer group (social organization) that places a high value (ideology) on drugs (technology). In order to be a member in good standing, to share a peer identity, the individual utilizes drugs and the associated paraphernalia. The education program only offers information as to why one should not use drugs; it does not offer status substitutes (social organization), it cannot alter the individual's need for identity or the values underlying the peer group (ideology), and it cannot provide material substitutes for the drugs themselves (technology). Indeed, coordinated efforts by several agencies making appropriate interventions into the cultural components would appear necessary if drug education programs or similar social problems are to be resolved.

Programs of career education offer an additional example. They are designed to foster knowledge and skills that enable the learner to complete a course of study and be prepared to assume a wage-earning or entrepreneurial status. Schools have traditionally provided such skills (technology) and knowledge (ideology) through industrial arts, vocational-technical, agricultural, and business education programs. In some cases, through nonformal alternative educational strategies, schools have begun to provide on-the-job or apprenticeship training in order to extend classroom learning to include demonstration and practice in the workplace. Few programs, however, have attempted to deal with the opportunity structure in order to foster employment for graduates. Thus, they have ignored the social organization component of culture, and the program's effectiveness is diminished.

If an objective of such career education programs is to provide opportunities for individuals actually to begin new careers in the areas for which they have received training, interventions in the ideological and technological components of culture must be accompanied by interventions in the cultural component of social organization. One strategy that may work satisfactorily in this regard involves planning career education programs at the workplace rather than in educational institutions. Even this approach, however, often meets with formidable obstacles, including child labor restrictions, labor union membership, declining labor demands in the economy, and so on. These obstacles do not detract, however, from the basic objective of the program—to provide skills and knowledge enabling an individual to secure a job. Where representa-

tives from industry and commerce feel they will benefit from cooperation in training programs and from subsequently hiring the graduates of such programs, the relationship between education and
work is likely to be productive. When institutional or individual
incentives from the education side are not matched with those
adopted by the workplace, however, the educational program falls
short of maximizing its efforts.

In all these examples, the need is clear for a multiple intervention strategy in order to increase the probability of achieving
individual, institutional, and societal goals. This linkage of education and the sociocultural environment points to the need in alternative education programs to go beyond the diffusion of knowl-
edge-skills-attitudes model typical of formal schools. Without
reinforcing behavior in the social, cultural, and physical environment by enabling the utilization of newly acquired behaviors, the
impact of education is often swamped or overpowered by other factors. Although the necessity for borrowing practices from the traditional schooling model should not be underestimated, such activities must be accompanied by other institutions and agencies in
order to provide the opportunity for new behavior to transfer and
become a characteristic part of the individual's life-style. Such an
approach demands that program planners be knowledgeable about
and concerned with the relationships among behaviors in a sociocultural system. The interdependence of human behavior is such
that simply providing information or skills in the "schooling" fashion may not be sufficient to alter and sustain new behaviors when it
is expected that those behaviors will be used to change traditional
practices in the wider environment.

In addition to intervening selectively in the learner's sociocultural environment, educators must assess the consistency between the experiences inherent in the education program and the
characteristics learners bring to the program. When the background
of the educators responsible for the curriculum is congruent with
the learner's sociocultural environment, this consistency is often
high. When either the educator or the learner represent different
sociocultural systems, however, consistency is often low, and the
potential for conflict and misunderstanding is high. Likewise, when
the learner must apply what is acquired through the education program in a different and distinct environment, the potential for conflict and inconsistency once again is high.

The conflict or misunderstanding in these situations can often be traced to the five learner characteristics mentioned earlier: the individual's knowledge, values, and predispositions; the individual's skills with which he manipulates his environment; the individual's way of coping with other individuals and of organizing for the achievement of objectives; language and the process of communication; and conceptual style or the organization of sense data. In each case, the educator must assess the congruence or consistency between the curriculum offered in the program and the characteristics brought to the program by the learner. For example, one might begin by assessing the individual's need to acquire new behaviors. One cannot assume that the learner will see a need to acquire new behavior simply because the educator, or some other individual, believes that the learner should do so. Since it is assumed that the impact of reinforcers will be directly related to the predispositions of need, the probabilities that the individual will want to engage in the acquisition of new behaviors are reduced considerably if they are not present. Knowledge and skills are likewise important variables because they reflect the individual's needs and wants and because they represent the experience and background the individual brings with him to the program. Another variable of potential concern is the way in which the individual is accustomed to relating to other individuals in his environment. If learning has been carried out through primary group processes or in dyadic relationships, the educator is wise to build upon such traditions. In the family, for example, older siblings may have considerable responsibility for socialization and child care, while parents remain somewhat removed. At the same time this variable may be important in determining who in the family and community has achieved or is ascribed decision-making authority and who can assist in supporting the objectives of the education program.

Language and conceptual style also are important characteristics in terms of learning. Because all dialects and linguistic codes are assumed to be functionally equivalent in relation to particular environments, it is appropriate for educators to become apprised of the standards and symbols inherent in their use. Educational programs must build upon the appropriate verbal and nonverbal modes of communication common to the learner in his environment. If second languages are to be introduced, considerable attention must be given to the consistent application of reinforcers between the education program and the wider environment. The final characteristic, conceptual style, has only recently received attention as a major learner variable. Cross-cultural studies conducted in several areas of the world have demonstrated that the ways in which individuals perceive and interpret reality may be a major catalyst or inhibitor to learning. Such investigations suggest that particular learner modes may be variably related to school achievement and in turn be derived from socialization practices in the family and community (Cohen, 1969). There is also some evidence to suggest that ethnic groups may be characterized by certain patterns of mental ability that remain constant across socioeconomic status levels (Lesser and others, 1965).

where to begin

I suggested in Chapter 2 that three broad categories of demands will be placed on educational institutions: relevance, efficiency, and equality. They were assumed to be associated with the three respective components of culture; thus, relevance was related to ideology, efficiency to technology, and equality to social organization. If one can assume that such relationships exist among these phenomena and, further, that one must adopt a multiple intervention approach to increase the probabilities that behavior change will occur, it is insufficient to build education programs around only relevance, efficiency, or equality. In effect, alternative educational strategies must make inputs into each of these demand categories because they are the educational channels, or ports of entry, into the components of the sociocultural environment. Among the criteria for making such interventions are the learner characteristics that emanate from, or cut across, the components of the model. Without addressing the learner's skills and predispositions that are brought to the educational process, the educational program is cut off from the environment and thus from the place where the characteristics emerge and are reinforced.

Where does one begin such strategies? The answer to this question depends on each population and environment. The first step is, therefore, to meet the learner in his or her environment. While there, one must assess community resources and gain insight into the individual and community life-style. By looking for the contingencies that reinforce behavior and by beginning to analyze their potential for achieving the learner's objectives, one finds that the locus of the educational programs will likely turn from classroom to community structures and community structures to the family. Although the process will need considerable organizational collaboration in order to ensure stability and consistency in the application of reinforcers, it is essential to begin where the learner spends his or her time. By joining forces with the needs and skills of the learner as well as the individuals and material with which he or she is surrounded, one can begin to differentiate between what the educators and others want for the learner and what the learner needs and wants for himself. Generalizations should emerge from these various perspectives and desires, and these are likely points for program initiation. Building on these common thrusts by working back and forth between the learner's needs and the learner's environment, one must be able to enlist the support of others and continue to intervene in the cultural components. During this process it is also necessary to ask continuously the following types of questions: Do the predispositions and values of others in the environment support the learner's needs (ideology)? Is the physical environment conducive to the objectives sought (technology)? Are the family and peer groups structured to offer assistance (social organization)? If the answers to these and many similar questions are affirmative, the educator may be achieving desired goals. If the answers are negative, it is likely that the interventions are inappropriate for the learner, the objectives, or the environment. One must remember, above all, that educational and community personnel are only attempting to increase the probabilities that selected behaviors are adopted and applied. We must be open, therefore, to the use of formal, nonformal, and informal educational modes in collaboration with community structures in order to increase such probabilities.

references

Averch, H. A., and others. *How Effective Is Schooling? A Critical Review and Synthesis of Research Findings.* Santa Monica, Calif.: RAND Corporation, 1972.

Brembeck, C., and Thompson, T. J. *New Strategies for Educational Development.* Lexington, Mass.: Lexington Books, 1973.

Cohen, R. "Conceptual Styles, Culture Conflict, and Nonverbal Tests of Intelligence." *American Anthropologist*, 1969, *71*, 828-856.

Cohen, Y. "The Shaping of Men's Minds: Adaptations to the Imperatives of Culture." In L. Wax and others (Eds.), *Anthropological Perspectives in Education.* New York: Basic Books, 1971.

Coombs, P., and Ahmed, M. *Attacking Rural Poverty, How Nonformal Education Can Help.* Baltimore, Md.: Johns Hopkins University Press, 1974.

Honigmann, J. J. *The World of Man.* New York: Harper, 1959.

Kunkel, J. *Society and Economic Growth.* New York: Oxford University Press, 1970.

Lesser, G. S., and others. *Mental Abilities of Children from Different Social-Class and Cultural Groups.* Monograph of the Society for Research in Child Development, Serial No. 102, 1965, *30*, No. 4. Chicago: the Society.

Litwak, E., and Meyer, H. J. *School, Family, and Neighborhood.* New York: Columbia University Press, 1974.

Mead, M. "Our Educational Emphases in Primitive Perspective." *American Journal of Sociology*, 1943, *48*, 633-639.

Scribner, S., and Cole, M. "Cognitive Consequences of Formal and Informal Education." *Science*, 1973, *182*, 553-559.

Williams, T. R. *Introduction to Socialization, Human Culture Transmitted.* St. Louis, Mo.: C. V. Mosby Co., 1972.

the relation between processes and values: an alternative function for evaluation

carl weinberg and rodney skager

Educational evaluation, as we know it today, is an offshoot of our social and political life. It exists primarily to meet a political need, the need to justify what we do in schools in order to receive additional funding for programs or to maintain present funding. It is only a slight exaggeration to suggest that, should external funding for evaluation be cut off this morning, most evaluators would be out of work before lunch. At the same time no similar activity would emerge to fulfill a similar function. This state of affairs suggests that the prime function of educational evaluation is to provide the consumer with evidence he can use to support a claim of some kind, either for funds or for the validation of an enterprise.

Those who support educational programs, state and federal

governments, require certain kinds of "output" or "product" data in order to be persuaded that their efforts are worthwhile. Many of the programs supported by government funding were initiated to improve the educational performance of nonwhite minorities. The key word in this expectation is "performance," and, when one talks about performance, one is led to only one kind of evaluation: "output" or "product" evaluation, which was discussed earlier (Chapter 5) by Skager. In deciding the kind of data that will satisfy the supporters of educational programs we also decide the emphasis of the programs themselves. Evaluation in this way biases the activities of schooling. When we inform educators about what counts in schooling, we influence what is done.

To cushion the impact traditional evaluation practice can have upon alternative forms of schooling, as well as to offer an alternative conceptualization of the kind of function that evaluation can fulfill, one must adopt an approach to educational evaluation that is explicitly value oriented. Views of evaluation, like evaluation itself, involve values. The intention here is to identify possible incongruencies between latent or real and stated or overt values about schooling and to assess the degree to which goals derived from the former are being achieved by the educational practices observed. This approach could be applied to conventional as well as alternative educational forms. It arises with the latter, however, because educational pluralism derives from a recognition that alternative value systems exist and that those value systems lead to alternative practices and alternative conceptions of what is desirable in schooling.

All conceptions of evaluation should be grounded in the relationship of learning products and processes to values or goals within educational contexts. Viewed in this light, evaluation can serve to help educators see what they are doing, what their assumptions about how schools should function actually are, and how these assumptions affect processes and, ultimately, products. In a broader context the function of evaluation can be seen as the clarification of theory and the further description of practice in order to assess the link between the two.

Evaluation should open rather than close the range of choices that educators have for making decisions about their tasks. If the evaluation process can be seen as being an assessment of congruence between processes and values, then evaluation practice ceases to maintain the supremacy of the status quo. If all we do is assess out-comes, then no one sees beyond the outcomes, particularly those that are traditionally assessed. The creation of alternative modes of schooling has made educators aware that things might be other than they are. The creation of an alternative model of evaluation capable of addressing alternative models of learning may help assure the continued viability of this learning.

the role of crises in revealing values

Some "new" sociological ideas are based on the assumption that a crisis calls forth energies that attempt to return an organiza-tional system to its normal state (Garfinkle, 1967). A useful tactic for learning about the value orientations of persons acting in an institutional context involves disrupting the operation of that con-text in order to observe the activities and attitudes that go into assessing the nature of the problem and "correcting" it. The notion is that any response to a crisis should reveal a real, rather than a token, mode of operation.

The distinction between "real" and "token" is important, for many school patterns are established to create a favorable image. At critical points, especially when the schooling process undergoes some sort of stress, from either inside or outside, real values usually emerge. A student council responds to strong student pressure in passing a more flexible dress code. If school administrators abrogate that decision, it appears that the values threatened were considered important enough to risk conflict and crisis. It becomes apparent that developing responsibility in students through participation in policy setting is secondary to maintaining control over certain areas of personal choice. A priority among values has been identified.

Ethical and practical considerations keep evaluators from creating problems for schools in order to observe how they are re-solved. The discussion that follows suggests that direct, neutral observation is seen as an ideal approach to the gathering of much evaluative information, although less direct and intensive methods, such as interviews, document analysis, and the like, are available.

Most schools are beset by large or small crises on a daily basis, and alternative schools are no exception. Often alternative schools fail because the process of normalizing is too difficult or because the modes of behavior practiced by school personnel in order to normalize appear contradictory to the value base on which the school was founded. In this instance, another crisis emerges on top of the first one: the staff becomes segmented, a serious split occurs, and students become lost in the shuffle.

focusing on educational structures that reflect values

Katz, in his insightful analysis of the historical roots of contemporary education, has demonstrated that entrenched bureaucratic structures have dominated education for more than a hundred years, unavoidably bearing the seeds of racism, sexism, and class distinction (Katz, 1971). If we seek evaluation strategies that do not serve this entrenched bureaucracy, then we must determine where educational structures fall on a continuum of value-based adaptations to the task of processing children. We suspect the typology proposed in Figure 4 will pinpoint critical issues behind much of the controversy that produced alternative evaluation strategies.

At the simplest level, organizational activities or functions in schooling can be located within structures that carry a value base. These structures correspond to the functional categories—organization, adaptation, allocation, socialization, and integration—suggested earlier by Weinberg (see Chapter 3). These comprise five important functions of schooling and, in themselves, represent no value disposition. We are suggesting, however, that the particular mode of achieving each of these functions can vary, depending upon the value base of each. And each variation should reveal the particular value system on which the adaptation is made.

The following sections expand this classification system for descriptive evaluation, discuss the possible points of comparison between one model of schooling and another, and provide some examples of what the focus on the proposed structures can reveal in an actual evaluation. The categories of our functional typology of educational structures are summarized in Figure 4.

Organization. The organization that characterizes a school or other kind of educational context refers to the way personnel are arranged in relation to each other. These arrangements constitute modes of handling functional problems such as decision making and the division of responsibility for taking care of the business of education. The range of adaptations to this functional requirement are

Functional Category	Structural Forms	
	Conventional	Alternative
Organization	Bureaucratic Authoritarian Hierarchical	Communal Democratic Egalitarian
Adaptation	Industrial Model Time-Space Limited Efficiency Centered Product Centered Teacher Centered	Community Resource Model Open Space Interest Centered Process Centered Student Centered
Allocation	Private Evaluation Universalism Unidimensionalism Certification Based	Community Evaluation Particularism Multidimensionalism Certification Free
Socialization	Extrinsic-Other-Directed Ethic (Morals and Skills) Homogenization Protestant Ethic	Intrinsic-Autonomy-Directed Ethic (Morals and Skills) Individualization Freedom and Responsibility
Integration	Extrinsic Satisfactions Institutionalized Goals Institutionalized Means	Intrinsic Satisfactions Personalized Goals Personalized Means

Figure 4. A Functional Typology of Educational Structures

presumed to cover a range of value dispositions about how educational tasks are best undertaken. The organizational structure we are proposing ranges from a conventional bureaucratic mode to an egalitarian communal mode. Other modes are theoretically possible, such as monarchical or dictatorial, or even what we might call "juvenocracy," where children make all the decisions, but these can be excluded until experience indicates that additional forms are required in our classification system.

Any form of schooling that has an organizational base falls somewhere between bureaucratic and communal in terms of organizational structure, based on several characteristics. Different schools can also be contrasted with respect to their relative positions on the scale. Part of the methodological task, aside from managing the problem of crisis response, is to generate indicators that would represent each of the particular stages given in the hypothetical model. This should only be attempted with the assistance of the school community in order to derive what is meant when members of the community speak about "democracy" or "responsibility" or "control." That is, schools may differ with respect to the particular activities used to implement a specific organizational style.

One important indicator along this dimension is that of *authority* or *control,* either within the school community or the classroom community. In dealing with mechanisms of control we would need to describe the kind and number of impersonal rules that are present in an organization, as well as the kinds of sanctions that are applied when rules are not followed. It is certain that, as schools are observed, a wide range of activities—both implicit and explicit, those that could happen as well as those that do—will be revealed. In this way we should be able to evolve a comprehensive evaluative framework for identifying the form of organization that is valued in a particular school context and assessing how well that form meets its own goals and standards.

The kinds of crises that would emerge logically in this category are those linked to the system management problems of either bureaucracies or communities. Values linked to the former appear as patterns of bureaucratic specialization. Crises occur when patterns of job specialization result in breakdowns in communication. Anyone who has ever tried to accomplish some task that requires dealing with a complex network of specialists has felt the strain and frustration of such a process. The alternative, however, personalizing the process, could easily result in a less efficient division of labor. As occurs in so many crises in this area, the choice is usually between making people happy and keeping the organizational machine running smoothly. In some instances the crisis stems from problems of communication between members of the same organization. Sensitivity training has evolved from this kind of organizational dilemma, in an attempt to have one's cake and eat it too— happy people functioning efficiently. In the case of communal organization, members of egalitarian-oriented groups have struggled and are struggling with problems involving differentiated authority and decision making. Anyone who has ever tried to apply a purely democratic principle to a decision-making problem is familiar with the numerous crises that emerge.

Adaptation. This particular structure takes in all of those activities and strategies that are employed in the educational context to accomplish whatever institutional goals dominate the consciousness of those involved in directing the process. If excellence is desired but not at the price (either of time or money) that districts or communities wish to pay, then the availability of resources will reflect this attitude. Quality education can only be called a goal to the extent that it has priority in a system. It is here that the value base of most educational processes associated with the adaptive function can be tested.

The two most popular adaptive modes of educational structures are the industrial or factory model, where resources are organized to obtain maximum output with minimum input, and the community resource model, where resources are organized for maximum availability to students. Skager, in Chapter 5, pointed to the relationship between contemporary conceptualizations of evaluation and the factory model of schooling. The activities that most prominently demonstrate the adaptive focus are associated with structures that aid the instructional process. Are students grouped homogeneously in terms of interests and ability for maximum efficiency or grouped heterogeneously in order to utilize the diversity within the student pool? Are classes based upon considerations of size (student-teacher ratio) or of activities? How is instruction located in time and place (school-limited, time-limited)?

Educational or instructional models, referred to in Chapter 5, are conceptual tools that help to define which adaptive activities relate most closely to the school's attempt to achieve a given goal. The Carroll model was useful in evaluating an alternative school that placed high priority on individualizing instruction (Carroll, 1963; Skager and others, 1973). Joyce's learning environments help isolate differentiated learning activities that can be described within a value framework (Joyce, 1973).

Other factors that distinguish modes of accomplishing the adaptive function are those reflecting an emphasis either on a product or a process. This is seen, for example, in the kinds of examinations that are given and the use to which the results of those examinations (grading, promotion, feedback, practice, and so forth) are put. The most distinguishing feature of the process-product dichotomy (if one talks about it as a dichotomy) is the dynamic of the teacher-pupil relationship. The product emphasis focuses upon an outcome of that relationship that must always be designated as an observable indication of progress. The process emphasis sees the relationship itself as a fundamental characteristic of the learning experience, independent of what specific learning outcomes emerge.

Another important question is, "Are all students learning the same subject matter at the same time?" Such an adaptation would allow us to presume that neither the school nor the classroom particularly subscribes to the notion that students learn best when they are allowed to work in their own way, at their own rate of speed, at times that are most comfortable. We are not making an argument for a best way, even though the alternative to the product, time-space-centered process, sounds more idealistic. We are suggesting, rather, critical ways of distinguishing and describing educational contexts within the category of *Adaptation*.

What kinds of crises might occur to help us describe the values underlying an adaptive structure? Two types are most likely to emerge: the first usually affects conventional contexts; the second, alternative contexts. Both are associated with the same consideration, efficiency. One is a crisis of not meeting achievement goals held by parents or administrators; the other is a crisis of trying to meet goals with either an insufficient budget or inadequate staff. What happens in conventional settings when there is parental pressure to individualize instruction? What happens in the alternative school when small teacher-student ratios cannot be maintained because of the inability to pay more teachers? Does the learning community deal with the problem by seeking solutions in the form of volunteer help, or assistance from parents, or does it acquiesce and allow class size to increase? What happens in a conventional public school when a teacher chooses new ways of grading, perhaps new ways of organizing a classroom? What kind of feedback does this teacher get? And what occurs in an alternative school when teachers require homework or dominate the classroom in teacher-centered ways? These are merely examples of a few of the events from which variations in adaptive structure can be derived.

Allocation. Another important function of schooling is that of allocation or the routing of learners through the system. The structures that have emerged to accomplish this take on particular forms and reflect a value disposition. We are concerned, in general, with those circumstances or conditions that underlie the process of turning out, as a result of schooling, a certain kind of person whose opportunities are prescribed by the nature of the paths into which a student is directed. Working backward to this function, we understand that society seems to require a number of different kinds of people to occupy different kinds of functional (and sometimes status) positions within the society. As an agent of society, schooling has assumed this responsibility, particularly in the last hundred or so years. The processes have not always been similar. The kind of elitist education, sometimes referred to as classical humanism, that characterized the earlier part of the nineteenth century did not see mobility as the intent of schooling. Some would argue that the long-range effects have not changed significantly to the present, even though the sorting processes differ in terms of the types of curricula and the highly differentiated occupational base of higher education.

How, then, do current allocation practices form the basis for providing us with our variables for evaluation? They differ basically according to the kind of internal evaluation, in the sense of assigning responsibility, that occurs in the school. Such evaluation may focus either upon the individual or the community. We can assess individual learners and assign them private evaluations which, in turn, determine their private mobility patterns, or we can make community evaluations where we focus upon the success of the educational enterprise in attaining its goals. Private evaluation implies that mobility to status positions or paths is based upon individual performance in a competitive system. Individual or private performance appears as private rewards, most of which are associated with the allocative process. Community evaluation pluralizes responsibility and is used as feedback for improving the instructional process for the total community.

Two value-laden dimensions characterize the process of allocation based on formal evaluations. One dimension concerns the extent to which different students are judged by the same kinds of standards, regardless of personal characteristics. That is, standards are applied either "universalistically" or "particularistically." The other is the variability that exists within the standards themselves. That is, do they exhibit "unidimensionalism" or "multidimensionalism"? This notion suggests that students can be evaluated in different areas of interest and their mobility can be based upon performance in these different areas. Currently, cognitive achievement constitutes the one dimension that is really important in conventional allocation patterns. The end product of this process is some form of certification of completion. The nature of that certification strongly influences the adaptation that students make to the process itself. Hollingshead's early work, *Elmtown's Youth,* describes a process where students opted for curricula having a higher status in terms of certification for college attendance, even when they had neither interest nor aspiration in that direction (Hollingshead, 1949).

Crises that emerge in the process of accomplishing the allocation function are usually those that center upon grading or other activities related to student evaluation. A familiar example is the claim raised frequently by minority students that college admissions tests are biased. Whenever a student claims an injustice based upon differences in personal experiences or interests, the teacher, the counselor, and others must react in a way that denies or admits the allegation. In several free schools students who were not graded began to complain that they did not know where they stood. When a student does not receive certification that he knows more than someone else, parents begin to worry that their child is not developing the competitive edge. These crises all relate to allocation.

One other allocation-related crisis can serve as an example of the way schools seem to react in order to normalize the crisis situation. There are many students, particularly today, who are not inclined to attain professional status in our society, even though their ability level is as high as that of students seeking professional careers. Do teachers or counselors discourage students when they choose automobile mechanics rather than engineering? Do they attempt to change the students' choices? We have seen students persist in personally unhappy careers as lawyers, teachers, engineers, or medical doctors simply because the system did not permit a student with high ability to be anything else. When pressure is exerted, and the student changes his mind as a result, the value base of allocative processes is evident in the reactions of members of the system.

Socialization. The process by which persons are socialized to membership in this or any society always involves two components —attitudes and skills. The only basis on which we can differentiate schooling models encompassing different perspectives is the degree to which the school forces students to adopt an ethic that is extrinsic to their subcultural socialization (family or community) and to their own proclivities. Conventional and alternative schools we have observed differ significantly in the process employed to instill values and skills as well as in the sanctions that are applied to maintain them. Conventional schools ordinarily utilize an extrinsic ethic grounded in tradition, while nonconventional schools often appear to focus upon an intrinsic ethic, looking toward the development of autonomous children. Conventional structures appeal to the student's regard for his own welfare; many alternative structures appeal to the student's regard for the community. In the latter case, some alternative schools do not have the wealth of punitive sanctions—grades, homework (as punishment), honors and awards, and actual corporal punishment—that conventional schools employ.

The questions on which we need to focus to derive the value base of different educational contexts are: What kinds of behaviors are punished or rewarded? And, on some scale of social prestige, What social skills and characteristics are emphasized? These and like variables can reveal the specific content of values associated with the socialization process attempted by educational institutions.

The kinds of crises that can and do occur in the process of socializing youth are as many as the areas in which this socialization takes place. Most of the so-called "crises" in conventional schools emerge at points where students reject the homogenizing process (conformity) that is expected and sanctioned. In alternative schools the crisis often emerges when individualism as an ethic spills over into the domain of others, disrupting their freedom. Some guiding questions might be: How often do students feel unjustly criticized, and how often do they react to such injustices? What are the grounds for complaint? What happens when someone who plays by the rules is not rewarded for doing so? Or the reverse, what happens when someone who does not play by the rules (for example, he cheats) is rewarded? To see the system at its revealing best, observe for a short time the dynamics in an early elementary school classroom when students are just learning the rules and how to play the games that confer rewards. Success is in part reflected by the number of complaints that behavior is not being rewarded. Once students arrive at an age where peer-group norms mediate the socialization goals of the institution, other kinds of crises emerge, particularly when the value systems clash. Take, for example, the teenage boy who decides to fight another boy so that his peers will not consider him a coward and who is then expelled from school for failing to report the problem to the vice-principal.

Many of the critical revelations of the values underlying the process by which students are socialized appear in the kinds of sanctions that are applied as well as in the behaviors that called forth the sanctions. We can assess punishment as a strategy, for example, without considering the rule that has been violated and has led to the punishment. As a description of process, what a system values is more realistically deduced by the activities chosen to achieve expressed value positions than by the value positions themselves.

Integration. In order for people to remain attached to an institution, they must either be required to be there, as in the case of a prison, or they must get something from it, or at least think they are getting something from it. Students who are perpetually truant and leave school at the earliest legal opportunity fall into the former category. We can say they have not been integrated into the school. Integration relates closely to the satisfactions of participants. It functions in the educational context to hold members within the system and assigns them differentiated roles. We have dichotomized the satisfaction dimension as *Extrinsic* versus *Intrinsic* satisfaction.

People, in order to be integrated into an institution, must like something about it and be able to find a place in it. Whatever the organizational arrangement of the school, the level of integration is reflected in the degree to which each member accepts his or her own place. In order to feel integrated in most conventional schools, one must accept the idea that the teacher is the appropriate person to make the rule. In many alternative schools, other organizational patterns require comparable compliance. When a school assigns significant, decision-making responsibility to students, the integration level is likely to be low for those who feel decision making is the teacher's responsibility.

Now, our formulation of the notion of satisfaction is contained within the framework of integrative structures. Conventional schools create the criteria by which participants are satisfied. Alternative schools may or may not. If one internalizes the standards of a given institution, he or she will achieve satisfaction to the degree that those standards are attained. The better a person internalizes the standards, the more complete the integration. If standards other than academic achievement prevail, satisfaction depends on attaining those other standards. Some alternatives could be showing curiosity, creativity, responsibility to the community, or utilizing resources.

In one sense we are suggesting that integration of participants is, indeed, an alternative criterion for evaluating in educational contexts. In order to assess the degree of integration, however, we need to define useful indices for integration. We begin with the simple idea that satisfaction with the goals and processes and one's personal involvement reflect integration, whether it be into a school or any other social institution. Then, using the educational context as the unit of analysis and the participants (administrators, teachers, students, parents) as the data source, we can discover the total level of integration, or level of satisfaction, within groups. If we then find out how participants feel about the goals and the activities of the school, we can evolve an evaluative description capable of including efficiency and product models, though it need not. The point here is that any operationalized model of schooling provides a means for assessing the extent to which members of a context perceive their integration into that context.

This is not far, by the way, from the more popular way in which the notion of integration has been used with respect to ethnic minorities and women. Because of the kinds of goals, processes, and ecological arrangements of schools, nonwhite minorities, people at a lower socioeconomic level, and women have been far less integrated into education than white middle-class males. This has been true on a number of grounds that can easily be converted into indices for integration. The following, we suspect, are generally useful questions:

1. *Meaningfulness*—To what extent do participants understand the process of which they are a part? How are activities linked to goals in particular?
2. *Importance*—How important do participants feel the goals and activities of the school to be?
3. *Isolation*—To what extent do others in the environment agree with the participants' perception of the way things are?
4. *Relevance*—To what extent are the goals and processes of the school congruent with the participant's sense of what is personally worthwhile and satisfying?

Using integration as a critical criterion in the evaluation of schools, one can compare different kinds of schools by utilizing the same criterion without violating the integrity of the school by evaluating it on criteria that it does not seek to attain. In this sense, the integration dimension is different from the others: it allows evaluative comparisons between schools having different value bases. There can be feedback to school personnel on the impact of the particular value configuration derived from the level of integration that members have achieved. If it is discovered that integration of members into a system is not an important value, invidious comparisons with schools that do value integration would not be made. It is unlikely, however, that any institution that does not value the integration of its members can survive.

Contrasting schools on the basis of the amount and kind of integration of their members does not require using output data that often ignore the possibility that standardized output is not valued equally by schools being compared. For example, the goals of one school place great stress on formal academic achievement, while those of another school stress the development of curiosity and independent learning.

Output or achievement data would not allow a useful comparison. The relevant evaluative question has to do with analyzing the activities of the school to determine the extent to which each school is operationalizing its *own* real values. In doing so, one can show that schools are really different in several ways, but one cannot say that one school is better than the other except in the sense of suggesting that one is better than the other at achieving its own goals. If both are successful, then approving one over the other is a function of agreeing with the underlying value structure on which the school is built.

It is also apparent that values can be opposed to one another, especially when activities aimed at implementing one value conflict with those that might be used to implement another. Resolution of this type of conflict reveals priorities. In the evaluation of one alternative school by Skager and his associates, repeated observations of certain children made it clear that genuine attempts to operationalize one of the two most important stated goals of the school frustrated the implementation of a second important goal that was initially presumed to be of equal importance (Skager and others, 1973). This interpretation of the empirical findings, in turn, pointed directly at the real, latent priorities of the school and helped greatly to explain why some of the participants had grown so dissatisfied.

One must also recognize the possibility of genuine, but inept, attempts to implement a given goal. That is, the frequency and intensity of actual activities suggest that the value base of an overt goal can be genuine, but the activities turn out to be ineffectual. One example of such an attempt can be seen in the failure of persistent efforts to create a communal-democratic organizational structure by involving students in decision making and planning at an alternative high school (Center for New Schools, 1972). When they were discussing this finding, the authors suggested that adolescents are primarily interested in participation and leadership within their own social structure, preferring to leave the tedium of school planning to adults. While this could be true, there may have been alternative means for involving significant numbers of students that were not tried at the school in question. This possibility, apart from helping to identify what is to be observed in evaluation, is the reason why relevant models, conceptions, and ideas about the educational process referred to earlier by Skager (Chapter 5) are useful. They suggest alternatives and provide possibilities against which observed activities can be compared.

using the proposed structures: an example

The evaluation of an alternative school mentioned earlier by Skager (Chapter 5) provides a means for testing the applicability of the five proposed structures (Skager and others, 1973). The evaluation was actually conducted before the above conceptualization was reached, but it served to call attention to the need for an alternative conception of the function of evaluation. The major findings of the study should, therefore, be interpretable within the structures discussed above, and, if this is done, it should help to concretize their meaning. To achieve this, it is necessary to look at both the school and the evaluation findings as a whole, rather than to concentrate on the application of the Carroll model as Skager did in Chapter 5.

The School. The evaluation was conducted during the initial year of operation of the first publicly supported alternative school in Los Angeles.* The school was funded by the board of education in response to a proposal developed by a group that was composed mainly of parents but that included at least one of the teachers who later joined the staff. Students, with the exception of kindergartners, were classified by grade level (K-12) primarily for purposes of record keeping. The school plant itself was located in a private facility not originally designed for the purpose to which it was being put. The student body was mixed ethnically and socioeconomically, although the group developing the proposal can be described as predominantly Anglo, middle class, and of a relatively high educational level.

In terms of teaching and learning activities at the school, students were roughly grouped into kindergarten, elementary (for most students the equivalent of grades 1-5), and secondary. Relationships between students and teachers were deliberately informal. The latter, for example, were referred to as "advisors." Students above the earliest grade levels were to plan their own individual weekly study and activity schedules and to assume responsibility for carrying them out. This might involve using materials at a learning center, asking for help or direction from an aide or advisor-teacher, and, for older children, attending more formal classes on topics selected by the student from various alternatives.

Students were free to move about, to approach adults at almost any time, and to begin or terminate activities at will. They were expected to be at the school site during the regular hours of the school day, although exceptions obviously had to be made for

---

*Now the Area H Alternative School of the Los Angeles Unified School District.

the many field trips incorporated into the curriculum as well as the numerous activities for secondary-level students held in private homes, partly because of serious overcrowding at the regular site. It is indicative of the general approach taken by the school that students were responsible for registering their own attendance. They recorded the time of their arrival or departure by signing a sheet posted in the yard adjoining the school structure.

With respect to the teaching-learning process, a corresponding emphasis was placed on individualization of instruction. Students could work alone, in small groups, with or without an adult, or in a tutoring relationship with a teacher, aide, or volunteer. Insofar as time and resources permitted, the staff attempted to provide alternative approaches for learning the same content. Finally, students at all age levels were often allowed to choose content, and older students were entirely responsible for selecting their own curriculum.

Organization and leadership at the school were democratized and, to a degree, spontaneous. To conform with district policy, there was a nominal principal who also served as principal of a nearby regular school. While obviously interested in, and supportive of, the alternative school, the principal did not attempt to interfere in the sense of making rules or influencing policy. Authority for the latter was formally vested in a coordinating council that incorporated students, parents, and staff. Regular staff meetings were also held on a weekly basis to deal with issues relating to instruction, utilization of staff, and sometimes discipline. An informal town meeting, open to the entire school community, was held as needed, for the general airing of issues. In general, individuals at all levels were expected to recognize and assume responsibility for carrying out school policy. The familiar "chain of command" was avoided.

The Evaluation. The evaluation effort was viewed by all parties, including interested members of the school board, as an effort to pinpoint strengths and weaknesses of the school and to guide planning, both for the school itself and for groups already developing proposals for additional alternative schools in the district. It was clearly understood that refunding for the next two years did not depend upon the findings of the evaluation, and this unusual situation helped to create an atmosphere of openness and cooperation between the school community and the evaluation staff.

The general strategy of the evaluation focused on the use of nonparticipant observation and interviewing. The former involved both formal (see Chapter 5) and informal observations of the instructional process as well as attendance at meetings of school participants. Those interviewed included instructional staff, parents whose children remained in the school at the end of the first year, parents who had withdrawn their children, and older students. Depending on who was being interviewed, questions focused on the goals and expectations of participants vis-à-vis the school, how various types of decisions were made, organization and communication, instructional decision making, and participants' level of satisfaction with various aspects of the first year of operation. Ultimately, the evaluation team was able to derive a perspective on critical areas of school functioning from the point of view of various categories of participants, and this perspective was used, along with observational data, to derive a number of conclusions about the school's effectiveness. How well, then, do the findings reported in the evaluation fit within the five structures of the typology? Very well, it appears, although two exceptions will be discussed later. What is most important is the way in which each of the first four structural forms (organization, allocation, adaptation, and socialization) developed in the school had a clear connection with satisfactions and dissatisfactions expressed by various members of the school community. In this sense the fifth dimension of the typology—integration—does appear to be useful as an alternative criterion for evaluation.

Organization. The brief description of the organizational and administrative structure of the school given above reveals an emphasis on communal governance, democratic decision-making processes, and egalitarian relationships between participants, including students and teacher-advisors. Interviews and observations of school meetings led to two conclusions that are pertinent here. First, in several important instances necessary policy decisions were either not made by the governing body of the school or, if made, were not communicated and carried out by individuals who presumably should have perceived their own responsibility. Second, an informal decision-making group coalesced in the resulting vacuum. Composed of three certificated staff members and two aides, this group obviously met an organizational need. And it eventually was able to exercise power far in excess of its numbers and to shape the school accordingly. Not only did this group make many of the day-to-day decisions affecting the functioning of the school, but it was often able to dominate decisions made by the policy group that represented all the participants of the school.

In terms of the model presented here, failures to make, communicate, or carry out decisions about school policy by the formal organizational structure of the school resulted in a series of crises. The development of an informal, partly covert, power structure (the members of which, it is significant, referred to themselves euphemistically as "the five-star generals") represented a spontaneous response to these crises. It is also evident, however, that the existence and mode of operation of this power group were at least to some degree inconsistent with the overt image of communal-democratic organizational style adopted by the school.

Integration (Organizational). About one-third of the parents interviewed who had withdrawn their children before the end of the school year cited dissatisfaction with the decision-making and administrative process as a major factor. These concerns, however, related primarily to efficiency and effectiveness. The most common reasons for dissatisfaction, both among parents who planned to remain and those who had withdrawn, related to the teaching-learning process of the school and its effect on their children. Many parents (and children) did not like what the school had become, and they either felt powerless to effect any changes through the formal organization or they did not choose to do so. In the integrative sense these individuals were indeed isolated in that they did not agree with the perceptions of other, more satisfied, participants, including the majority of the staff of the school, especially the informal decision-making group that ultimately exercised so much influence.

Adaptation. The way in which the school set about carrying out its function as an environment in which children were to learn fits the Community Resource Model very closely. Most instruction went on in an "open space" environment. Materials at learning centers were designed to elicit student interest and to provide alternatives within the same content area. The entire school community appeared to be deeply concerned with the learning process. Many participants, including teacher-advisors, saw traditional schools as caught in a race for "results" that disregarded the importance of the teaching-learning process itself.

Systematic observations of the instructional process plus information derived from interviews provided mutually consistent images of adaptive structures at the school. Repeated observations of elementary-level students classified by teachers as being either very high in perseverance or very low in perseverance with regard to studying and learning revealed that the latter spent the overwhelming proportion of their time in informal play or passively inactive. On the other hand, most students classified as high in perseverance spent a substantial amount of their time engaged in some sort of formal learning activity. They also received considerably more attention from the instructional staff because they were more willing to approach adults to ask for help or direction and to demonstrate what they had accomplished. These observations helped greatly to verify statements made by parents and staff, especially evaluative statements about the instructional process itself.

The instructional staff tended, in general, to wait until individual children expressed interest in learning something before providing help. This is not to say that they made no attempt to find ways to motivate children who were low in perseverance. Learning materials were provided, and suggestions were offered; force or more subtle means of coercion were seldom, if ever, used. The final decision of whether or not to study was left up to the child. In discussing this policy, the instructional staff generally expressed confidence that virtually all the students would ultimately decide on their own to participate in learning activities.

This approach was consistent with the school's overall policy of encouraging the development of traits of independence and self-direction by assigning responsibility for learning to the students themselves. This emphasis on autonomy, of course, reflected the kind of socialization ethic the school hoped that the learners would choose. Many students appeared to accept that responsibility and to utilize much of their time in productive learning activities. Many others did not.

Integration (Adaptive). Probably no other single characteristic of the school led to stronger, more prevalent feelings of dissatisfaction among some participants than the strategy of leaving the decision as to when and what to learn up to the learner. For a significant subgroup of students this meant that the adaptive function of the school was not carried out. Many parents concluded that their children were not learning. Representative comments from parents whose children withdrew from the school illustrate the nature of the dissatisfaction. They said:

"It's up to the child to plug in."

"The school felt if he was not ready to learn they would leave him alone."

"Nobody cared . . . she would feel ignored."

"He was not willing to put himself forward and attract the advisor's attention."

These and other statements from interviews clearly reflect concerns about isolation and irrelevance on the part of some parents and their children vis-à-vis the adaptive structure of the school.

Other parents saw the school in a different light, depending primarily on how their own children appeared to react. Even among parents who reported that their children would remain in the school, however, similar concerns were often expressed, although not as frequently or as intensely.

This kind of dissatisfaction amounted to a crisis, or a series of crises, for the school. Among parents of children withdrawn at the end of the first year or earlier were a number of the most active of the original founders. Some of these individuals expressed considerable resentment toward members of the staff and parents who had shaped the school into a form that their children could not accept. Others felt that the school was fine for some children, but not for theirs.

The reaction of the school staff, as well as that of the parents who agreed with them, was consistent and firm. Several staff members suggested that the school could not be everything for everyone and that the first year had involved some sorting of participants. The strength of commitment by the staff to the development of independence and autonomy in children through the assignment of responsibility obviously reflected strong underlying values.

Allocation. It is not surprising that the allocative structure of the school tended toward modes of evaluation that were multidimensional and particularistic. That is, students gained approval and were seen by staff as doing well to the degree that they manifested interest and involvement in something of their own choosing.

Such a stance with respect to the evaluation of what students are doing was inevitable given the school's emphasis on autonomy and individual responsibility.

It is perhaps significant that the allocative structure of the school did not emerge as a central aspect of the study in the sense that the adaptive structure did. In many respects the form of the school could be seen as a reaction to negative aspects of traditional schools. Evaluation of students was, accordingly, deliberately deemphasized and usually informal, even subtle. Grades had to be recorded in conformity to district policy, but grades were not important at the school or with most parents. Approval was conferred upon individual students whenever possible, and disapproval was avoided when possible, except when aggressive or acting-out behavior on the part of some students disrupted the activities of others. No member of the evaluation team recorded instances of overt disapproval for failure to undertake or complete schoolwork, although this may have occurred in some cases.

Allocation (Integration). Possibly because of the deemphasis on formalized mechanisms for evaluating students and the fact that virtually all the participants acceded to such deemphasis, the allocation structure did not appear to be associated with events that might be described as critical. Some teachers did express concern about not being able to keep track of the progress of each learner assigned to them as advisees, as well as dissatisfaction with the way in which children were (or were not) recording their own progress. Some parents, especially among those who had withdrawn their children from the school, expressed dissatisfaction about not getting feedback on the progress of their children. Overall, however, issues relating to allocation were not critical factors in the integration of participants at various levels.

Socialization. Socialization has to do with making choices. We are, in effect, asking about the kinds of choices the school appeared to be trying to get students to make. The results of successful or unsuccessful socialization are inevitably reflected in the way in which the students responded to the organizational, adaptive, and allocative structures of the school. In this sense what we can conclude about socialization has in part been anticipated. At the organizational level there were signs that adults at the school wanted students to be responsibly involved, not just passively participate. Student members were included on the coordinating council, for example.

We have already noted the school's emphasis on individual choice as far as the time, place, and nature of all types of formal learning activities were concerned. Actual statements by teachers make this dramatically clear:

> "The idea here is that the children choose what they are interested in learning. . . ."

> "The learning center should function by itself, with just somebody there to offer assistance to the kids who need it. . . ."

> "If they want to do something they have to initiate it themselves."

These statements, confirmed in the systematic observations conducted by the evaluation team, clearly imply that the school wanted the students to choose to learn autonomously and independently. It can even be said that this value was so fundamental to the staff of the school that it became acceptable for students, who were not ready or willing to make that kind of choice, to avoid most or all learning activities. While it was assumed that eventually all students would choose to learn independently, the immediate priorities were obvious.

Finally, the deemphasis on grades or other formal means of evaluation such as tracking, noted in the discussion of allocation, reveals an emphasis on the development of intrinsic, instead of extrinsic, systems of reward.

Socialization (Integration). A random sample of half of the secondary-level students was asked about involvement in decision-making processes at the school. Only a handful indicated any interest. Of the few who had been involved earlier in the year, most had withdrawn. For whatever reason—student indifference, adult resistance, the fact that the meetings were long and probably boring for the adolescent—students were not making the choice that the school ostensibly desired. It is unfortunate that the information collected in the evaluation did not focus sufficiently on this issue to determine whether the latent values of many adults actually lead them to behave in such a way as to discourage participation by students.

With respect to adaptation, it has already been reported that some students chose to learn independently and others did not. The willingness of the instructional staff to wait until the latter were "ready to learn" was a major source of dissatisfaction among many parents and students. Students who were not involved in learning were often noisy and sometimes disruptive. Although the staff exerted control when such problems became severe, there was considerable tolerance up to that point. Many members of the staff, parents, and students expressed dissatisfaction with this situation, although some attributed the problem primarily to inadequate space.

The information collected in the evaluation was, unfortunately, not very helpful in determining the extent to which individual learners had developed internalized, intrinsic systems of reward. Certainly many of the younger students were informally observed to be very eager to gain the personal approval of certain teachers or aides. In no case did parents, teachers, or students express a desire for greater emphasis on grades, contests, or other impersonal external systems of reward.

Exceptions. As indicated earlier, two findings do not fit within the proposed structures. First, the school site was overcrowded and otherwise unsuited for many school activities. While this situation created a variety of problems that at times approached crisis level, its lack of relevance to the model proposed here removes it as an area of concern.

The interesting exception lies in the fact that nothing has been said about scores on achievement tests, the central focus of most evaluation reports. Students in the school did take the regular battery of tests administered in late spring under the testing program mandated by the state. It was found that the average student at most grade levels made normal progress from prior baselines. For example, second-grade students, most of whom had been tested the previous year in regular schools of the district, made slightly more than one year of progress on grade equivalent scores. Overall, the picture was one of normal growth in reading and mathematics achievement.

The testing results, apparently of primary concern to most administrators and members of the board, were of little or no significance within the school or, for that matter, in the evaluation itself, although the results were duly reported. This is not to suggest that parents, teacher-advisors, and many students were not concerned about traditional academic achievement. A number of parents, for example, indicated that their children had been withdrawn because they were not making sufficient progress academically. In a number of instances it was the children themselves who first expressed concern in this regard. Other parents were confident that their children were progressing academically. In the face of direct evidence available to the participants, scores on standardized tests, arriving in any case after the school year was over, contributed little or nothing to impressions already formed.

This is not to say that the proposed evaluation model in any way excludes achievement test data. In the present case such data were simply not relevant to the integration of the participants as far as the adaptive function of the school was concerned. If the *only* evidence available to participants vis-à-vis academic achievement of students had been test scores, the situation might have been different. The direct evidence available to parents, teacher-advisors, and students determined their function in the school long before test scores were available. In this sense one could argue that traditional evaluation measures, such as standardized achievement tests, are most meaningful for those farthest removed from the situation being evaluated.

conclusion

The proposed model does appear to provide a means for structuring the evaluation of an educational community. It is meant to help the evaluator see the community as being composed of groups of participants whose satisfaction may vary depending on how the various functions of the enterprise itself are carried out. It sees the community itself, like any other social organization, as striving to integrate its participants in the sense of convincing them that the processes in which they engage are meaningful, important, understood in the same way by other participants, and relevant to themselves. The level of satisfaction expressed by participants with respect to each organizational function reflects the degree to which those participants perceive themselves as integrated.

The model is pluralistic, as it must be if it is to address alternatives. It in no way suggests that integration into one framework is better than integration into another, although its use might reveal that the integration of certain types of participants is less likely in one situation than in another.

The model, while it accepts satisfaction of participants as a universal criterion, does not lead to the subjectivization of evaluation in the sense that it is simply a kind of popularity poll. Virtually all types of data now collected in typical evaluations are potentially relevant, as long as they either reflect directly the integration of members or help to explain why members are, or are not, integrated into the institution. Attitude tests (if valid in a given situation) have the potential for reflecting integration. Achievement measures, insofar as they measure something that is important to participants, are also relevant. But direct measures—systematic observation, interviews, and the like—are more important. Statements by participants about satisfaction cannot ordinarily be taken at face value without obtaining evidence to confirm or refute such statements. In this way the model seems to open the door for the collection of types of data that often have been ignored as evaluators rushed to make superficial comparisons between fragmentary output characteristics of learners.

references

Carroll, J. B. "A Model of School Learning." *Teachers College Record*, 1963, *64*, 723-733.

Center for New Schools. "Strengthening Alternative High Schools." *Harvard Educational Review*, 1972, *42*, 313-350.

Garfinkle, H. *Studies in Ethnomethodology*. Englewood Cliffs, N.J.: Prentice-Hall, 1967.

Hollingshead, A. B. *Elmtown's Youth*. New York: John Wiley, 1949.

Joyce, B. "Humanistic Education: Monoism vs. Pluralism." In C. Weinberg (Ed.), *Humanistic Foundations of Education*. Englewood Cliffs, N.J.: Prentice-Hall, 1973.

Katz, M. *Class, Bureaucracy, and Schools*. New York: Praeger, 1971.

McClelland, D. C. "Testing for Competence Rather than for Intelligence." *American Psychologist*, 1973, *28*, 1-12.

Skager, R., and others. "Evaluation of the Los Angeles Alternative School: A Report to the Board of Education of the Los Angeles Unified School District." Los Angeles: Center for the Study of Evaluation, U.C.L.A., 1973.

Skager, R., and Russock, R. "Four Alternative Schools: 1973-1974." Research and Evaluation Branch, Los Angeles Unified School District, Report No. 339, April 1974.

satisfaction: an alternative criterion for school success

gary d. fenstermacher

This chapter argues that schools are successful insofar as they provide for the attainment of satisfaction by pupils, teachers, and parents. Satisfaction is here conceived as a criterion for the successful
pursuit of any educational activity undertaken in schools. Pupils,
teachers, and parents are considered to be the primary participants
in the process of schooling, and as such they should achieve satisfaction in their attempts to fulfill the aims of schooling. The argument
for these views is based primarily on the organizational nature of
formal schooling: because the school is an organization, it functions
optimally when it provides its primary participants opportunities to
experience satisfaction as they discharge their responsibilities and
commitments to schooling.

   No mention is made of the kinds of satisfactions that people
ought to derive from schooling. Rather the argument rests on the
view that an individual's search for what is satisfying to him is part
of the meaning of "becoming an educated person." Because, in our

society, formal schooling comprises so much of the educational process, the school should provide participants with opportunities to learn what is satisfying to them. Schooling is an educative experience to the extent that it promotes inquiry into what are and should become satisfying experiences for human beings to seek, explore, and attain. To specify here the kinds of experiences that ought to be satisfying to participants would terminate the participant's own inquiry and would turn education into a form of indoctrination.

But saying that the search for satisfaction is educational and explaining how it is possible for this search to occur in schools are two very different things. A school is not always able to do what is morally right or pedagogically sound just because it would be the morally right or pedagogically sound thing to do. Schools are something more than the good people who occupy positions there. They are organizations, and as such they frequently function differently from the ways right-thinking people may want them to behave.

schools as people and as organizations

Much of the literature on formal education in the Western world falls into one or the other of two categories: that which discusses schools as an aggregate of different populations of people, and that which discusses schools as organizations or institutions. Generally speaking, the writing of educational psychologists, instructional theorists and technologists, curriculum specialists, and textbook writers tends to focus on the people in schools. The people, again generally speaking, are the pupils, the teachers, and the administrators.

Sociologists, anthropologists, revisionist historians, and management theorists, on the other hand, tend to focus less upon the people in schools and more upon the phenomenon of schooling. They talk about such things as groups, subcultures, authority patterns, latent and manifest functions, and institutional change. This bifurcation between people and organizations is, of course, artificial. It is very difficult to make explicit reference to one without making implicit reference to the other. Yet it is cause for some amazement to note how frequently the implicit reference, be it people or the organization, is ignored by educational thinkers. One need not search long to discover, say, an educational psychologist making a recommendation for the behavior of teachers that takes no account of the organizational realities of the school. And it is not difficult to locate an organizational theorist who recommends an administrative structure without knowing what the effects will be upon the learning of children in the school.

People and Organizations Act. Because we are the people, most of us have some difficulty comprehending the phenomenon of organization. We can see the trees, but not the forest; the classrooms, but not the university. But the organization is there. Etzioni (1964, p. 1) states the case succinctly:

> Our society is an organizational society. We are born in organizations, educated in organizations, and most of us spend much of our lives working for organizations. We spend much of our leisure time paying, playing, and praying in organizations. Most of us will die in an organization, and when the time comes for burial, the largest organization of all—the State—must grant official permission.

Schools, like business, government, and hospitals, are organizations (Dreeben, 1973; Bidwell, 1965; Goslin, 1965). As an organization, the school is something in addition to a simple collective of persons performing the roles of student, teacher, counselor, principal, and so forth. Hall (1972, p. 12) asks "whether or not organizations have an existence of their own, above and beyond the behavior and performance of individuals within them. The question becomes, 'Do organizations act?' " He answers in the affirmative. To perceive schools as organizations is to see something that is not visible when one simply studies the individuals in them. It is not so much that the whole is greater than the sum of its parts, but that the sum can act differently from its parts and, in so doing, can affect the actions of its parts.

The People-Organization Interaction. If the people and the organization are different phenomena, and if both act in ways that influence one another, then what can be done to control this interaction so that both function to optimize the goals of the system? It is difficult to grasp the meaning of the question, much less answer it. The enormity and influence of organizations have come upon us so quickly, and we have been pressed so tightly by academic and pedagogical concerns, that the question hardly makes sense. Yet the question must be reckoned with. Many of the accusations hurled at mid-twentieth-century schooling center around the people-organization interaction: Why are the schools rigidly bureaucratic? Why can schools not share decision-making power with the community? Why are the schools denying minorities equality of opportunity? Why is the administration of schools not in the hands of local teachers and principals?

It is unfortunate that educators appear to be making little progress in answering these questions. The failure, I believe, is partly accounted for by our unwillingness to attend to the interaction between people and organizations. We focus attention on either the people in the system, or the organizational character of the system, but not on the relationships between the two. As stated earlier, educators seem to fall into two categories: those who ask people-focused questions (such as, "Are these teachers any good?") and those who ask organization-focused questions (such as, "Is this school any good?"). The two interrogators infrequently ask questions of one another.

the conventional criteria for success

People-focused school evaluators seem to concentrate on output variables. Organization-focused school evaluators stress input variables. Some variables studied by people-focused evaluators are:
1. achievement (performance) levels of the pupils
2. number of graduates entering college
3. job placement record of graduates
4. number of scholarship recipients
5. scores earned by students on college entrance examinations.

Evaluators who stress the organizational characteristics of schooling tend to focus on such variables as:
1. per pupil expenditure
2. size and diversity of the physical plant
3. number of volumes in the library
4. credentials of the teaching faculty
5. academic and vocational curricula and programs
6. scope and variety of extracurricular programs
7. salary scales for certificated personnel.

Most school personnel are familiar with these two categories of evaluation variables. When site visitation teams arrive at the school for accreditation, they generally gauge the success of the school on input, organization-focused variables. State legislatures, taxpayers, and parents, on the other hand, seem to take more interest in output, people-focused variables. Those who advocate accountability, behavioral objectives, and assessment of performance are concerned with output. By and large these advocates focus exclusively on pupils; they take an interest in teachers, budgets, books, and equipment only to the extent that these resources affect the performance of pupils.

Input-Output Interaction. One would think that if school evaluation divides so conveniently into two foci that there must be some sort of relationship between them. For a long time, educators assumed a relationship—a causal one. The better the input, the better the output; the quality of output varied proportionately with the quality of input. But recent exhaustive studies deny this causal relationship (Coleman and others, 1966; Averch and others, 1972). Inputs provided by the school seem not to affect output. The factors affecting achievement of pupils are, rather, parental background, family income, and neighborhood, all three of which are intertwined.

Although their accuracy is not yet clearly demonstrated, these research findings seem to be leading many educators to neglect input variables that can be directly controlled by the schools and to focus almost exclusively on output variables. Such a move might be salutary were it not for the fact that, for most of us, considerations of organization and input variables are almost equivalent. A decision to neglect input variables is tantamount to a decision to neglect the organizational characteristics of schools. If indeed this state of affairs is coming into existence, then concern for the people-organization interaction will diminish considerably. This would be an unfortunate consequence, for it is clear that the organizational facets of schooling are there, they are powerful, and they do affect the people who are participants in the school.

In sum, contemporary efforts to evaluate the success of schooling concentrate on either assessing organizational input or pupil output. Those who focus on input believe that people accommodate to and are governed by the structure, functions, and resources of organizations. But empirical research does not support a causal relationship between input and output, at least not in regard to schooling and achievement of pupils. Those who focus on output care little about the organization as an independent phenomenon; they believe it accounts for a minimal variance in achievement of pupils. But again research calls into question the degree of impact that people-focused evaluators believe instructional treatments can have. Furthermore, many persons are increasingly uncomfortable with the mensuration mania of output evaluators. There is an emerging recognition that the drive to measure everything is a drive to maximize quantitative variables while ignoring qualitative phenomena. Some sort of mechanism is needed to forge a substantive relationship between input and output, between people and organization. Several scholars and educators have thought that satisfaction might be the vital link.

linking people and organizations

In the pell-mell rush to measure output, on the assumption that the really vital and causally relevant inputs are beyond the control of the schools, we commit a logical blunder. If, as the research claims, the critical inputs (family, income, neighborhood) are beyond the reach of the schools, then why bother to measure output? What can the schools do about it? If output is foreordained and predetermined by factors that do not directly involve the schools, what reason is there for measuring it in the schools?

Bane and Jencks (1972) are two researchers who have concluded that the critical input variables are external to the school. In contrast to many other researchers, they followed their investigations to a logical conclusion (p. 41, emphasis in original): "[Our] findings have convinced us that the long-term effects of schooling are relatively uniform. The day-to-day internal life of the schools, in contrast, is highly variable. It follows that *the primary basis for evaluating a school should be whether the students and teachers find it a satisfying place to be.*"

Bane and Jencks draw this conclusion on what seems to be the "There are no better alternatives, so why not do it?" position. The input variables that effect desired educational outcomes are beyond the reach of the school; consequently, the school might as well do something else that is worthwhile. Why not provide satisfaction for pupils and teachers?

But suppose satisfaction were the outcome of choice rather than inevitability. Suppose that, rather than saying that the satisfaction of teachers and pupils is about all we can expect to attain in schools, we positively affirm that satisfaction is a desired educational outcome. What kind of a difference would this change of perspective make? One very important difference is that it would reestablish the salience of organization as a major phenomenon of schooling. "The problem of modern organization is thus how to construct human groupings that are as rational as possible, and at the same time produce a minimum of undesirable side effects and a maximum of satisfaction" (Etzioni, 1964, p. 2).

Acknowledging satisfaction as a desired outcome of schooling may be a means to gain control of the people-organization interaction. Satisfaction is a people-focused outcome, but it is an outcome that is almost exclusively controlled by organizational considerations (Flizak, 1968; Hartley, 1966; Hornstein and others, 1968). If satisfaction were adopted as an intended outcome of schooling, it might serve as a critical link between the needs of individuals and the demands of an organizational setting.

This beneficent state of harmony between individual needs and organizational realities is, unfortunately, much easier to describe than to effect. Homans (1974, p. 227) gives the reason in a single sentence: "Remember first that satisfaction is at best a slippery concept." Yet its potential importance for schooling justifies a modest analysis of the term, to which I shall now return.

Satisfaction and Group Functions. Goslin (1965) follows Parsons in drawing a distinction between groups that function expressively and those that function instrumentally. Expressive groups "exist primarily or wholly for the enjoyment of their members and have no goal beyond this" (p. 132). Instrumental groups exist for the accomplishment of some purpose over and above the simple enjoyment of members; these groups make specific role demands on members in order to get a job done. This distinction between expressive and instrumental groups is useful for clarifying the place and purpose of satisfaction in education.

If we assume that schools do or should consist primarily of expressive groups, then satisfaction must be understood differently from what would be the case if we assumed that schools are made up of instrumental groups. In the case of the expressive group, satisfaction of members must be considered a central goal of the group.

This point of view characterizes much of the popular reform and humanistic literature on education. The purpose, or at least a key purpose, of schooling is to promote satisfaction for members of the group.

The popular reform view of satisfaction is quite different from the view of satisfaction offered by Bane and Jencks (quoted above). Whereas the reform view constitutes an intentional and considered adoption of satisfaction as a most worthy aim of schooling, the Bane-Jencks view is (seemingly) one of satisfaction by default. To Bane and Jencks, satisfaction is something that the schools ought to generate for members since they are unable to produce other apparently more appropriate or important outcomes. But to the popular reformers and humanistic educators, satisfaction is an outcome to be regarded equally with or more highly than other outcomes. Bane and Jencks appear to argue that the organized groups comprising the school should be realigned from instrumental to expressive because the instrumental function strives for unattainable ends. The reform position is that the groups ought to be expressive in the first place because the real purposes of schooling require it.

Thus those who have argued for satisfaction as a value in schooling have done so by treating it as a kind of outcome. In so doing, they have not succeeded in bridging the gap between people and organizations; they have merely substituted one output variable for another. Instead of determining school success by measuring the cognitive achievement of pupils, they would have us measure the affective satisfaction that pupils gain from the school experience. The popular reform and the Bane-Jencks views represent a shift in school functions from instrumental to expressive. Because they conceive of satisfaction as an aim (outcome), these agents of change have not yet provided a means for establishing supportive relationships between participants and the school organization. But they have been extremely effective in establishing the centrality of the satisfaction of participants to the nature and purpose of education. What must now be done is to show how satisfaction can provide the basis for linking people and organizations. The link is established by conceiving of satisfaction as a criterion rather than an aim.

an alternative criterion for success

If satisfaction is considered a criterion, it is something one must experience while in pursuit of an aim. If in the course of attempting to achieve some aim the participant does not experience satisfaction, then the aim cannot be considered successfully accomplished. Thus school groups may function instrumentally, that is, in pursuit of objectives other than the satisfaction of members. Note that because a group is in search of an objective other than satisfaction, this effort does not mean that members of the group forgo satisfaction. It is both conceivable and probable that members can experience satisfaction in the pursuit of aims other than satisfaction itself. Indeed, experiencing satisfaction in pursuit of an aim is precisely what is required when it is held that satisfaction is a criterion for the attainment of aims.

Distinguishing Aims from Criteria. Some simple examples should aid in understanding the differences between aims and criteria. When you are running a race, your aim is to win. But how do you know you won? The criterion for winning is to cross the line or break the ribbon first. If your aim is to paint a red house green, the criterion for having done it is that an observer can see only green and not red when he looks at your house.

Suppose the school sets the aim of increasing reading scores in each grade by one and one-half grades for the year. Thus, if a child reads at the 2.1 grade level, you as the teacher are being asked to advance him to 3.5 during the year he is in your grade. In order to determine your success, criteria are established. Usually the criterion for an aim such as this one is the student's passing a standardized test with a composite score of 3.5 or better. If the student meets or exceeds the criterion, you have achieved the aim set by the school.

An aim is a goal, an outcome, a destination, a place you want to get to (Dewey, 1916, 1961, chap. 8; Peters, 1967, pp. 5-8). In order to determine whether an aim has been reached, criteria are needed to assist in the decision. The criterion case for satisfaction requires that the attainment of satisfaction by participants be a criterion for determining whether any aim of schooling has been achieved. The criterion case differs from the popular reform case for satisfaction in that the latter makes satisfaction itself an important and worthy aim of schooling. In the criterion case, satisfaction is not itself an aim, but rather an experience people must have when striving toward the successful achievement of an aim. Thus the criterion case provides for the instrumental functioning of school groups by allowing for the formulation of ends beyond the mere enjoyment of members of the group. The criterion case differs from the Bane-Jencks position because the former positively affirms the propriety of satisfaction as a criterion, while the latter seems to value satisfaction as an aim only because the schools are powerless to affect achievement and equal opportunity outcomes.

This attempt to distinguish between aims and criteria and to set criteria for aims is by no means unique. In *Democracy and Education* (1916, 1961, pp. 104-106), Dewey wrote on "the criteria of good aims." But satisfaction of participants was not one of his criteria. In 1916, the year of initial publication of *Democracy and Education,* organizations were neither consequential nor problematic features of social systems. They are today, and our criteria for aims should account for their imposing salience in the social systems of schools.

defining satisfaction

It is at this point that the final connections among satisfaction, participants, and organizations can be made. For the moment I shall stipulate (and will defend later) that the primary participants in the organization we call a school are teachers, parents, and pupils. In contending that satisfaction is a criterion for the successful attainment of aims, I am holding that the organization must be designed and managed to provide sources of satisfaction for its primary participants. Tables of organization, divisions of labor, authority patterns, administrative decision making, resource allocation, personnel retentions and promotions should all be managed so that the three groups of primary participants can attain satisfaction as they pursue the fulfillment of the aims of the school. If satisfaction is not experienced by the primary participants, the criterion will not have been met, and thus the aim will not have been achieved. Before exploring the implications of this position for each of the groups, it is imperative to clarify the meaning of the term "satisfaction."

Some Semantic Difficulties. The term "satisfaction" has at least two important semantic characteristics: it is vague, and it is ambiguous. Many people are put off by these properties of words, believing that vagueness and ambiguity are shortcomings, deficiencies in our language. It is true that these semantic characteristics frequently cause trouble, but communication would not be possible (to any great extent) were they not features of our language. If every word we used could have but one meaning, and precise application were required in every case, we would need many more thousands of words than are presently found in unabridged dictionaries. Imagine our plight if "bald" could refer only to a person with 600 or fewer strands of hair; if "love" could mean only an emotion experienced when in the presence of a spouse; if "community" referred only to a group of persons who are inhabitants of a geographical area not greater than three square miles.

Much useful discussion is cast aside because the discussants erroneously conclude that nothing worthwhile can come from building arguments that contain vague or ambiguous terms. Thus it is that "satisfaction" is often depreciated as a worthwhile basis for inquiry into human affairs. Fortunately, not everyone shuns slippery words, else "democracy," "justice," "beauty," "mind," and "wisdom" might have disappeared from our lexicons centuries ago. So long as the semantic properties of such terms are recognized and respected, no case is weakened by their inclusion into argument. Ambiguity can be resolved, and vagueness can be confronted directly by the careful stipulation of meaning.

The term "satisfaction" is ambiguous in that it has more than one meaning. Note these different expressions: "Now that you've done it, I hope you're satisfied!" "I really don't get much satisfaction out of it." "It was a genuinely satisfying experience."

In the first sentence, "satisfaction" means something different from what it does in the other two sentences. Its meaning involves some sort of reparation or compensation for injury. Recall the romantic days when the offended noble drew his sword while saying, "I demand satisfaction." The demand is for atonement; it is an order to make amends.

In the second and third sentences, the meaning of "satisfaction" involves gratification, the experience of pleasure. But there are nuances to be distinguished here. The second sentence is a simple report that the person does not get any pleasure out of doing whatever he is doing. The third sentence is more than a report; it is a judgment. It is a claim that the experience was not only a source of pleasure, but was valuable and rewarding to the person. More is involved in this third case than merely getting on the other side of a rare porterhouse steak. There are good feelings about oneself, a pride in accomplishment, an experience that endures beyond the occurrence of the event.

It is this third meaning of "satisfaction" that is germane to the argument of this paper. To contend that satisfaction should be a criterion for attainment of goals is to contend that the attainment should be a worthwhile experience, a source of pride, a valuable and enduring activity for the persons who worked toward its accomplishment. Satisfaction in this third sense does not mean mere hedonistic pleasure, momentary gratification, or some simpleminded version of happiness.

This brief discussion of possible meanings helps to resolve the ambiguity of the term "satisfaction." It should be clear that, as the term is used in this chapter, it does not imply atonement, compensation for wrongdoing, or quick gratification. Rather, the meaning chosen here entails pride, fulfillment, enduring gratification, and a sense of personal worth. But these terms are themselves quite vague; resolving the ambiguity of "satisfaction" does not clear up the inherent vagueness of this term. This lack of precision would ordinarily be taken care of by amplifying the preferred meaning, making that meaning precise and discriminating.

Adjudicating Claims of Satisfaction. But it would be unproductive to concentrate on formulating a carefully delineated definition. From the standpoint of participants in an organization, a precise definition of "satisfaction" is not nearly so important as understanding how to adjudicate claims of satisfaction. No one can count on participants' adopting someone else's definition of "satisfaction," and so it is futile to devote great effort to formulating a precise definition that few will heed. The more critical concern is how to determine the adequacy of satisfaction for any participant. Not only will the participants in any one of the three primary groups (teachers, parents, pupils) make different claims of satisfaction among themselves, but the claims among groups will be different. Some mechanism is needed to decide on the legitimacy of the various claims.

The recognition that claims of satisfaction must be adjudicated is a recognition that there will be conflict between primary participants and primary participant groups. That I explicitly accept the inevitability of conflict and value its existence in an organization clearly removes me from at least one camp of organizational theory: the Human Relations position of Elton Mayo and Kurt

Lewin (see Etzioni, 1964, chap. 4). The Human Relations theorists posited that one of the primary aims of the organization is to provide satisfaction for participants. Conflict was considered destructive, alien to the goals of the organization. The Scientific Management school also eschewed conflict, believing that productivity was enhanced when employees were "happy" (a view of satisfaction already rejected in this chapter). The Human Relations advocates distinguished themselves from the Scientific Managers by believing that satisfaction of participants was an end in itself, while the Scientific Managers thought it a means to optimal production—a distinction evocative of the differences between expressive and instrumental groups. Both the expressive functioning of groups and the Human Relations school of thought seem to undergrid some of the literature on alternative education, especially that of the popular reformers (Denison, Silberman, Kohl, and many others who emphasize joy, love, happiness, and harmony). The differences between these views and the criterion case for satisfaction is that the latter does not espouse satisfaction as an end in itself. The criterion view recognizes and values conflict as an inevitable outgrowth of individuals interacting with one another, and it acknowledges the need for organization as a mechanism for channeling conflict and generating opportunities.

Because conflict is inevitable, some procedure is needed to adjudicate among conflicting participant claims to satisfaction of various participants. For example, a parent might contend that he experiences great satisfaction when his child achieves. The parent understands "achieve" to mean getting the highest possible marks in reading, mathematics, science, and social studies. On the other hand, a teacher claims he will experience satisfaction if he is allowed to develop the skills of critical inquiry in children. The teacher says he needs to abandon the traditional marking system because it retards free expression and promotes a "right answer" syndrome. Yet another conflict arises when the pupil contends he will find satisfaction in doing something other than reading, mathematics, science, and social studies. This conflict represents an instructional opportunity; it is the beginning of an exploration into what persons do value, what they may value, and what they ought to value. In order to capitalize on the opportunity, there must be a means available for each participant to subject his claim to scrutiny, and to legitimate his claim for the other claimants.

Four conditions for adjudicating claims of satisfaction will be suggested here. I trust it will be understood that this effort is exploratory and tentative, as there appear to be no previous attempts to deal with satisfaction in just this way. A participant's claim to satisfaction is considered legitimate to the extent that it meets all four of these conditions:

1. The claimant can explain or show how his own growth and development will be enhanced by this opportunity for satisfaction. For example, a pupil who believes that model-building would be a source of satisfaction says, "In order to construct this model successfully, I will have to search for reference works, learn to draw blueprints, and solve several mathematical and architectural problems."

2. The claimant can defend his claim on ethical or moral grounds. For instance, a parent contending that she would experience satisfaction if her daughter were admitted to a particular program of study says, "Justice requires that my daughter be given this opportunity since she has clearly demonstrated her potential to succeed." Or a teacher who wants to devise his own materials says, "The maximum benefit will accrue to the greatest number of my students if I can design materials unique to each of them."

3. The claimant can show that his claim is appropriate and related to the aim being pursued. Citing studies or research in support of one's position is one way to justify the appropriateness of a claim. As an illustration, a teacher who wishes to adopt bilingual instruction says, "Six studies indicate that reading skills in a second language are markedly improved by a bilingual approach to language arts." Rational argument, the simple giving of reasons, is another way to establish appropriateness. Thus, "The community is requesting bilingual instruction, I speak the native language and have had training, and pupils say their satisfaction will be enhanced if instruction is in the mother tongue."

4. The claimant can show how the opportunity to pursue his claim furthers the attainment of the aim. If, for example, the aim is to promote the physical health and well-being of pupils, and a teacher claims he can experience satisfaction by involving his class in the reconstruction of the playground, including building new equipment, he might say, "By redesigning the equipment and constructing three new pieces, more pupils will be able to play, more muscles will be involved in play, and more children will want to work on the equipment."

Applying the Criterion of Satisfaction. Late in 1973 a predominantly black, inner-city junior high school in Los Angeles published the results of its efforts to develop goals for the school. Ranked first by the parents and third by the school staff was the aim of critical thinking and effective problem solving (the staff ranked mastery of basic skills first, while parents ranked it sixth, thus putting this aim in third place). Given the criterion case for satisfaction, the question that participants must now ask is, "Will striving for the attainment of this aim provide opportunities for satisfaction?" Since parents and teachers ranked this aim high, the answer to the question appears to be in the affirmative (although one primary participant group, pupils, apparently were not asked to rank the top ten goal choices). The second question is, "How can satisfaction be attained in pursuit of this aim?"

Each participant group should be given the opportunity to come to grips with these questions. Each participant group is entitled to specify ways in which it may gain satisfaction through working toward fulfillment of the aim. The task of the administration is to guide the organization so that opportunities are provided to participants for realizing legitimate claims of satisfaction. Legitimacy of claims of satisfaction is determined by application of the conditions set forth in the preceding paragraphs. Thus the organization, which as has already been pointed out has a force of its own beyond the individuals who function in it, has as one of its central purposes the coordination needed to assist participants in goal-setting tasks, and the provision of opportunities for satisfaction in the realization of these goals. This view of administrative responsibilities is similar to a position taken by Carl Rogers (1969, p. 208): "The task of the administrator is to so arrange the organizational conditions and methods of operation that people best achieve their own goals by also furthering the jointly defined goals of the institution." Rogers may not assent to the criterion case for satisfaction in all its details, but there is agreement between the criterion position and Rogers on the proper functioning of administration. Among the central mechanisms for optimizing the interaction between people and their organizations is the provision by management of conditions for goal setting by participants and the attainment of satisfaction by participants.

If there are no means whereby participants can experience satisfaction in pursuit of the school's aims, then (according to the criterion case) the aim should be abandoned as incapable of being successfully achieved. If a criterion for winning the race is breaking the ribbon first, but no entrant can break the ribbon, then no one can win the race. If attainment of satisfaction is a criterion for achieving an aim, but no participant can experience satisfaction, then the aim cannot be achieved.

Yet another dimension of the criterion case is the identification of the three primary participant groups. All three groups—teachers, parents, and pupils—must perceive that there are ways for each of them to experience satisfaction in the realization of mutually agreed upon aims. By stipulating that all three groups must have opportunities to experience satisfaction, conflict is made more likely. But this conflict is viewed as a healthy and appropriate outcome of the coming together of different human beings for what they perceive as a common purpose. The first step in conflict resolution is the assessment of the legitimacy of the claims of satisfaction. This step is achieved by requiring the various claimants to subject their claims to the conditions previously identified. A large measure of conflict will be overcome as participants attempt to legitimate their claims. The dialogue among participants during the legitimation process will further reduce conflict by revealing avenues of compromise and consolidation. But there probably always will be some inconsistencies and contradictions among claims. Many of these can be differentially accommodated by administrators (parents can pursue a course of action that is fulfilling to them, while teachers pursue a different course, and pupils yet a third course, all three of which jointly promote attainment of the aim).

Suppose that an agreed upon aim is to develop skills of pupils in the wise use of leisure time (an aim ranked second by the junior high school parents, and tenth by the teachers in the study previously mentioned). The parents state that they will experience great satisfaction if their children respond positively to suggestions that they read books, visit a cultural event, or work at a hobby. Teachers report that they would experience satisfaction in pursuit of this aim if they were relieved of some pressure to prepare pupils for standardized tests, and if they were provided resources to engage pupils in various hobbies. Pupils report they would get satisfaction from choosing their own activities, being free to reject those activities suggested by teachers and parents. Though there are some clear sources of conflict here, there are many broad areas of agreement. There are also several clear stipulations on what is required of the organization if it is to provide each group with opportunities for satisfaction.

Because the criterion case for satisfaction, if implemented, will engender conflict and make heavy demands on the school organization, why should anyone believe that it is worth the trouble? What justifies the criterion case as an appropriate and proper conception of the way schooling should function? The criterion view of satisfaction has been explained and illustrated, but thus far there has been little justification for the view. It is time to see how well the criterion case can be defended.

justifying primary satisfaction for participants

"When I think about school, I am struck not by any special ideas, observations, philosophies or theories but by the sounds of human beings: their orders and pleas, their anger and obedience, their crying, their silence" (Cottle, 1973, p. 5). Whatever else a school is, it is a place where people are charged with relating to other people in productive and beneficial ways. This relationship should provide for the education (in the broadest and best sense of the term) of the people in the school. But because schooling takes place in an organizational setting, it is possible that the people and the school function at cross-purposes. To prevent this, the organization should function in a manner that supports its participants, and the participants need to know what they can ask for and expect from the organization of which they are members. The contention here is that the organization can function to promote and maintain satisfaction of members, and participants may reasonably expect the organization to provide it. But two fundamental questions are still unanswered. Why are parents, teachers, and pupils the organization's primary participants? Why is the satisfaction criterion a good mechanism for facilitating the interaction between primary participants and the organization? I shall try to answer each question in turn.

Why Parents? Some may think it unusual to identify parents as primary participants in schooling. But parents probably have more legal, moral, political, and practical reasons supporting their legitimate involvement in education than any other constituent group.

First, there is the oft-quoted but little regarded section of Article 26 of the Universal Declaration of Human Rights of the United Nations Charter: "Parents have a prior right to choose the kind of education that shall be given to their children." Because of the manner in which formal education is structured and financed, this right must mean more than that the parents have a right to choose the school their children will attend. It is a right, a *prior* right, to choose *the kind of education* their children shall be given. But how do parents exercise this right in these times of organized schooling? What means and mechanisms do parents have at their disposal to act on this right? Pitifully few, it seems. The decision of the state that schooling shall be compulsory for all children is, in many ways, an abolition of the right to choose the kind of education the child shall be given.

The criterion case for satisfaction is a means of partially restoring the parental right. It requires (for more than legal and moral reasons, as will be shown) that the parent have a voice in the aims of schooling, by stipulating that the pursuit and accomplishment of school aims must be a source of satisfaction to parents. If parents cannot obtain satisfaction from such pursuit and attainment, the effort of the school must be regarded a failure.

A second reason for identifying parents as primary participants is social and political. The school serves an extremely important function as a local association in which parents may involve themselves as citizens. After examining trends toward totalitarianism and causes of alienation in society, Nisbet (1962) concludes that the ability of a nation to sustain a democracy is based upon the diffusion of power in local, grass-roots associations. He believes the United States has to an extent unwittingly abandoned its commitment to democracy through the destruction of intimate associations and the consequent flow of power to the state. He says (p. 54):

> Our present crisis lies in the fact that whereas the small traditional associations, founded upon kinship, faith, or loyalty, are still expected to communicate to individuals the principal moral ends and psychological gratifications of society, they have manifestly become detached from positions of functional relevance to the larger economic and political decisions of our society. Family, local community, church, and the whole network of informal interpersonal relationships

have ceased to play a determining role in our institutional systems of mutual aid, welfare, education, recreation, and economic production and distribution.

Assuming Nisbet's thesis to be sound (and I do), one must perceive the school as having the potential to be an intermediate association with strong ties to parents. Thus it can serve to retard alienation and to diffuse power more broadly. But if schools isolate their constituencies, particularly parents, as they often do, they promote alienation. If isolated from such intermediate-level associations as the school, parents will attempt to overcome their alienation by calling upon the state to enforce compliance to their needs. If and when the state acts, it does so by assuming power previously vested at a more subordinate level. If the cycle occurs frequently enough, the preponderance of power eventually comes to rest with the state, and then both the parent and the school may find it far more difficult to obtain action on perceived needs.

By requiring that parents experience satisfaction in their intercourse with schools, the organization is called upon to respond directly to parental needs. The satisfaction criterion becomes a means of allowing the parent to maintain association with the school, a means of calling upon the organization to respond to concerns, information, ideas, and pleas.

The third and final reason for considering parents as primary participants is the need for their own education. Parenting is a skill, a frame of reference, a set of attitudes, beliefs, and values. It is as legitimate an educational subject as teaching, farming, manufacturing, and nursing. The school has an opportunity to promote the growth of children and parents simultaneously by including parents as primary participants. In his analysis of what is needed to promote a developmental approach to schooling, Piaget (1974, p. 84) says, "The school has everything to gain by knowing what the reactions of parents are, and the latter find increasing advantage in being initiated into the problems of the school."

But one does not gain access to an organization simply because others think there is warrant for participation. The organization must be structured so that it can accommodate and assimilate its participant communities. In this respect, I believe Kvaraceus (1971, p. 75) errs somewhat when he states that he has a "prejudice toward the P.T.A. as a waste of time as currently organized and directed."* If indeed the P.T.A. is a waste of time, it is not solely the fault of the P.T.A. Almost any parent can testify to the difficulty of becoming a part of decision making in the schools. The organizational basis for parental interaction simply is not available. In order to establish effective involvement, the organization must be held accountable for participatory criteria. Satisfaction is one of them.

Why Teachers? I assume that no special argument is needed to establish the primary participant status of teachers. What is required is justification for the position that teachers are entitled to satisfaction as primary participants. Grace (1972, p. 107) sets the stage for a defense of this position: "It can be argued that modern educational systems in bringing the pupil rightly to the centre of the stage may have pushed the teacher too far into the wings. . . ."

In this era of assessment of measurable outcomes, we appear to be defining teaching solely in terms of learning. At one time it was said that intelligence is what I.Q. tests measure; soon we shall be able to say that teaching is what pupil performance tests measure. To define the role of the teacher totally in terms of the pupil is to distort the person who is a teacher. Grace's study (1972) of role conflict among teachers in England led him to the conclusion that "there is a need for 'planned change' in educational organizations which monitors the consequences of innovation not solely in measures of learning achievement or pupil reaction but also in terms of teacher reaction and teacher satisfaction" (p. 107).

One way to establish the independence of the teacher from the learner is to entitle teachers to make unique claims against the organization—unique in the sense that teachers may seek satisfaction from the organization in ways that may not automatically and necessarily yield satisfaction for students. This statement does not imply that teachers may either neglect the needs of pupils or ignore their interests. It simply establishes the right of a teacher to function as a person while performing in an occupational role. It also implies that a school is more successful if it enhances the satisfaction of teachers than if it does not.

*So as not to quote Kvaraceus out of context, I should note that he goes on to say (p. 75), "I have come to view the National Congress of Parents and Teachers as the most unused and misused resource in the country and have at times attempted to point to ways to harness the potential of this giant organization."

Why Pupils? Again it seems that no argument is needed to support the view that pupils are primary participants, but some reasons are required to defend their right to satisfaction. This point of view has been presented effectively by neo-humanist and alternative educators (Holt, Denison, Borton, Neill, Kozol, Friedenberg, Rogers, Silberman, and Weinberg in Chapter 3 of this volume). While it is clear from the preceding argument in this chapter that there are substantive differences between the criterion case and some neo-humanist positions on education, there is no disagreement with the conditions of schooling as the neo-humanists and popular reformers have described them. Pupils are morally entitled to a voice in their education, it is educative in itself for them to have and express this voice, and the aims of schooling are furthered by permitting the expression and listening attentively to it.

But morality, pedagogy, and organizational theory aside, there is another compelling reason. The same reason given for parents: alienation. By disenfranchising the pupil from the organization in which he has participant status, he becomes victimized, isolated, and helpless. He sees little alternative but to cop out. "The schools have become one of the most potent breeding grounds of alienation in society. For this reason it is of crucial importance for the welfare and development of school-age children that schools be reintegrated into the life of the community" (Bronfenbrenner, 1974, p. 60). But how is this transformation of the school to take place? One way to start is to acknowledge organizational characteristics and establish criteria for their functioning. The criteria, however, must accommodate all the primary participant groups in the school, parents, teachers, *and* pupils.

Where Are the Administrators? No mention has been made of administrators as primary participants, and yet they are the key to maintaining interaction between the organization and its participants. The administrator's task is to manage the organization so that primary participants have, among other things, opportunities to experience satisfaction. Does this task make the administrator a primary participant? Does the administrator have the same right to satisfaction as parents, pupils, and teachers?

I have no ready answers to these questions and can only suggest why the questions pose some difficulties for me. There are at least two ways to view the case of satisfaction for the administrator. One is to contend that the administrator is entitled to satisfaction, but of a kind different from that experienced by the other primary participants. The administrator's source of satisfaction derives from the satisfaction experienced by others. That is, the administrator takes satisfaction from being able to provide an interactive environment wherein pupils, teachers, and parents experience satisfaction. Thus the administrator may claim satisfaction, but its source is derivative rather than primary.

A different view is that of the administrator as a coequal primary participant along with the pupils, parents, and teachers. According to this view the administrator may make claims of satisfaction of the same (primary) kind as are made by other participants, and these claims may conflict with others just as those of parents may conflict with teachers, teachers with pupils, and so forth. But this second view, while possibly more just and fair, poses problems involving conflict of interest. If the administrator is a coequal primary participant entitled to make his own claims of satisfaction, can he not at the same time manage the organization so as to promote his claims over those of other primary participants? Would not the administrator be more likely to attend to the needs for satisfaction of others if he were obligated to seek his own sources of satisfaction in the successful opportunities for satisfaction provided to others?

The two views are almost paradoxical. That they both may appear plausible is due perhaps to the incredibly rapid organizational development of American schooling, without a corresponding change in the training or role perception of the school administrator. In smaller schools the principal may also be a teacher. In many European schools the headmaster or headmistress is more than an organizational facilitator; he or she often plays a vital role in curriculum planning or instructional decision making. But in large schools and school systems in the United States administrators manage complex organizations. They are deeply enmeshed in tables of organization, divisions of labor, committee structures, salary scales, compliance with statutes, and a host of other duties only minimally related to substantive curricular and instructional matters.

It seems that to the extent that the administrator is a creature of the organization he is obligated to seek his sources of satisfaction derivatively, that is, from making it possible for others to experience satisfaction. But to the extent that the administrator engages in curricular and instructional concerns along with other participants, he is entitled to make and legitimate the same kinds of claims of satisfaction as the other participants. But in this latter role, the administrator is barred from intentionally biasing the organization toward the fulfillment of his own claims. Thus, the administrator in a complex organization pays a price for stepping out of the role of organizational facilitator: he becomes a peer to other primary participants. To what extent administrators are free to move back and forth in roles, and to what degree they are capable of keeping these roles distinct, I do not know. It does seem clear, however, that the administrator cannot claim primary participant status ex officio. Whether he is entitled to make substantive claims of satisfaction should perhaps be dependent on the role he must or chooses to play in the school.

Why Satisfaction? On what basis was satisfaction selected as the criterion for assessing the success of schooling? What makes satisfaction different from other criteria? Is satisfaction really an alternative to conventional criteria for determining success? These questions call for a summary and conclusions.

While the argument may seem complex and diffuse, it is actually a fairly simple thesis. The complications arise from the need to explain, clarify, and defend the basic propositions. The basic propositions are:

1. Schools are organizations.

2. Organizations and their participants are different phenomena; each act, and each interact with one another.

3. The conventional criteria for the success of schooling stress either organizational or participant variables, but neglect considerations of interaction between the two.

4. Many alternative and humanistic reform movements attempt to rectify what they perceive to be the failure of schools by reformulating the aims of education or schooling.

5. The mere reformulation of aims fails to account for the participant and organizational nature of schooling because it merely changes the desired outcomes without specifying the changes required in the participant-organization interaction.

6. To influence the participant-organization interaction, it is necessary to specify what participants may legitimately expect from their organization, and to specify what the organization as organization might reasonably provide its participants.

7. Satisfaction, defined as enduring gratification yielding a sense of worth and pride in accomplishment, is both a reasonable and educative expectation for participants and a possible and educative provision by the organization.

The idea that interconnects these seven propositions is the distinction between satisfaction as an aim and as a criterion. The criterion case allows the school to pursue aims other than satisfaction, but holds that participants must experience satisfaction as they pursue and achieve these aims. By analyzing satisfaction as a criterion, one creates a link to support interaction between people and organization. The organization is charged with functioning in a manner that provides opportunities for participants to experience satisfaction, while participants are charged with making claims of satisfaction against the organization. Both participant and organization must act to adjudicate claims and to set aims against which claims must be legitimated. The criterion case for satisfaction is a means of establishing the kind of school environments shown to be effective by recent work on educational change (see Williams and others, 1974; Culver and Hoban, 1973) and is an instance of what environmental design theorist Robert Propst (1974, p. 609) had in mind when he said: "When we go to work or when we go to school we go with some expectation that we will be part of something of consequence. The degree to which we are able to participate, to contribute, to be known and valued, is a major measure of human satisfaction."

If no primary participant experiences satisfaction, then an evaluation of the school must conclude that its effort is a failure. But to the extent that the satisfaction criterion is attained, the school may be considered a success. Even though the aim may not be fully achieved, the school may be successful insofar as the attempt to achieve the aim provided satisfaction. It is clear that many of the major aims of education can never be fully achieved; we set them not because we believe we can reach them, but because they give focus and direction to our work. Our success then is not determined by whether we fully accomplish the aim, but by what happens to us during the journey toward fulfillment. If on this journey we can learn what we value and what others value, if we can make our institutions work on our behalf, if we can forestall the alienation of parents, pupils, and teachers, and if we can learn to resolve conflict in order to work for mutually held goals, then much success will have been achieved. The major injustice of this era in education may be that we have convinced ourselves that there can be no satisfaction until the goal is reached, and thus we make no claims for it until the journey ends. But it never does.

references

Averch, H. A., and others. *How Effective Is Schooling? A Critical Review and Synthesis of Research Findings.* Santa Monica, Calif.: RAND Corporation, 1972.

Bane, M. J., and Jencks, C. "The Schools and Equal Opportunity." *Saturday Review,* 1972, *55,* 37-42.

Bidwell, C. E. "The School as a Formal Organization." In J. G. Murdoch (Ed.), *Handbook of Organizations.* Chicago: Rand McNally, 1965.

Bronfenbrenner, U. "The Origins of Alienation." *Scientific American,* 1974, *231,* 53-61.

Coleman, J. S., and others. *Equality of Educational Opportunity.* Washington, D.C.: Government Printing Office, 1966.

Cottle, T. *The Voices of School.* Boston: Little, Brown, 1973.

Culver, C., and Hoban, G. J. *The Power to Change: Issues for the Innovative Educator.* New York: McGraw-Hill, 1973.

Dewey, J. *Democracy and Education.* New York: Macmillan Paperbacks, 1916, 1961.

Dreeben, R. "The School as a Workplace." In R. M. W. Travers (Ed.), *Second Handbook of Research on Teaching.* Chicago: Rand McNally, 1973.

Etzioni, A. *Modern Organizations.* Englewood Cliffs, N.J.: Prentice-Hall, 1964.

Flizak, C. W. "Organizational Structure and Teacher Role-Orientation." *Administrator's Notebook,* 1968, *17*(2).

Goslin, D. A. *The School in Contemporary Society.* Glenview, Ill.: Scott, Foresman, 1965.

Grace, G. R. *Role Conflict and the Teacher.* London: Routledge and Kegan Paul, 1972.

Hall, R. H. *Organizations: Structure and Process.* Englewood Cliffs, N.J.: Prentice-Hall, 1972.

Hartley, H. J. "Educational Bureaucracy, Teacher Orientation and Selected Criterion Variables." *Journal of Educational Research,* 1966, *60,* 54-57.

Herriot, R. E., and Hodgkins, B. J. *The Environment of Schooling: Formal Education as an Open Social System.* Englewood Cliffs, N.J.: Prentice-Hall, 1973.

Homans, G. C. *Social Behavior: Its Elementary Forms.* Rev. Ed. New York: Harcourt Brace Jovanovich, 1974.

Hornstein, H. A., and others. "Influence and Satisfaction in Organizations: A Replication." *Sociology of Education,* 1968, *41,* 380-389.

Kvaraceus, W. C. "Fantasies in a Place Called 'School.' " In A. H. Passow (Ed.), *Reactions to Silberman's Crisis in the Classroom.* Worthington, Ohio: Charles A. Jones, 1971.

Nisbet, R. A. *Community and Power.* New York: Oxford University Press, Galaxy Book, 1962.

Peters, R. S. *Ethics and Education.* Palo Alto, Calif.: Scott, Foresman, 1967.

Piaget, J. *To Understand Is to Invent.* New York: Viking Press, 1974.

Propst, R. "Human Needs and Working Places." *School Review*, 1974, *82*, 609-616.

Rogers, C. R. *Freedom to Learn*. Columbus, Ohio: Charles E. Merrill, 1969.

Williams, R. C., and others. *Effecting Organizational Renewal in Schools: A Social Systems Perspective*. New York: McGraw-Hill, 1974.

transition:
toward alternatives

john i. goodlad

The reader is asked to turn to the typology of educational alternatives discussed in Chapter 1 and displayed in Figure 2. The bottom right-hand cell depicts both the widest array of alternatives and the Utopian ideal of the individual's drive for knowledge and skills being satisfied within the framework of a learning society. Within this cell or extrapolated from it to the right and off the chart lies an indeterminate number of educational possibilities. A rich array for all other cells already exists or at least has been envisioned by someone. Although examples in the bottom row are difficult to find in practice, they can be described. Summerhill, for example, fits the description of the middle cell.

It appears, then, that we are not lacking in alternatives to the conventional in education. Although the search for the new and, one would hope, better will continue to be challenging, it recently has diminished sharply and will maintain a lower profile for some years to come. The challenge is to make what already is envisioned more widespread, to accelerate the pace of change.

This chapter is addressed to the problems of effecting a transition from those forms and practices conventionally characteristic of the common school to those educational opportunities best suited to human variability in a pluralistic society. The locus is the United States in a world context; the time span is the balance of this century. Although the several authors of this volume approach the subject of educational alternatives from different perspectives and disagree on some assumptions and somewhat more on specifics, they are agreed on a sense of direction: the desirability of moving toward the right-hand and lower boxes of Figure 2.

The next section examines some of the formidable barriers to reconstructing schools and creating alternatives in and out of them —especially the malaise of helplessness. Then, there is a section on how schools as social systems might move from self-preservation to a condition of greater responsiveness to their larger cultural context, to their own problems and needs, and to solutions for dealing with them. The chapter concludes with a brief look at alternative roles for schools and the interface between these and an increasingly educative society envisioned for tomorrow. Much of what has gone before in the volume reappears in the fabric of this concluding chapter.

the prospect for alternatives

Given the current rhetoric regarding open classrooms, alternative schools, free schools, and the like, one might readily conclude that an almost irresistible momentum designed to loosen up the schooling enterprise has built up. This is not the case. As a matter of fact, most of the signs suggest quite the contrary. Considerable concern for whether the schools are doing a good enough job, couched in the familiar language of pupil achievement in the three R's, never goes away and implies staying with or returning to what we have had. The hand of restraint comes on stronger at some times than at others and is coming on strong right now.

Whether or not the schools are doing better or worse than a decade ago or three decades before that actually has little to do with these themes of criticism. As La Belle points out in Chapter 8, our schools are inextricably woven into the fabric of our culture and are much more affected by it than they influence it. The schools not only suffer from general societal malaise, but also

receive more than their share of the blame for it, largely because of the popular myth that the schools were and potentially are powerfully countervailing agencies. The fact that research increasingly suggests otherwise does not destroy the myth; it merely attests, in the eyes of many critics, to the present inadequacy of schools. They can be made better by toughening them up, rather than seeking new ways, goes the argument, and this, in turn, can be done best by prodding the teachers. The problem having been grossly oversimplified, the solutions are simplistic.

The fact that these tides of primitive simplicity in regard to our schools are virtually endemic to our culture, waxing in visibility with events such as Sputnik and a variety of economic crises, and that they presently are moving once again toward flood level is not in itself cause for alarm. In the normal course of events, they wane again, rolled under by fresh waves of change or at least the rhetoric of change. The danger lies more deeply embedded in the structures, technologies, and sanctions employed to establish one set of ideas over another.

The reader is advised at this point to refer to La Belle's heuristic model of culture in Chapter 8. A dynamic, free society presumably keeps in some reasonable balance of enlightenment and development the three major cultural elements conditioning human behavior. It should, consequently, stop short of converting controversial ideologies into procedures backed by laws or of placing sanctions on public institutions that do not adhere to them. Such practice amounts, in effect, to making laws out of what should be options in the intellectual marketplace and then adding punishments to enforce them. It is ironic that education—presumably the classic stronghold of competing ideas—falls prey to this serious inroad on our freedoms. And it is regrettable that this cultural disease can be traced even to the Supreme Court of the land (witness the busing issue).

But let me be more specific. This country's educational enterprise has benefited richly from a productive tension between what might be classified, on one hand, as the humanistic view and, on the other, the behavioristic. I concluded the Preface to this volume by saying how fortunate we are to have able spokesmen for both views. The two positions need each other. Some states are moving currently toward so-called teacher accountability plans which tip the scales in favor of teaching toward behavioral objectives that presumably would assure fulfillment of general state goals. There is a pseudoscientism here which, when carried to excess, understandably would invoke a strong, countervailing corrective from the more humanistically oriented side of the dialogue. This is as it should be in a free society.

The danger, however, lies in legitimating what still falls considerably short of science by endorsing it with state laws and then backing up this endorsement with the threat of economic sanctions. No longer is there free and open choice in the marketplace of ideas when this happens. The result can only be the elimination of alternatives and a steady erosion in teachers' willingness to innovate.

This, in itself, is dangerous. But there is a greater danger. Accountability plans that are sharply focused on pupil achievement and, in turn, on teacher performance designed to produce it leave teachers naked and exposed. Lacking clear-cut directives as to what to do when pupils score at the fifteenth percentile on standardized reading tests, teachers feel themselves threatened. The most natural and most readily accessible source of help and strength often is the union or state and national associations possessing the collective clout teachers lack as individuals. The union or state teachers' association now bargains with other power groups as to the ideas that should prevail. The sanctioning of ideas by power adds no special truths to them. In fact, the search for truth, equity, or "what is best for the children" sometimes characterizing early rhetoric soon is lost in the struggle to place power over power.

If the scene of battle were removed from the local school and community, there might be some net gain, since those closest to where teaching and learning take place could go about their business in some peace. But this is not the way events proceed. The constituency in the politics of education ultimately and fundamentally is local, whatever the power struggle in state and national capitals. There are parent groups, teacher groups, administrator groups, all with their chosen representatives sifting and screening what comes back to fuel the home fires. As a consequence, those who must work together to reconstruct the schools and to create educational alternatives are sharply divided, becoming antagonists in a struggle having little to do with good education. In such an environment, alternatives and the search for alternatives are not likely to flourish.

One of the most serious blocks, then, to moving toward more options to promote educational development from cradle to grave is the substitution of political negotiation for the exchange of ideas. In some urban settings, the situation may have progressed beyond the point of recovery; in most places, a choice still is possible. "The real choice is now clearly in the hands of those who have the power —including teachers' associations. Will they continue to play by the old political power game that can only lead to violent collision, or will they lead in creating a ball game in which the individual teacher, parent and student become the major cooperating players?" (Fantini, 1974).

A second and related major block to the attainment of alternatives on a widespread basis concerns the way in which certain traditional values have been built so thoroughly into the means of schooling. Many of these already have been dealt with in previous chapters: goals expressed almost exclusively in terms of achievement in subject matter rather than, for example, satisfaction on the part of all involved (Chapter 10); content, textbooks, and progress of pupils geared to graded expectations and structures (Chapter 7); and evaluation not only geared to norms derived from these goals but also serving to teach the value of achieving in them and, indeed, only in them (Chapters 5 and 9). To attempt to introduce hands-on programs in vocational education, the arts, or the health sciences is to run the risk of having to measure success on the basis of paper-and-pencil tests.

Almost all the regularities of schooling interlock in such a way as to preserve and teach a set of values into which students, teachers, administrators, and parents are quickly socialized. Difficult as it is to invoke serious discussion of educational ideas in any dialogue on schoolkeeping, it is infinitely more difficult to change these regularities. Countervailing practices are effectively blocked, co-opted in such a way as to blunt their innovative character, or given the kiss of death by being adopted in name only. The court of last resort in resisting change often is the seemingly innocent question, "What does research say about it?" when, of course, there can be no answer to such a question until the alternative has been tried and tested. If a trial is granted, the criterion for testing usually is drawn from assumptions underlying threatened old practices rather than the new. Sarason points to these regularities in the culture of the school, our general lack of knowledge about them, and failure on the part of reformers to take them into account as major deterrents to educational reform (Sarason, 1971).

It is generally assumed that the large, bureaucratic structures of public schooling create these regularized constraints, and, no doubt, they contribute significantly. But this falls far short of being a full explanation. For example, many kindergarten classes of the K-12 graded school come reasonably close to descriptions of what might be considered exemplary (Goodlad, Klein, and Associates, 1974); whereas nursery schools independent of "the system" appear not to be marked by innovation or a thrust toward better ways (Goodlad, Klein, Novotney, and Associates, 1973). Alternative and "free" schools, if they survive more than a year or two, seem to fall quickly into conventional patterns or to develop new rigidities (Chapter 1). Replacing one rigidity with another may be an improvement, but it does not extend the range of choice (Chapter 6). Schools have difficulty in initiating change and especially in maintaining a significant, self-renewing momentum. It is regrettable that there has been little sustained inquiry into these phenomena, and such as exists is of recent vintage. The creation of dynamic human settings is one of the most challenging problems of our time and is proper work for educators (Sarason, 1972).

A third block to opening up alternatives and to gaining access to them lies in our tendency to equate a conception of school that is time and place bound with education. Even though, for example, we sought to go beyond school in this volume, we found ourselves constantly coming back to this singular institution which automatically comes to mind whenever the word "education" is spoken. Although, as stated at the beginning of this chapter, many alternatives have been conceptualized, and a significant array has been tried, the pieces lie scattered about. Comprehensive conceptualizations are lacking, and rarely have more than a small handful of innovative arrangements been put together at one time and in one place —rarely enough to change the familiar character of schooling.

Thinking more comprehensively and, ultimately, acting on the basis of a broader perspective could easily double the array of resources available for use on school time as well as provide an equal amount of time for nonschool educational activities without seriously intruding on such "idle" time as most humans seem to desire. Observations show that pupils in the upper elementary years are engaged in repetitious rituals performed with minimal cerebral activity by slow and fast learners alike (Goodlad, 1975). That part of the brain presumed to be stimulated by novelty—sometimes referred to as Magoun's brain—cannot conceivably be stirred very often. At least the high school student is stimulated by the demands of adjusting to the personalities of several different teachers each day. But the student in the last three years of elementary school hears daily only two or three adult voices and frequently only one. The nature of the subjects changes only slightly from hour to hour since almost all constitute a conversion of physical or social realities in the larger world into "the language arts," a conversion into abstraction singularly characteristic of schools. The real world lies waiting to be confronted and dealt with for educational purposes if only schools would shake off their shackles.

Similarly, schools must shake themselves loose from the nine-to-three syndrome in thinking about educational opportunity and ways to enhance it. By the age of thirteen, a young person has spent about 6.9 percent of his life in school; by seventeen, about 8.3 percent. This is hardly enough time either for rectifying the malaise of the surrounding society or for achieving the noble goals we set for our schools. Even after accounting for sleeping (which constitutes between 35 and 38 percent of a person's time), there remains a good deal of time for eating, recreation, idle time, and the rest. One need not look around very much to become aware of the fact that much of this time is spent in dulling boredom from which most people, young and old, would prefer to be rescued.

The possibilities for rescue are almost endless, and they are, for the most part, outside of schools, not in them. They require an educational approach to human engineering: that is, rethinking existing institutions, human and natural resources, places of meeting, and each potentially new setting, with educational potentialities in mind. Television is an obvious example. By the age of seventeen, a young person has spent 9 to 10 percent of his life before a television screen—that "glass-faced bastard" of *The One Hundred Dollar Misunderstanding* which has cut off discourse in many a household. Television is, however, a powerful educational tool; we need to think of it as such. But this is not the place to open up these possibilities. Many are discussed in previous chapters; aspects of the human engineering involved are discussed later in this one.

Of the many obstacles to change toward alternatives in education, one more needs attention here. It is perhaps the major one blocking constructive progress in so many realms of need—ennui, despair, feelings of impotence or helplessness—call it what you will. It is a malaise of the human spirit that deprives the world, perhaps

fatally, of the energy now so badly needed for the task of leadership and followership involved in reconstructing our institutions
and, indeed, society.

Everyone seems to be waiting on everyone else when not
blaming someone else. Of course our teachers are at fault. And our
close neighbors. And our far ones. But these facts do not change
anything. It may be comforting to jump our minds over a few decades to contemplate the golden future some educational futurists
would have us anticipate. But this does not help much either, and
the chances are pretty good that they are wrong anyway. The critical need is to line up our self-interests with reality. The reality is
that our self-interests—all of our self-interests—are going to be
served very badly in coming years unless we set about redesigning
the setting of which each one of us is a part. It is in the very best
self-interest of educators to reconstruct their institutions and to
transcend them in the process of creating new ones. To begin to act
in this enlightened self-interest is to begin to overcome our ennui.
We should spend only a little time redefining our goals. This distrac-
tion is too convenient, especially when we know what they are
anyway. And there is no point in waiting "until the data are in"
because hardly anyone is gathering the kind we need. We will, undoubtedly, want to spend a little time contemplating whether it is
worth beginning, whether there is any hope. Some of us will want
to look around a little, too, to see if there is a ready blueprint.

The rapidly accumulating body of literature subsumed under
the theme of futurism provides no clear picture either of what we
might reasonably anticipate for a tomorrow several decades away or
of how to achieve the future of our choice. There simply are too
many imponderables. A sizable chunk of this literature is, consequently, a kind of pseudoscientific soothsaying.

Nonetheless, two divergent themes emerge from it all, whether it be from the sensational or the more thoughtful, responsible
statements. One is the ever-recurring rhetoric of hope: humankind
in its limitless capacity for creative responsiveness shall overcome.
Peace, freedom, health, and food for all are just over the next hill,
around the next bend, beyond the present crisis. This is the literature of Utopia. It is the literature favored by educators, perhaps
because without such hope there is little place for educators, viewed
in their most idealized roles. The second theme constitutes the literature of despair. Extrapolating from the present, we are on the road

to hell, whether or not it be paved with the literature of Utopia. Some recent literature in this vein sees us barely making it into the twenty-first century and then going under about 2050.

But few, if any, of even the most pessimistic writers of this scenario are prepared to accept it, when forced to take a position, just as the very young cannot accept their mortality or understand the nature of their immortality. For example, Heilbronner, whose assessment of the future is anything but cheering, has this to say:

> The human prospect is not an irreconcilable death sentence. It is not an inevitable doomsday toward which we are headed, although the risk of enormous catastrophes exists. The prospect is better viewed as a formidable array of challenges that must be overcome before human survival is assured, before we move *beyond doomsday*. These challenges can be overcome—by the saving intervention of nature if not by the wisdom and foresight of man. The death sentence is therefore better viewed as a contingent life sentence—one that will permit the continuance of human society, but only on a basis very different from that of the present, and probably after much suffering during the period of transition [Heilbronner, 1974].

Pushed far enough, cautious optimists and conditional pessimists ultimately seem to find a common denominator put nicely by Norman Cousins: "Nothingness is conceptually impossible" (Marlin, 1974). What is conceptually possible is a road around and beyond doomsday. Difficult though this conceptualization clearly will be, working out its implementation will be even more so, and for the latter we may need "the saving intervention of nature."

These last two sentences could be interpreted as suggesting some master plan for dealing with what threatens us on a global scale, which simply is not feasible in any meaningful detail or in any early future. Rust (Chapter 7) is, no doubt, right in stressing the need for national priorities to give way to global ones, but this will not happen soon. The many states that have not yet experienced the potency of full nationhood are not likely to sacrifice their ambitions for a blueprint of the sovereignty of humankind. In the name of nationalism, some peoples will tolerate, indeed cheer patriotically, extravagant exploitation by dictators whose life-style surpasses those of the richest industrial barons. We are likely to see, for a time, the continued exercise of strong political power by the nation-state. Indeed, if some of the most critical decisions are to be made soon enough, there must be strong national governments capable of making decisions to save mankind. "The nation-state may all too seldom speak the voice of reason. But it remains the only serious alternative to chaos" (Calleo and Rowland, 1973).

While a blueprint for tomorrow is not feasible, it is possible to lay out alternatives and make better choices in all of the major realms of human culture, choices that transcend boundaries of many kinds simply because they represent the enlightened self-interest of those on all sides. Such a perspective is applied more readily to the technological component of the cultural trilogy determining human behavior than to the other two (see Chapter 8). For example, fear of there being no gasoline and, therefore, no demand for automobiles, much more than the impassioned plea of environmentalists, will cause manufacturers to produce autos with half the present need for gasoline. The "better" decision, in the self-interest, is clear. In the process, the rhetoric of the industrialist and the conservationist will be scarcely distinguishable. Cry "hypocrisy" if you will. Traits of human character will not change much in the next twenty-five or fifty years, and by then it may be too late. *The key to change is for decisions made in the interests of self to coincide with the commonweal—or, conversely, for the commonweal to be perceived as coincidental with the advancement of self-interest.*

Even though the grand schema eludes us, it is possible to anticipate some of the consequences of decisions made in one cultural realm on others. Prerequisite, of course, is an essential awareness of the systemic nature of things, today on a global scale. It is estimated that cutting in half the gasoline consumption of all cars driven in the United States would make this country virtually self-sufficient in oil. Conceive of the implications of this for the role of this country in world affairs. The critical question then becomes whether the central principle of change cited above can work at the national level. That is, can certain basic conditions essential to the self-interests of the nation-state and the commonweal be served simultaneously? Unless this question is answered affirmatively much more often than negatively during the rest of this century, the future will be bleak, indeed.

Much will depend on more intangible things than even rational decision making in enlightened self-interest. Most important among these is the nature of that Man celebrated in the literature of Utopia. Without cultural contingencies to reinforce freedom and dignity, is there any hope for autonomous man in a society so aversive that we must change it almost in its entirety, some say, to stave off doomsday? On this issue there are no clear choices; there is only hope. And, perhaps fortunately, hope is like religion: if it can be understood, it is no longer hope.

But hope can be converted into challenge, and challenge can be converted into specific activities. It becomes useful in our situation, to develop a point of view called by Cousins "consequentialism"—the recognition that whatever one thinks, says, or does has consequences extending to all (Cousins, 1974). The concept joins with the teaching of Teilhard de Chardin. It offers an alternative to both that invidious feeling of helplessness to shape our collective destiny and the escapist tendency to enjoy one's own unpolluted island while the world destroys itself. Increased awareness of the consequences rather than the mere existence of our individual and collective selves may stir just enough of us to contemplate and respond to the fact that ours is the opportunity, the privilege, to enter upon the greatest adventure faced by Man—his own survival. The challenge is as old as Man, but the specifics are so fresh that only a few have begun to align them with their self-interests.

reconstructing schools

It is in the self-interest of teachers, administrators, students, and their parents that schools be reconstructed so that they become more satisfying places. What constitutes "satisfying" is for those who work there and send their children there to determine and make functional. Fenstermacher already has addressed the problem of defining what gives satisfaction or is satisfying (Chapter 10). It is something to be determined by those most intimately involved with the setting.

Those most intimately involved with the setting of the school are the principal, teachers, and students. Parents are at a once-removed level of intimacy; they do not live there five or six hours each day. Their interest, participation, and, therefore, satisfaction are, consequently, of a somewhat different order. They expect, of course, to be heard in matters of intent and must have some legitimate medium or forum through which their wishes are communicated. And they should be informed—and, in turn, take the time to be informed—about what goes on in schools and about what is proposed for educational change generally. But whether they should participate in determining the day-to-day routine of schooling is something about which I have considerable reservation.

Much current rhetoric appears to be based on an assumption that closes the issue: participation in all the affairs of the local school is a parental right. I have reservations about how much parents should be the determining figures in the total lives of their children, and I include in these reservations the extent to which determination of their children's education is desirable. I stop short of their participating in determining the daily character of the school workplace, except for being informed and given reasons (not gobbledygook and exhortation). I prefer to leave the regularities of schooling to teachers rather than my fellow parents—especially those who once taught, some of whom by virtue of having done so seem to have a penchant for hanging around the place a good deal and for claiming a special voice in school affairs. Since the teachers still are responsible, I know whom to hold accountable and even where to find them when I want them.

It is as difficult to generalize about parents as it is to generalize about teachers. However, just as university professors are more conservative about higher education than about politics, parents assume their most conservative stance when family matters are at stake. And so I do not want the affairs of the school to be dominated by family self-interest. Many parents who complain about the rigidity of schools merely want to substitute their own brands of rigidity, just as the Pilgrims wanted to establish their own brand of religious conformity. For them to go off to establish their own schools with a small band of believers may seem harmless enough but I am not much in favor of this, either—and especially not if it is to be with tax dollars.

My reasons will become clearer as this chapter progresses. Suffice it to say now that I do not believe that the creation of little school enclaves is in the best interests of children in a pluralistic society and, indeed, of a pluralistic society. I remember only too well a university administration that denied me an experimental school to explore educational alternatives for *all* but that, shortly after 1954, was quite prepared to open such a "private" school for a segment of that community. I believe not in *an* alternative education for children, nor even in alternative options that exclude other alternatives, but rather in education that guarantees exposure to a wide array of alternatives—education in and through alternatives. More than alternative schools, we need more alternatives in and out of schools. One of these alternatives is the opportunity to go to school with others from diverse backgrounds whose parents often prefer similarity, not dissimilarity. One of the basic advantages of a pluralistic society is the right to be educated in the human race, a right to be upheld by the courts when families will not do so.

The wealthy make sure that their children go to certain private schools, not just because they perceive them to be academically better (although their rhetoric will stress this reason) but because they incorporate certain values in their policies, regularities, and promotional brochures. These schools hold and attract their clientele because they adhere to these values and do not innovate in regard to them. They innovate only in fringe areas or when what they stand for is not at all threatened. They proclaim their independence, but are in no way independent to do as they wish and especially are not independent of their alumni upon whom largess and future clientele depend.

Current interest in free and alternative schools is not devoid of similar elements. Traditions are lacking; beginnings usually are marked by strong expressions of educational philosophies that are supposed to be markedly divergent from an oft-exaggerated articulation of what characterizes public schools. For some parents, such schools actually serve as way stations between public schools and private schools which for various reasons were rejected earlier but which are more readily accepted after initially high expectations for a newly created alternative school have faded, much of the disenchantment resulting from inability to agree on *a* philosophy.

The creation and management of alternative schools by small groups of families marked by socioeconomic similarities constitute a formidable threat to equity and to equality of educational opportunity (indeed, such activity only postpones the necessary reconstruction of the educational system, school by school). The problem of equality was perceived by the Working Man's party in the 1820s which proposed that children be removed from parents and placed in boarding schools by the age of two, before the differential effects of family status already would have done their work (Lipset,

1970). A major task of education in a free society is to provide all with a maximum opportunity to overcome the inequalities of birth in the course of seeking maximal development of personal potential. The proposal to send children at the age of two to state-financed and state-controlled boarding schools bruises the parental sensitivities of most of us, but the Working Man's party made an effective point.

Another major task of education is to develop understanding of what it means to be a self-governing citizen in a free, self-governing political community. Some of those parents who want to run their own "alternative" schools within and supported financially by the public school system—and some of those educators who advocate that they do so—dangerously redefine the concept of community. Hutchins (1972) states the problem:

> *Brown v. Board of Education* had the unintended effect of promoting a new definition of the community. The community was no longer everybody; it was not united for the common good of all. The community became people of my race, my neighborhood, my economic class. The rhetoric of the community now asserted that the school belonged to the community as redefined. "Pluralism" became a popular war cry. The black and white racists, the poor and the rich, the city dweller and the suburbanite all demanded that the school their children attended should be theirs. . . . The neighborhood school, meaning a school that ignored the existence or importance of the wider political community, became a sacred object. This is not what *Brown v. Board of Education* meant.

An immediate effect of this distortion in the meaning of community and of local control of education is segmentation and segregation. In the long run, the concept of *public* school—in the sense of belonging to and helping to promote the public interest—is lost.

We do not yet have an acceptable alternative to public schools. If the problems pertain to rigidity, "mindlessness," inappropriate evaluative criteria, lack of options, and the like, as many serious reformers and proponents of alternatives claim, the rational alternative would appear to be their reconstruction.

Reconstruction must assure interpretation of those broad goals articulated by the state. This is a process for the citizenry—not just parents but all citizens—and one for which they must be held responsible and accountable. What must be guarded against is the formulation of expectations that are little more than the extension of family and parochial interests, often made legitimate, as Hutchins points out, in the name of pluralism. Local constituencies act responsibly when they recognize and respond to an ever-widening sense of community.

It is up to principals, teachers, and students to reconstruct school settings for purposes of fulfilling these purposes. Determining the routines by means of which each school functions is not a task for parents, although they might participate in a variety of appropriate ways. Given a choice between my neighbor and a certified teacher running my child's classroom, I shall choose the latter every time—and sleep much better knowing that the former is not messing about there (other than as an aide directed by that teacher) while I am engaged elsewhere. Should the teacher abuse the post and human sensibilities in the process, I shall carry my dissatisfaction to the appropriate authority. But I shall not interfere with the teacher's authority to make instructional decisions. Above all, I shall fight against sharing these decisions with my neighbor for fear of raising the process to a dangerous level of partiality and, indeed, incompetence. Being a *good* teacher is a full-time job.

How then might this reconstruction proceed? The starting point is the local school, the largest *organic* unit for educational change (Goodlad, 1972). Anything beyond it is superstructure, useful for support and communication but overly bureaucratic when it perceives itself to be the operating agency for the conduct of schooling. The larger system should attempt to articulate new possibilities, infuse ideas possibly relevant to the needs of individual schools, and provide the results of independent analyses of what other schools currently are doing. When it seeks to do much more than this, the system's function soon shifts to self-preservation and self-aggrandizement, to the point of using up for these selfish ends resources that belong in the local school.

Fulfillment of this principle pertaining to the individual school means that there are not district-wide reading programs, for example. Rather, the district espouses the importance of reading as one of the inalienable rights of each child and seeks to provide unequivocal support and resources geared to the peculiarities of the student population of each school. Decentralization of authority and responsibility includes giving to the local school funds for this purpose, not determining what the school needs and spending money for it, perhaps in the name of (false) economy.

Lay citizens serve on the "body of responsible persons" defined by Joyce as essential to the continuous planning and appraising required for school renewal (Joyce, 1969). Ideally, the persons on this body are sought out because of their recognized wisdom and leadership ability and are persuaded to take the posts. Use of the position to enhance political ambitions is discouraged. This body seeks to interpret state goals and to articulate them in such a way as to suggest the scope of and the priorities among school activities. It seeks neither to determine the final choice of specific content in the social studies, for example, nor the instructional procedures to be used.

Principals, teachers, and students maintain a variety of dialogues regarding what they perceive the role of the school to be, sometimes seeking clarification from and making suggestions to the body of responsible parties; the structure and ongoing conduct of their workplace, including the use and modification of facilities; available curricular programs and materials; and procedures for carrying out the instructional process. Although dialogue on such matters is part of the daily milieu, it does not stop with talk. Dialogue must lead to conscious, articulated decisions; these to actions; and the results of actions must be appraised. And then the cycle is repeated (Bentzen, 1974).

Each school is a functioning unit in a network of schools—communicating, visiting, sharing ideas—to assure stimulation beyond the ability of single schools to be self-motivating. Schools can and do become ingrown, self-centered, and provincial. Principals need to share with other principals who are experiencing similar problems; it is a lonely job otherwise. Teachers need to see what peers in other schools are doing, to learn from and to teach one another. There are not only the very tangible benefits of getting new ideas and learning new techniques but also the more intangible ones of feeling a part of something bigger: traditions, a profession, a worthy human endeavor, and shared hope.

But even this is not enough to assure continuing self-renewal at the level of the local school. There needs to be a kind of neutral agency, a hub, whose sole reason for existence is to give moral and material support to each school and to assure effective communication, use of resources, and expert help among schools. Teachers do not have time to know about or to screen among the hundreds of books written each year in their own and related fields. Nor is it easy for them to select from the outpourings of new curricula and materials. A hub of the kind envisioned here can do much of this for them, organizing what is available but leaving final choices to teachers. A hub can serve to bring together teachers who want to share and teachers who want what their peers have to give. Significantly, it can provide a kind of serendipity—unexpected benefits in the form of encouragement to try and, indeed, legitimation of the right to fail. For, without assurance of support in failure, educators are unlikely to innovate.

There must be pedagogical service stations to assure the development of those specific skills which teachers want to perfect—and they do, indeed, wish to do this—after having had some exposure to the class of a teacher demonstrating what they wish to acquire. Since the best source of help is other teachers who are doing it, these teachers should be freed from classroom responsibilities temporarily in order to staff a pedagogical service station focusing for a few days or weeks on individualizing instruction, using learning centers, teaching word-attack skills, or whatever. When the demand is met, the staff moves back to their classrooms, and a new group takes over. The concept is not unlike the English teacher centers now at various stages of development. Continuous updating of teaching skills is absolutely essential to teachers' well-being and the health of the enterprise. It is ironic that teaching is the largest enterprise in this country for which in-service training fails to be provided for at the time and cost of the industry. We reap what we sow.

There is nothing particularly novel about what is proposed above. If there is anything unique, it is in the way the pieces are conceived as a composite whole. My colleagues and I in |I|D|E|A| developed and tested these ideas as hypotheses in a strategy for school improvement conducted in the League of Cooperating Schools, a network of eighteen schools in Southern California (Goodlad, 1975). Elements of the strategy are now contained in the |I|D|E|A| Change Program being employed by more than a thousand schools across the country.

Our research showed that all of these elements are essential if schools and those in them are to be reasonably self-renewing, certain components being more important than others at different cycles or stages in the change process (Culver and Hoban, 1973). We also found that high-level development of dialogue, decision making, action, and evaluation (DDAE) seemed to go hand in hand with high morale of teachers, high professionalism of teachers, and high feelings of power on the part of teachers. All these, in turn, with high DDAE, appeared to go hand in hand with an array of positive attitudes of students toward their schools. Put together, these feelings of teachers and pupils might well be defined as satisfaction (Goodlad, 1975).

It is interesting that, as teachers grew in these characteristics, they became more open with parents and their communities, the dialogue increasingly extending outward. Parents became more interested in school affairs, the base of participation as aides, for example, broadening from a few to a large number of parents. As many as 150 per week assisted in this way in one school of 500 pupils. We have evidence that parents sought to cross district lines to enroll their children in league schools, to move to league school attendance districts, and, when one or the other of these alternatives was not available, to "smuggle" their children into the "out-of-bounds" schools. Call this satisfaction, if you will.

The thesis we sought to test in the league developed in my mind after twenty years of observing and participating in change that failed to take account of the school as a social system in its own right or, perhaps more important, to focus on it as the unit for and of reconstruction. To put the matter simply, the school with its principal, teachers, and students is the key unit in educational change and, *under certain conditions,* can become self-renewing. The conditions are those pertaining to the role of the district, the processes within the school, and the support systems surrounding it suggested above. Taken together and worked toward, the foregoing propositions constitute both a beginning point and a sense of direction in seeking a more comprehensive educational environment which, in its most complete realization, becomes the learning society.

alternative scenarios for alternative education

Space limitations prevent my endeavoring to conceptualize a variety of ways in which the structures, contents, and processes of reconstructed schools might differ from the conventional ones we know. Chapters 1 and 7 suggest some of the possibilities. Describing these and many more in detail would require not just another chapter but another volume. The purpose here is, rather, simply to sketch two somewhat different scenarios for a combination of schools and other educational options we could have in a relatively near future, let us say around 2000. All the components have been described elsewhere; they need to be put together in systemic form, as suggested by La Belle in Chapter 8.

One scenario suggests a comprehensive role for a much-changed and extended school. The school becomes essentially a concept rather than a place, more or less guiding utilization of a host of settings for learning twenty-four hours a day. As merely an extrapolation from our current six-hour-per-day school, it would be a bureaucratic monstrosity going far beyond the extremes against which some have railed and proposed as alternate the complete de-schooling of society. But this is not necessary if the reconstruction of schooling proceeds somewhat as suggested on previous pages. Stress on considerable local initiative and absence of state laws designed to legitimate certain competing ideas rather than others would encourage open competition among views and the periodic correction of excesses. The other scenario suggests a sharply limited role for the school as just one of many institutions providing options for choice.

There is no reason why, in the future, both scenarios and a variety of alternatives between them and options within them should not flourish side by side in our society. Some are more appropriate to certain communities than to others. For example, most educational futurizing that invokes the use of a wide variety of institutions outside of schools is more easily realized in urban settings. Rural communities seem more likely to move toward the school as the center of educational, recreational, and cultural life. For urban communities, much enlightened human engineering must occur before they will be able to provide many safe educational adjuncts to or extensions of schools.

What follows is based on the assumption that these scenarios will not result in performances as a result of efforts only to improve education. Rather, educational changes will follow or accompany changes in the larger society. Planners and policy makers must be convinced, however—and educational processes should play a role here—of the importance of building educational provisions into the process of environmental change. This may prove to be the most difficult and unlikely proviso in seeking to create educational alternatives.

It is to be hoped that, before all of us choke to death in our own pollutants, we will begin to redesign our cities, beginning at the core. It will be necessary to relocate any heavy industries now located there, all but a few service-type businesses, and most housing. Open parks and bodies of water will replace them. As quickly as funds permit, art galleries, museums, theaters, a few hotels, some housing for the elderly, and some hospitals will be constructed, with open space maintained always in excess of what is built upon. All of this will be a shift away from present policy with respect to parks and recreation areas, for example. Current policy favors the young and affluent who are able to reach remote preserves with cars and campers. It is in the city that the quality of life must be restored.

Emphasis on housing and care for the elderly is part of a process of recognizing the need to stimulate and provide for our most neglected group. They will not lack for association with young people because the young will be attracted to the central city and, indeed, the elderly will serve, in part, to educate the young in the ways and artifacts of their cultural community. Hotels will provide temporary accommodation for artists, speakers, and entertainers who come to provide their services in the cultural and recreational facilities.

City planning will revert to an old but neglected idea: the green belt. Moving outward from this inner core, one will encounter wide green belts completely encircling what lies within. Scattered about in each green belt will be recreational facilities of many kinds. In each populated segment will be those cultural and educational facilities requiring personal interaction more than access to precious artifacts of the kind maintained, with other things, at the city's central core.

Wide spokes of green will radiate out from the city center. Through them will run fast trains elevated above the ground. These will stop at each green belt where they will be met by minicars serving adjacent neighborhoods. Limited stops for the master trains in a coordinated system of transportation will assure quick access to the core from homes at the periphery. There will be no charge to passengers, assuring equality of access to most parts of the total city.

The horsepower of automobiles will be sharply restricted by law; the convenience of public transportation and the absence of parking spaces at the city's core will limit their use.

The use of computer terminals on a large scale will occur first in homes, largely bypassing schools in the early stages of becoming established everywhere. With the home as the prime market, the terminals will have prices equivalent to those of today's television sets. The terminal will provide not only a conventional television screen but also a responsive one for interacting with a variety of educational programs. News of all available cultural events will be frequent and as readily available as news of the weather is today. Computerized consoles will become available free of charge in many public locations including schools, and, from them, all citizens will receive information on what currently is available for educational exploration. Providing these services will be normal operating procedure for what are now radio and television stations.

Lessons taught by humans and machines in every conceivable subject and activity will be available, just as classes in aerodynamics, surfing, skiing, tennis, painting, singing, playing the piano, yoga, transcendental meditation, bridge playing, and knitting are available today. Although there will be many more classes than today, the critical differences will be in legitimation, as we shall see below, and ease of access. There will be no age barriers; young and old will participate side by side. Teaching one another will be taken for granted.

Obviously, these strokes are broad. As stated earlier, the chances are about as great that we will be looking into the abyss of doomsday instead, but "Nothingness is conceptually impossible." And, if we are to achieve these possibilities, A.D. 2000 probably is an optimistic date. If we are not well on the way by then, however, it is doubtful that we ever will be.

Scenario One: The Schooled Society. One scenario, then, is for all of the educational components to be encompassed by something called school. There would probably be a commissioner of education and culture with broad powers to guide the development and utilization of the educational possibilities inherent in all of the city's resources. Many of our museums, galleries, and, indeed, in some places even libraries (although the last decade or so of enlightenment in this sector is encouraging) are custodial and archival. But in the scheme envisioned here, a significant part of their public support would depend on availability and service for educational purposes. Similar expectations would prevail for YM and YWCA buildings, recreational halls, and the like, most of which now go unused for large portions of the day. Similarly, school buildings would be brought into twenty-four-hour use, seven days a week.

The transportation lines radiating outward like spokes of a great wheel would divide the city into pie-shaped educational districts, each supervised by a deputy. Each of these units, consequently, would embrace whatever socioeconomic differences prevailed from the small segment nearest the inner core to the outside rim of the pie. Financial resources for education would be equally distributed throughout, that handwriting having been written on the wall in the 1970s. There would be no busing to assure racial or ethnic integration. Everyone would be bused or, rather, carried on a train or minicar for part of his education, more in later than in earlier years.

A school building would be the base of operation and the planning center in making educational provision for the surrounding community. But it would be only one of many settings used throughout the day and might very well not be the site for some students for long periods of time. At the level of the local school, the body of responsible parties described earlier would have access to all the educational resources of the immediate and larger community in planning the total offerings available to the successive groups of students entering and moving through the institution. Within this framework, teams of teachers would work with groups of children enrolled in a nongraded phase of schooling embracing three or four years of time—early schooling, intermediate, and so forth.

In the earliest phase, children would tend to stay together in multiaged family groupings, since the important learnings are those acquired socially: learning to get along with peers and adults, exploring and sharing things together, examining all of these relationships in a search for the meaning of selfhood within the context of a group. Later, children would begin to move out from the family group to develop special interests and talents in company with individuals from other school-family groups. But children would continue to return to the base group for purposes of sharing and for finding personal meaning. A child should always be able to return to where he was before without fear or embarrassment. Later, more and more time would be spent in other settings with and without other students, in alternative educational settings and workplaces. School would become, indeed, a concept but not *a* place.

There are many possible alternatives within the broad scenario laid out above. The essential concept is a thoroughly schooled society, with schooling extended to encompass a wide array of alternatives but with school as a place diminished in significance. School and education become more nearly synonymous than is the case today.

Scenario Two: A Restricted Concept of School. Another scenario calls for a much more sharply limited school. Again, there could be many alternative versions. One involves a combination of school as a place and a completely open voucher system by means of which one spends educational voucher coupons as one wishes. Choices are in no way monitored by school. Certain core learnings are the responsibility of a place called school. A small child might divide his time between such a place, from which he and his cohorts would venture out from time to time into the larger learning society, and some kind of home environment, as is the case today. Perhaps 10 percent of the young child's nonschool, nonhome educational experiences would be "purchased" in the educational marketplace. The vouchers for this purpose would be given to each child; those receiving the vouchers in payment for educational services would turn them in to the appropriate authorities for cash derived from state and federal taxes. By the age of twelve or so, a child might be receiving 50 percent of his education through the use of such vouchers. By this age he would also probably have arrived at some sort of agreements with his parents as to what proportion of the vouchers were spent independently of parental wishes. Vouchers distributed equitably to each person would, in essence, serve as coin of the realm in determining the educational diet of the individual. A family might pool vouchers (adults would have them, too) to purchase an array of lessons, plays, musical performances or whatever, stored on tape by profit-making educational companies for replay at the convenience of users via television or computer terminals.

Although I am opposed to the use of voucher plans for the creation of entire schools (which would, in the words of a strong advocate, "destroy the public school system as we know it"

[Jencks, 1965]), there are interesting possibilities in the modified plan proposed here. The school becomes responsible for only core learnings rather than the entire range of educational possibilities. Much career education might be done in work settings, as would a good deal of personal or vocational counseling by persons or institutions with less of a vested interest in schools.

With core learnings not left solely to the jurisdiction of the home nor scattered among an array of specialized agencies, there remains ample opportunity for dispatching those traditional interests of the state in the commonweal. One needs no great insight to realize that survival in the future will call for a general drawing back from the self-destructive course on which humankind is embarked. Enlightened self-interest must extend far beyond the limited boundaries of family or communal life. In time of stress, families tend to pull the wagons into a tight circle; understanding and compassion extend not far beyond. If self-interest is to extend beyond the family, it would be folly to leave responsibility for broadening it to that group. But perhaps the state, in its most enlightened self-interest, will come to see the need to educate for a mankind perspective as part of our common learnings (Goodlad and others, 1974).

Another virtue in the plan described above is allocation of the vouchers to the individual who then exercises personal preferences. Such an arrangement recognizes that long-standing duality in educational aims expressed earlier: the individual and the larger society. It is recognized, of course, that parents would tend to serve as proxy for the young child, but they would do so as one administers a trust; ownership cannot be revoked. In a learning society, educational vouchers might well replace money in helping to develop independence and a sense of potency in the young.

There are, of course, troublesome difficulties with any voucher scheme. This one, however, avoids some of the most obvious: the regulation of entire schools eligible for voucher payments; the establishment of a bureaucracy to establish and administer standards; and the elimination of the humanizing role of the common school —that is, the process of humanizing the essential lore of the human race for popular consumption. Also, problems of discrimination and indoctrination are somewhat lessened, but by no means eliminated. The problem of what enterprises are eligible still looms large.

We are left, of course, with the challenging question of determining core learnings for each successive phase of schooling. But this is, indeed, a lesser problem than prevails today. Rather than having to provide within the narrow confines of school a range of offerings approximating human diversity (which is impossible), as well as some approximation of what should be common to all (a concept that gets short shrift), we confront only the latter. The problem is still a tough one, but it is clear and need not become fogged up by considerations of electives, majors, minors, and the like.

Many readers will conjure up a vision of the three R's for the school-based core learnings, but I am not at all sure that these will be the most vital selections a few years from now. They can be learned more efficiently, individually, conveniently, and with less sex bias and emotional tension via machines than through the intervention of human teachers. Because a child's freedom to use the larger environment without them is restricted, however, perhaps one phase of schooling will devote part of its time to assuring that these learnings occur. Nonetheless, the central core is more likely to involve the higher literacies defined by Chase as "the ability to use relevant processes for selection of goals and activities; the ability to select and use means appropriate to learning and other goals; the capacity and the disposition to apply aesthetic and ethical criteria to the manner in which activities are performed; the capacity to respond to an increasing range of phenomena and relationships with understanding, appreciation and appropriate overt action" (Chase, 1966). These learnings are enhanced by interaction with others and benefit from the guidance of an adult mentor. Teachers who are good at selecting and arranging knowledge and little more will be redirected into the programming of material for self-selection on automated devices.

The central function of school, then, will be to further the search for synthesis and integration. "The essential philosophical quest is for integration—which is to say, the need to bring together rational philosophy, spiritual belief, scientific knowledge, personal experience, and direct observation into an organic whole" (Cousins, 1974). The search for how best to provide for this integration will require that the reconstruction of schooling be a never-ending process. The learning society cannot be a static one, with all the contingencies determined, refined, and in place.

The Deschooled Society. The preceding scenarios, with their various alternative scenes and acts, are not improbable ones for the United States and many other countries. None of the elements is new or unenvisioned. The parts simply have not been put together —and certainly the necessary reconstruction of our cities and schools has not taken place. Progression into another scenario involving no places called school, even on a reduced-time basis, is not difficult to envision, either. In fact, 10 percent school and 90 percent on vouchers for an eighteen-year-old would come very close. There is really no need, then, to take up space with a detailed description, since conceptual extrapolation from what has been described is relatively easy, although the logistics would be somewhat complicated.

The successive scenarios for many countries would be quite different, however, the problems being less ones of deschooling than of continuing to school. If, for example, the goal is to attain universal literacy quickly, the construction and staffing of schools may be one of the least effective alternatives available. Attaching some form of literacy training to the workplace may be both cheaper and more efficient. La Belle already has touched on at least some of the issues and possibilities, and there is a growing body of useful literature on the subject. The educational futures of societies not yet schooled is a subject that, unfortunately, must be eschewed here.

Deschooling in the United States and other countries with comprehensive, bureaucratized educational systems is less a matter of envisioning the possibilities than of determining the desirability and feasibility, at least within this century. Regarding feasibility, the problems of logistics appear less formidable than those of habit, attitude, and convenience. Rusch, for example, experienced goodwill and almost universal cooperation in seeking to use community resources for the busload of children constituting a kind of school (Rusch, 1974). But whether such cooperation would prevail were hordes of young people to be turned over to workers and workplaces for their education remains a question to be answered through audacious, large-scale experiments. It is interesting that Rusch found that there was a need for quiet places to read and for spaces suited to discussion, which he found in libraries and YW or YMCA buildings. If there were not enough such places in a deschooled society, we might find ourselves once more building them and be well on our way to schooling society once again. Perhaps school is one of the things we would invent if we did not already have it.

The desirability of deschooling everywhere is, however, the more troublesome issue. It may be that the most educated and most affluent segments of humankind have about run the full course in their search for developing (and indulging in) individuality, at least until we put that larger setting called the world in much better order. What is required, I think, will not be found through escape to far-off exotic places, because we already have made them part of the problem. Nor will it be found in backyard gardens, although many of us may find ourselves growing them. And it certainly will not be found in the backyard bomb shelter or its equivalent, carefully stocked to maintain one family until the air clears.

Many who favor deschooling assign the family a large but ill-defined educational role in a deschooled society (sometimes in a manner similar to the way the Constitution delegates educational responsibility to the states), at a time when the family is in considerable disarray. It is interesting to note that many of the proponents are well-educated liberals whose ability and willingness to provide education according to the most enlightened self-interest probably are considerable. But I am worried about those whose actions and neglect constitute the largest cause of children's deaths, injuries, and neglect. And I remain distrustful of the ability of most families to educate for the common welfare in the times of stress ahead that will call for a combination of self-discipline and large-scale rational planning. We must be educated to understand that each of us is part of a world ecology and to develop a considerable awareness of the consequential character of individual behavior. None of us runs the course alone, no matter how much we value and seek our autonomy.

Movement must be toward the creation of more educational opportunities and easier access to them. I would resist placing the schools in charge of options in the larger society or as gatekeeper monitoring who and how one gets to them. I must opt for the rest of this century, at least, for a schooled nation, with schools to be reconstructed at the local level, with each seeking a balance between education for responsible membership in the family, local, state, and world community and education for personal fulfillment. This prospect cannot be contemplated with unbridled optimism, but contemplating other alternatives provides little satisfaction.

references

Bentzen, M. M., and Associates. *Changing Schools: The Magic Feather Principle.* New York: McGraw-Hill, 1974.

Calleo, D., and Rowland, B. *America and the World Political Economy.* Bloomington, Ind.: Indiana University Press, 1973.

Chase, F. S. "School Change in Perspective." In J. I. Goodlad (Ed.), *The Changing American School,* pp. 290-291. Sixty-Fifth Yearbook of the National Society for the Study of Education, Part II. Chicago: University of Chicago Press, 1966.

Cousins, N. *The Celebration of Life.* New York: Harper, 1974.

Culver, C. M., and Hoban, G. J. (Eds.). *The Power to Change.* New York: McGraw-Hill, 1973.

Fantini, M. D. *What Is Best for the Children?* New York: Doubleday, 1974.

Goodlad, J. I. *The Dynamics of Educational Change: Toward Responsive Schools.* New York: McGraw-Hill, 1975.

Goodlad, J. I. "Staff Development: The League Model." *Theory Into Practice,* 1972, *11*(4), 207-214.

Goodlad, J. I., Klein, M. F., and Associates. *Looking Behind the Classroom Door.* Rev. Ed. Worthington, Ohio: Charles A. Jones, 1974.

Goodlad, J. I., Klein, M. F., Novotney, J. M., and Associates. *Early Schooling in the United States.* New York: McGraw-Hill, 1973.

Goodlad, J. I., and others. *Toward a Mankind School: An Adventure in Humanistic Education.* New York: McGraw-Hill, 1974.

Heilbroner, R. L. *An Inquiry into the Human Prospect.* New York: W. W. Norton, 1974.

Hutchins, R. M. "The Great Anti-School Campaign." In *The Great Ideas Today,* pp. 154-227. Chicago: Encyclopaedia Britannica, 1972.

Jencks, C. "Is the Public School Obsolete?" *The Public Interest,* 1965 (Winter), 27.

Joyce, B. R. *Alternative Models of Elementary Education.* Waltham, Mass.: Ginn & Co., 1969.

Lipset, S. M. "The Ideology of Local Control." In C. A. Bowers, I. Housego, and D. Dyke (Eds.), *Educational and Social Policy: Local Control of Education.* New York: Random House, 1970.

Marlin, W. "Norman Cousins in Person." *Christian Science Monitor,* November 5, 1974, 5.

Rusch, C. W. "MOBOC: A Mobile Learning Environment." In G. J. Coates (Ed.), *Alternative Learning Environments.* Stroudsburg, Pa.: Dowden, Hutchinson and Ross, 1974.

Sarason, S. B. *The Creation of Settings and the Future Societies.* San Francisco: Jossey-Bass, 1972.

Sarason, S. B. *The Culture of the School and the Problem of Change.* Boston: Allyn and Bacon, 1971.

index

269